Multinational Corporations

MULTINATIONAL CORPORATIONS

The Problems and the Prospects

A study prepared by the Graduate Institute of International Studies, Fairleigh Dickinson University.

Second Edition Revised

Nasrollah S. Fatemi,
Gail W. Williams
and Thibaut De Saint-Phalle

SOUTH BRUNSWICK AND NEW YORK: A. S. BARNES AND COMPANY
LONDON: THOMAS YOSELOFF LTD

A. S. Barnes and Co., Inc.
Cranbury, New Jersey 08512

Thomas Yoseloff Ltd
108 New Bond Street
London W1Y OQX, England

Library of Congress Cataloging in Publication Data

Fatemi, Nasrollah Saifpour, 1911-
  Multinational corporations.

  Includes bibliographical references and index.
  1. International   business   enterprises. 2. Corporations,   American.
  I. Williams, Gail W., joint author.
II. Title
HD69.I7F33   338.8'8   75-29728
ISBN 0-498-01879-2 (cloth)
ISBN 0-498-04097-6 (paper)

PRINTED IN THE UNITED STATES OF AMERICA

Contents

Preface

A book on the *Multinational Corporations, Their Problems and Prospects,* is likely to be out of date next year, in this changing world. Any general book, such as this, in a field of scholarship where research is active, must suffer from attrition, if it is not revised. It is not just that the advancing research adds new data and ideas but events in both the developed and developing nations are changing commercial relations and perspectives and introducing a wholly "new economic order" with new prospects and new problems. Since the first edition of this book was published and sold out in 1975, there have been radical changes in the attitudes, actions, and relations of the host countries.

In the developing countries, foreign direct ownership is increasingly regarded as a form of neocolonialism. In the United States the concern of some members of Congress against the investment of the petrodollars and possible take-over of American businesses by the OPEC nations is but another instance of the same bias. Revelations of political payments by MNCs have compounded the prejudice. In ten months, twenty-two new bills against foreign investments have been introduced in the Congress ignoring the fact that the total direct foreign investments in the United States is less than one-tenth of American investments abroad. While five years ago multinational investments in foreign countries

7

were mostly direct investments and foreign controlled, the new trend is toward joint venture, licensing arrangements, cooperative agreements, investment by contracts, and profit sharing arrangements based on the control of the host country.

At the United Nations a code of ethics has been recommended and a multinational commission has been established. The OECD Commission has codified new guidelines regulating the operation of the multinational enterprises.

Whether all these attempts to regulate multinational corporations and restrain the host governments will produce a fair deal within the canon of the new economic order remains to be seen. However, this search for a unified general rule of cooperation between the multinational and host countries suggests that, in the future, realism, reason, and facts about multinationals may replace the past fantasies and fictions.

In this revised edition a number of changes have been made including an addition of the final chapter that centers on the new developments of the last twelve months. For the preparation of this last chapter we are grateful to Mr. Thibaut de Saint-Phalle for his valuable assistance and contribution.

N. S. Fatemi
G. W. Williams

Graduate Institute of International Studies
Fairleigh Dickinson University

Acknowledgments

The authors are deeply indebted to Fairleigh S. Dickinson, Jr., for his encouragement and his valuable advice at many stages in the preparation of this book, and for his generous financial support of all the research projects of the Institute of Graduate Studies at Fairleigh Dickinson University.

We would also particularly like to thank Dr. Jerome Pollack, President of the University, for his moral support; Dr. Peter Sammartino, Chancellor of the University; the Honorable David Van Alstyne, member of the Board of Overseers; Mr. James Grant, Vice President in charge of Research at C.P.C.; Professor Johan Galtung, of the University of Oslo; Dr. Zuhayr Mikdashi, of the American University of Beirut; and various other friends for their effort in reading the manuscripts and making helpful suggestions.

We are also indebted to Miss Dian Brown and Miss Grace Keefe for their valuable research work, to Mrs. Audrey March for her work in proofreading, and to Mrs. Sandra Asdoorian and Mrs. Marion Johnson for their work in typing.

Introduction

For three years, several Congressional committees have been investigating the multinational corporations' activities both at home and abroad. Several thousand pages of pro and con reports concerning the multinationals have been produced as a result of these investigations. Half a dozen bills have been introduced in the Senate of the United States.

The United Nations Economic and Social Council, in a resolution adopted unanimously on July 28, 1972, requested the Secretary-General to appoint a group of eminent persons to study the role of multinational corporations and their impact on the process of development, especially that of developing countries, and also their implications for international relations, to formulate conclusions that may possibly be used by governments in making their sovereign decisions regarding national policy in this respect, and to submit recommendations for appropriate international action.

In a report of more than a thousand pages, the United States Tariff Commission told the Senate Committee on Finance that the rapid growth of the multinational corporations and their private influence on many aspects of world trade since the end of World War II has had a profound influence upon the economy of the United States and other countries, and accordingly poses many political, legal, economic, and social issues of considerable importance.

Not only are diplomats at the United Nations and government officials in Washington showing great interest in the multinational corporations, their operations, and their impact throughout the world, but their unprecedented expansion has evoked a strong interest among scholars, the mass media, and the general public. While much information and understanding have been gained from this surge of interest, the complexity of the subject and the controversy that surrounds it require serious analysis, lest fantasies should prove more appealing than facts and emotions stronger than reason. "Multinational corporations, which are depicted in some quarters as key instruments for maximizing world welfare, are seen in others as dangerous agents of imperialism." The basic facts and issues still need to be disentangled from the mass of opinion and ideology and a practical program of action still awaits formulation.

The studies of the Senate Committee on Finance, the reports of the U.S. Tariff Commission, the research of the Department of Commerce, and the deliberations of the United Nations on this subject reflect the preoccupation and currents of thought of the times.

The attack and adverse publicity aimed at multinationals and the political and social dimensions of the problem of multinational corporations are only too apparent. The present involvement of the Congress and the United Nations in the operations of the multinationals was in fact prompted by incidents involving a few corporations. The concern, publicity, and excitement occasioned by the revelations of these incidents, the oil crisis, and worldwide inflation proved that the multinationals both at home and abroad are facing criticism, suspicion, and uncertainty.

"Despite the considerable and transnational power which

multinational corporations possess, they, unlike governments, are not directly accountable for their policies and actions to a broadly based electorate. Nor, unlike purely national firms, are the multinational corporations subject to control and regulation by a single authority which can aim at ensuring a maximum degree of harmony between their operation and public interest. The question at issue, therefore, is whether a set of institutions and devices can be worked out which will guide the multinational corporations' exercise of power and introduce some form of accountability to the international community into their activities." [1]

The multinational corporations have definitely contributed to world welfare. They have been partly responsible for the rebuilding of war-ravaged Europe and the development of resources of many developing nations. Their ability to tap financial, physical, and human resources all over the world, their capacity to develop new technology and skills, and their managerial supremacy to translate resources into specific outputs have proven to be outstanding. The important contribution of multinational corporations to the growth of the developing nations was recognized by the United Nations General Assembly in 1970 and their assistance for the second development decade was unanimously requested. Their productivity, efficiency, reduction of risks, and their global role in economic development were commended. Yet, their predominance, their size, their monopolistic structure, and their response to a small segment of the population in developing nations are considered the cause of suspicion and the source of tension.

On the national level, there has been a serious concern about the implications of multinational corporations on United States trade, labor technology, investment, and balance of payments.

The purpose of this research is to analyze some of the

different aspects of the multinationals, and to examine the charges and countercharges and to try and find some answers to the following:

1. The degree of freedom that multinationals should have, or the extent of regulations that should be imposed on present operations and future growth.

2. The effects of the massive influx of American capital into other countries on the balance of payments, exports, and employment in the United States.

While the positions of those whose concern is the relationship of labor to management and its place in the world has been touched upon many times, it has, however, not received sufficient attention to the extent for which we hoped. In a future study the entire matter can, of course, be complacently dwelt with based upon predetermined sets and biases. Any document, however, that purports to be a scholarly approach to a major worldwide phenomenon cannot treat this matter either lightly or unfairly. A prime suggestion that I will make, therefore, is that it be part of a third volume of the trilogy consisting of this book and commencing with *The Dollar Crisis*, written in 1963, and now in the process of revision.[2]

The future volume alluded to above should include with the detailed study, the position of labor and the effect that multinational corporations have or could have concerning it. Also should be included are such things that arise from discussions in the present volume:

1. The causal relationship between public policy in the various nations and the multinationals.

2. The ability of the multinational corporations to bend with changing political circumstances both in the framework of time and in broadly philosophical terms.

3. A true study of those who guide the decisions in multinational corporations toward their country of citizenship and as long-term guests in host countries.

4. Relationships with the nations of the so-called third world.

5. The relationships affecting corporate interests and far more national interests in relationship to countries with planned economies, centralized ministerial control of economic decisions, and the host of other differences that exist between Western Europe, the United States, and many other countries; particularly those countries which are rather loosely termed as being philosophically and structurally communistic.

One of the most difficult questions to answer is the extent to which multinational corporations affect other destinies; or, phrased differently, are they a causal factor or the effect of the immensely changing conditions of our times?

It would be inappropriate to thank Dr. Fatemi and his colleagues at length because, in the first instance, it would be impractical to express sufficient appreciation in a very few words. Lengthy documentation in a foreword is frequently, perhaps usually, not read. I would conclude, therefore, with a simple expression of thanks.

Fairleigh S. Dickinson, Jr.

Notes

1. United Nations, Department of Economics and Social Affairs, *Multinational Corporations in World Development*, 1973, p. 2-3.

2. N. S. Fatemi, Thibaut de Saint Phalle, G. Keeffe, *The Dollar Crisis*. Teaneck, N.J.: Fairleigh Dickinson University Press, 1963.

Multinational
Corporations

1.
The Historical Development of United States Multinational Corporations

The forerunners of American transnational enterprise in the early nineteenth century consisted largely of individual entrepreneurs investing for the most part in Canada and Mexico. Milling, mining, and the manufacture of transportation equipment were the industries predominently developed by American direct investments abroad. One of the first sizable American direct investments was in the Panama Railroad chartered in 1849 and built with $5 million of American capital.[1]

By 1850 there were fifty large corporations in the United States, and half of them had significant overseas operating interest including branches for manufacturing and distributing their products. The second half of the nineteenth century saw an increase in the American manufacturing firm looking to supply a foreign market. By the 1890's Singer, Standard Oil, General Electric, National Cash Register, and American Bell all had overseas operating interests.

While it is often pointed out that the size of direct investment abroad was negligible as compared with today's large-scale investments, by 1914 United States' direct foreign investment of $2.65 billion comprised 7 percent of the United States Gross National Product. In 1972 direct investment of $94 billion was 8 percent of the GNP.

Barriers to international trade following World War I led United States multinationals to increase their investments abroad, particularly the automotive and associated industries. By 1929 the United States direct investment totaled $7.2 billion, and there were 1,057 foreign manufacturing subsidiaries of United States enterprises, 446 of which were in Canada.[2]

Until the 1930's most countries paid little attention to the capacity of multinational corporations to cross international boundaries. Except for purposes of trade, few theoretically reasoned it necessary to impose restrictions at national boundaries. During the depression years American private investments abroad were halted, and the United States Government did very little either to give investors the assurance and support they sought, or to provide much needed capital throughout the world.

In the mid-thirties attention was directed toward national policies to increase output and employment internally. As nations began to recover from the depression years and to plan economic goals and priorities, they were confronted by corporations that could operate across national boundaries, institute policies, and undertake activities that could frustrate governmental efforts. Direct foreign investment was throttled and languished until after World War II.

At the end of World War II, the United States Government undertook the major commitment to help rebuild the war-torn nations of Europe and Japan. It was generally considered that the 1946 loan to Britain and France and the Marshall Plan would provide ample assistance for the reconstruction and rehabilitation and recovery of trade in Western Europe and Japan. By 1950 industrial output in most of these countries was at the same level as in 1938. Furthermore, the multilateral trade accords negotiated in Geneva (1947) and Annecy (1949) seemed to signal reductions of the barriers to world commerce.

The sudden sharp devaluation of the pound sterling, and the weakness of the French franc in September 1949, brought into the open the need to reassess the economic situation of Western Europe and to find means for furnishing further assistance. The United States at that time, with its vast productive capacity, was "the only country of any size which has almost complete freedom of action in the field of international economic policy."[3]

On October 31, 1949, Paul Hoffman, addressing the organization for European Economic cooperation, called for an integrated recovery program: "The substance of such integration would be the formation of a single large market within which quantitative restrictions on the movement of goods, monetary barriers to the flow of payments, and eventually all tariffs are permanently swept away."[4]

Despite all these statements, the major difficulty in revitalizing multinational trade was the inadequate supply of dollars. The decline of Britain's economic position, and the needs of Western Europe to finance large import surpluses even with Marshall Plan aid, caused a continuing disequilibrium in the trade accounts. Britain and Western Europe were no longer in a position to finance large exports of capital goods.

The United States position as a producer and creditor was looked upon as unparalleled in strength, and her investment policy assumed prime importance. The administration in Washington began consultations with various business groups to determine why private capital was not moving abroad. The

National Association of Manufacturers pointed out that the private capital would not be exported unless the host nations guaranteed the rights claimed by the private investor, including the right to transfer earnings into dollars and exemption from discriminatory taxation.[5]

By the end of 1949, the Truman Administration was convinced that the emphasis in Europe and Japan must shift from government spending to organized means for the international movement of technology and private capital.

On March 31, 1950, President Truman asked Gordon Gray to undertake an assignment and recommend ways and means for a United States course of action to stimulate international development. The Gray report of November 10, 1950, stated that private investment is the most desirable method for helping other countries:

> It must be recognized that there are now substantial obstacles to an expansion of such investment. The present international tensions are a controlling deterrent in those areas where an actual military threat exists. In other areas the obstacles are largely due to actions or expressed unfriendly attitudes of other governments toward foreign capitals, political instability, fear of government control or expropriation and economic difficulties, particularly those resulting in exchange restrictions. There is also an unwillingness on the part of the United States investors to engage in foreign investment owing to past unfavorable experience in some countries, and the high rates of return available to capital in this country. Thus United States foreign investment has been almost altogether direct equity investment by United States corporations, with direct marketing or supply interest in foreign countries, and is likely to remain so for some time to come.
>
> A lack of basic services, port facilities, roads, power facilities, sanitation facilities, irrigation, etc., is also a bar to many types of private industrial development. The need for improving such facilities in the underdeveloped countries is enormous, and they are usually prerequisites to other investments. But construction of such facilities is usually not attractive to private enterprise because even though they are productive, they usually do not yield to direct financial return, or yield one only over a long period of time.[6]

The Gray report, for the first time, suggested that in order for American investors to receive assurance and encouragement to risk their capitals abroad, the government of the United States should press for the negotiation of investment treaties which could protect investors against nationalization, non-convertibility, and expropriation. Furthermore the Gray report suggested:

> Careful study should be given to the desirability and possibility of promoting private investment through tax incentives in areas where economic development will promote mutual interest, but where political uncertainty now handicap United States private investment. [7]

The report concluded that there were definite limitations on the extent to which private investment could be encouraged. It therefore recommended that, for several years, the Export-Import Bank lend $500 million annually to the countries which need American technology and machinery.

Following the Gray Report, President Truman realized the difficulties confronting his administration in persuading American investors to invest their capital in other countries. True to his characteristics, he never gave up his search for a solution to the problems of the nations in search of foreign investments.

In December, 1950, he asked Nelson Rockefeller, then Chairman of the Advisory Board on International Development, to continue the study of the private investments abroad and recommend ways and means by which the administration could help investors to make up their minds. Furthermore, Mr. Truman asked the Rockefeller study group to address themselves "specifically to the consideration of desirable plans to accomplish with maximum dispatch and effectiveness the broad objectives and policies of the Point-Four Program."

The Board, after studying the situation, made several major recommendations:

1. There were some 33 international agencies operating in the economic field and 23 United States agencies with some foreign operations. It was suggested by the Rockefeller group that all the 23 agencies should be unified and centralized into one overall agency, headed by a single administrator, reporting directly to the President.

2. The Board supported the Gray Report that $500 million a year be made available for loan to the countries seeking American technology and machinery but lacking dollars to pay for them.

3. The Board recommended the establishment of an International Development organization to which the United States would contribute $200 million for capital. The organization's operation should be international under the management of the International Bank in Washington.

4. The flow of capital to the rest of the world should be tripled. In order to accomplish this objective, tax incentives and bilateral treaties guaranteeing the protection of the private capital and convertibility of their profits were suggested:

> At present, return from investments abroad after all taxes are deducted are not sufficient to offset the great risks of business failure under strange conditions, exchange risks and other extraordinary risks of foreign investment. This is especially true in view of the counter-attraction of domestic investment, which offers high returns and less risks. Moreover, the payment of the United States tax on top of foreign taxes, puts the United States company operating abroad at a competitive disadvantage against local and other foreign companies.[8]

5. Income from foreign investments abroad should be free of the United States tax to the extent necessary to stimulate the flow of private capital to underdeveloped areas. In the

case of corporations, the Board recommended the adoption of the principle of taxing income from business establishments abroad only in the country where the income is obtained. To ensure the investors, Congress should authorize in bilateral tax treaties a provision that would guarantee this principle.

6. The Board recommended that commercial treaties between the United States and all the countries seeking investments from the United States should be negotiated. In these commercial treaties the following points, stated by Congress in the Act for International Action, should be recognized:

> Capital investment can make a maximum contribution to economic development only where there is understanding of the mutual advantage of such investment and where there is confidence ... and respect for the legitimate interests of the peoples of the countries in which the investment is made and of the countries from which the investments are derived ... It involves confidence on the part of investors that they will not be deprived of their property without prompt adequate and effective compensation, that they will be given reasonable opportunity to remit their earnings and withdraw their capital, that they will have reasonable freedom to manage, operate and control their enterprises, that they will enjoy security in the protection of their person and property, including industrial and personal property and non-discriminatory treatment in taxation and in the conduct of their business affairs.[9]

7. The Board did not recommend insurance of the capital invested abroad by it but suggested that $100 million of the loan and guarantee authorization of Export-Import Bank be earmarked to "underwrite for a fee the transfer risk on new foreign debt obligations purchased by private United States investors."[10]

8. In the opinion of the members of the Board one of the greatest obstacles to foreign investment in many countries was the lack of local capital; therefore it was suggested:

> Create an International Finance Corporation as an affiliate of the

International Bank with authority to make loans in local and foreign currencies to private enterprise without the requirement of government guarantees and also to make non-voting equity investment in local currencies a participation with private investors. This proposal should be viewed as a means not only of making capital available initially for foreign enterprises but also as a means of arousing interest in a particular foreign country for investment in business.[11]

The Rockefeller Study tried to confirm the ideas expressed in the Economic Cooperation Act of 1948 the purpose of which was "to promote world peace and the general welfare, national interests, and foreign policy of the United States through economic, financial, and other measures necessary to the maintenance of conditions abroad in which free institutions may survive and consistent with the maintenance of the strength and stability of the United States."[12]

The United States emerged from World War II as the strongest economic power in the world. The heavy infusion of government spending and private capital investment during the war period successfully extricated the national economy from the depression of the 1930's and turned the United States into an arsenal for the nations fighting against Germany and Japan. In the decade 1938-48, the United States gross national product had nearly tripled while its exports had quadrupled. Of all the major industrial powers of 1939, only the United States survived the war with its industrial plants intact and its productive capacity immensely expanded.

The period between 1945 and 1952 confronted the Truman Administration with a number of significant policy issues:

1. There was great concern that, if the rest of the world could not regain its economic health, there would be a sharp drop in the demand for American goods which would result in a severe recession or depression.

2. There was also great fear over the future of Western Europe and the development of stable governments in the war-ravaged countries of Europe. This second concern was significantly heightened as the Soviet aggressive intention in Eastern Europe became apparent. Communism was seen as a monolithic movement antithetical to U.S. interests and institutions.

The governmental measures to alleviate some of the economic problems of Western Europe through the Marshall Plan was helpful but not enough. The underlying rationale of the Marshall Plan was that growing and expanding economies raised the probability that stable governments would evolve. A growing economy provides expanded resources for government operations as well as lowering political dissatisfaction among the population. "This accelerated economic growth was to be accomplished by a massive capital infusion into Europe to replace capital destroyed during the war.

"This infusion of capital goods was to be supplied by the United States thereby helping to hold up the postwar demand level in the United States domestic economy. In the longer run the rebirth of the economies of Europe and Japan also held the prospect for a greater expansion of world trade."[3] The development of world trade and a private investment system to support it were part of the long-run recovery process in Europe and Japan.

The motivations of the United States in establishing the Marshall Plan and the private investment policy in Europe and Asia are still being argued. "It is enough for our purposes here to record that the United States undertook a major program—economic, political and military—designed to aid the U.S. economy in its transition to peace-time production, and forestall any plans by the Soviet Union to directly or indirectly absorb the countries of Western Europe."[4]

The centerpiece of this strategy was first the Marshall Plan and then the private investments which led to multinational corporations.

The initial program of private investment and the government guarantee was modest in scope and the U.S. Government only guaranteed equity convertibility. Only twelve corporations applied in the first year. Later, as a result of Gordon Gray's Report, the guarantee was extended to loss through expropriation or confiscation. In 1951 the guarantee program was revised and attached to the Mutual Securities Act of that year. But, despite all these steps, the private investors' response was both slow and inadequate; therefore President Truman established another study group, the Paley Commission.

On January 22, 1951, President Truman appointed a commission to study the natural resource needs of the United States and their relation to the industrial development and trade expansion of friendly nations. On June 2, 1952, William S. Paley, the Chairman of the Commission, submitted to the White House a comprehensive five-volume report entitled *Resources for Freedom*. The report discussed the resource needs of the United States industries up to the year 1975, the availability of materials, the possibility of a shortage of certain natural resources in the near future, the problems of private investments in foreign countries, opportunities for domestic and foreign trade, the supply of energy for economic growth, and technology and investment opportunities. Furthermore, the Commission's report elaborated on some of the real problems faced by investors in natural resources:

> In almost all foreign countries minerals can be extracted only after obtaining government permission. In countries where the subsoil is owned by the state, the government concedes the privilege of working government property. In other countries although the owner of the surface enjoys some rights in the subsoil, the privilege

of mining or drilling depends on contractual permission from the state.[15]

Then the report continued with the explanation of how the investors' rights depended on a concession which the host government could terminate at will. In most countries the investors had to face the problem of management, employment, the convertibility of their profits, and arbitrary taxation.

The Commission recommended investment treaties between the United States Government and the recipients of private investments. The insurance of private investment was also suggested.

In areas of taxation the Commission proposed that:

1. The corporation be permitted to elect annually between the per-country and overall limitation, or the foreign tax credit.

2. The income of overseas branches be exempt from taxation until the income was remitted to the United States.

3. Foreign subsidiaries of the multinational corporations be allowed to file consolidated returns as domestic corporations.

4. The expending of capital costs in resources be permitted investors in foreign subsidiaries by obtaining a credit against dividends received.

The Commission also gave consideration to the question of exempting foreign income from United States tax, but decided against it.

Before any significant action could be taken on the Paley Report, the Truman Administration was replaced by the Eisenhower Administration, which transferred all the foreign aid programs to the new Foreign Operations Administration. With only 53 contracts for convertibility guarantees written, totaling $39.6 million, with expropriation guarantees totaling only $1.6 million, and applications pending totaling a mere $69.2 million, the program was still in its take-off stage and very few big corporations were ready to risk their capital abroad. Insurance by the Federal Government had been written only for 17 countries, 13 of them in Europe.

On August 7, 1953, at the request of the Eisenhower Administration, a Commission of Foreign Economic Policy was established consisting of five Senators, five Representatives, and five Presidential appointees. Clarence B. Randall was appointed Chairman, and Lamar Fleming, Jr., Vice--Chairman. The duties of the Commission were:

"To examine, study, and report on the subject of International Trade and on enlargement consistent with a sound domestic economy, our foreign economic policy, and the trade aspects of our national security and total foreign policy, and to recommend appropriate policies, measures, and practices."[16]

The Commission made a trip to Europe to obtain firsthand information concerning the capital needs of Western Europe. Inside the United States the Commission had 27 long meetings and heard 64 witnesses. Several study groups were established by the Randall Commission to interview businessmen and experts and to prepare papers for publication.

The Eisenhower Administration was careful to draw the members of both commission and study groups from the ranks of the internationalists and economic isolationists. It insisted that a compromise report acceptable to both groups should be produced. But to nobody's surprise, the Commission members could not resolve their differences and, as a result, the report bristles with majority and minority statements.

The Commission first recommended that the foreign aid and technical assistance programs be continued. As far as private investment abroad was concerned, the Commission

believed that it was too little, and therefore it suggested that
steps must be taken to increase the flow of capital from the
United States to friendly nations.

The Commission thought that the reason for the small
flow of private capital abroad was the concern of investors
over the unstable political, economic, and military situations
in Western Europe and other areas of the world. These
difficulties could be overcome if the foreign countries would
provide a secure "legal status for private capital and enterprise, domestic as well as foreign. United States investors can
hardly be expected to venture into countries' aid fields which
local capital and enterprise consider unattractive or insecure.
On the other hand, the United States investors will venture
into areas with political and economic stability which provide
fair and equitable treatment—and with it—an opportunity for
reasonable profit and assurance of remitting earnings."[17]

The Randall Commission also recommended:

1. That the U.S. Government continue to use the treaty
approach to establish rules for the protection of investments.

2. That the United States Anti-Trust laws acknowledge the
rights of each nation to regulate trade within its own borders;
but it should be made clear to all the countries hoping to get
private American investments that any laws restricting production or marketing arrangements would discourage the
United States businessmen in investing abroad.

3. The United States Government should establish a new
policy placing primary reliance on private investments for
assisting economic development abroad. Furthermore, the
Government should reduce the spending of tax money and
convince the foreign countries that the era of free aid was
over.

4. The Government, through a tax reduction of 14 percent, must encourage American corporations to invest in the
countries where the climate for capital investment is favor-

able. Removal of certain restrictions on the foreign tax credit should be given serious consideration. The 10 percent ownership requirement for crediting the foreign taxes of a foreign corporation should be eliminated. The interpretation of "in lieu of" income taxes must be liberalized and the overall limitation on foreign tax credit should be eliminated.

5. The Commission also recommended that the corporations be allowed the option of treating any direct foreign investment, either as a branch or subsidiary, for United States tax purposes.

6. The program of guarantee of "expropriation or convertibility of exchange be given a further period of trial and, during this period, guaranty coverage on a discretionary basis should be authorized against the risk of war, revolution and insurrection of new investments abroad."

7. The Commission also believed that the International Bank and the Export-Import Bank had an important role to play in financing the development of Western Europe and Japan. In cases of urgent political need for foreign financial assistance it was suggested that Export-Import loans be authorized, "although the risks might not be strictly bankable."

8. It was recommended that tariffs or import restrictions on raw materials should be determined on economic grounds. "The most effective contribution which the United States Government can make to the development of foreign sources of raw materials in which we, and the free nations are deficient generally, is to follow policies favorable to private investment abroad and to advocate among nations adherence to principles and practices hospitable to foreign investors."[18]

The Commission emphasized that the problem of tariff policy in the United States is directly and indirectly related to investments abroad.

Concerning trade with Communist nations, the Commission suggested that as long as it did not jeopardize the military security the United States should not object to trade between the West and the Soviet Bloc. They favored an embargo on goods sent to China and North Korea.

9. The Commission recommended direct subsidy to the merchant marine so that American shipping would be able to compete with foreign countries.

10. The Commission recommended that certain measures be taken to encourage the expenditures of American tourists in Western Europe and Japan.

Another important report on American investments abroad was the Report of the National Industrial Conference Board prepared by J. Frank Gaston at the request of the President's Committee for Financing Foreign Trade. This report was different from the other reports because it was based entirely upon a survey of 178 corporations representing about 90 percent of the direct foreign investments by American companies. Sixty percent of the companies responded to the survey and the results were published in April, 1951.

According to the results of the survey the problems facing the investors ranked in the following order:

1. Exports or import quotas.
2. Limitations on remittance of profits and convertibility.
3. Control of the capital investments by the recipient countries.
4. A genuine need for social legislation.
5. Lack of trained native administrators and technical staff.
6. Lack of roads, harbors, railroads, storage facilities, housing, hospitals, and shopping facilities for employees.
7. Multiple exchange rates.
8. Inadequate power facilities for the new industries.
9. Foreign restrictions on importation of personnel from investor countries.
10. Instability of regimes, fear of nationalization and expropriation.
11. Unequal treatment before the law with respect to property holdings, etc.
12. Requirement for reinvestment of earnings. (It should be pointed out that in all countries only .09 percent mentioned the require-

ment for reinvestment of earnings. There was a breakdown by regions and the highest percentage of companies reporting the problem was for Asia: 1.2 percent.)

There was variation in the ranking of these factors according to countries, though export and import quotas were rated first for every area; limitation on remittance of profits was second for all but Africa (where it ranked third), with a lack of trained personnel being ranked second. Of the all countries group, 51.4 percent reported export and import quotas as problems—the eighth ranking factor; inadequacy of housing was reported by 9.9 percent of the groups.

Three of the first four problems, export-import quotas, limitations on remittance profits and control of capital movements, were all sub-parts of the foreign exchange controls section in the questionnaire. The fourth, burden of social security legislation, was among the labor problems; the fifth, lack of trained personnel, was also under the labor problem subheading. It was interesting to discover that 21 percent reported no problems with regard to their investments.

Despite all the proliferation of recommendations, Presidential messages, and policy papers, private capital outflow between 1950 and 1955 was only 10 percent higher (in constant dollars) than it was in the period 1924-1929. Furthermore, most of this capital was invested in petroleum, bauxite, lumber, and other mineral resources in Canada, Latin America and the Middle East.[19]

The Eisenhower Administration, in response to many requests from Europe and Japan, on March 30, 1954, and January 10, 1955 sent two messages to Congress asking for additional authorization to encourage the flow of private investments from the United States:

The whole free world needs capital; America is its largest source. In that light, the flow of capital abroad from our country must be stimulated and in such a manner that it results in investment largely by individuals or private enterprise rather than by the government.

An increased flow of United States' private investment funds abroad, especially to the underdeveloped areas, could contribute much to the expansion of two-way international trade. The underdeveloped countries would thus be enabled to acquire more easily the capital equipment so badly needed by them to achieve sound economic growth and higher living standards. This would do much to offset the false but alluring promises of the Communists.[1][2]

The Eisenhower policy in regard to foreign assistance was based mainly on private investments. To achieve fruitful results, the President emphasized maximum freedom and facilities for investments abroad. The rationale behind this policy was that the free flow of private investment, instead of foreign aid, across national boundaries is beneficial to the United States and to the world economy. Furthermore, it was believed that "the international investment process was improving the world's allocation of resources to the mutual benefit of parent, host, and other countries. Foreign investment also contributes to U.S. national income and helps stimulate U.S. exports".[2][1]

Notes

1. Mira Wilkıns, *The Emergence of Multinational Enterprise: American Business Abroad from the Colonial Era to 1914.* Cambridge: Harvard University Press, 1970, p. 23.

2. *U.S. Branch Factories Abroad,* Senate Document No. 258., 71st Congress, 3rd Session. 1931, Table 4.

3. Douglas C. Abbott, Canadian Minister of Finance, in a speech made in Washington, D.C., September 7, 1949, *New York Times,* September 8, 1949.

4. *New York Times,* October 31, 1949.

5. A report of National Association of Manufacturers, *Capital Export Potentialities after 1952,* New York, March, 1949.

6. Gordon Gray, *Report to the President on Foreign Economic Policies,* U.S. Government Printing Office, Washington, D.C. November 10, 1950, pp. 61, 62.

7. Ibid, p. 62.

8. Nelson A. Rockefeller, *Partners in Progress, A Report to the President* by the U.S. International Development Advisory Board, March, 1951, p. 79.

9. Ibid, p. 81.

10. Ibid, p. 82.

11. Ibid, p. 83.

12. *Report of the Committee on Foreign Relations, United States Senate*, 93rd Congress, First Session, October 17, 1973: Government Printing Office, Washington, 1973.

13. Ibid, p. 2.

14. Ibid, p. 3.

15. William S. Paley, *Resources for Freedom*, A Report to the President, Vol. I, June, 1952, pp. 64-65.

16. E. R. Barlow and Ira Wender: *Foreign Investment and Taxation*, Englewood Cliffs, N.J., Prentice-Hall, Inc., 1955, p. 86.

17. Clarence B. Randall, *Commission on Foreign Economic Policy*, "Report to the President and the Congress," Jan., 1954, pp. 18-19.

18. Ibid, p. 40.

19. Raymond F. Mikesell, *Promoting United States Investment Abroad*, National Planning Association, Washington D.C., 1957, p. 2.

20. *The President's Message to Congress*, January 10, 1955.

21. Janet Bancroft, Congressional Research Service, *The Multinational Corporation*, Library of Congress, December 20, 1972. p. 8. See also *United States International Economic Policy in an Interdependent World*. Report to the President submitted by the Commission on International Trade and Investment Policy, Washington D. C. July, 1971, p. 173.

2.
The Evolution of the Multinational Corporations

The reasons or underlying motives for the rapid growth of United States direct investments abroad during the later 1950's, apart from the Eisenhower Administration's encouragement, were numerous and they varied according to the type of investment. To clarify other factors underlying investment decisions in this area it is helpful to classify direct investments abroad by function:

1. Investments to develop foreign sources of raw materials and semi-manufacturers for American industry: petroleum, bauxite, iron ore and other minerals; primary metals; wood pulp and newsprint; and other industrial commodities including products of tropical agriculture.

2. Investments to promote the distribution and sale in foreign markets of goods produced in the United States or by direct-investment enterprises such as those of the petroleum companies in the Middle East.

3. Investments to provide services in foreign countries. These include direct investments in public utilities, transportation and communication, hotels, and various other service industries.

4. Investment in foreign manufacturing enterprises.[1]

Major factors, aside from the pressures and promises of the Truman and Eisenhower Administrations, to induce United States corporations to establish or expand manufacturing facilities in foreign countries, included the following realities:

1. Tariffs, import quotas, and currency controls which, especially before 1960, severely limited foreign markets for American-produced consumer goods.

2. Reduced transportation rates on locally produced goods and, in some cases—especially in the United Kingdom and Germany—substantially lower costs of production.

3. Excess capacity in most of the durable goods industries of this country which led many firms to look to foreign lands for more attractive investment opportunities.

4. Anticipation of higher profits from manufacturing enterprises in countries whose economies have been growing at a much more rapid rate than that of the United States.

5. Foreign trade barriers. The creation of a European Economic Community, and desire to benefit from the elimination of internal tariffs in an expanding market area.

6. The international role of the U.S. dollar. Restriction of nonresident convertibility for the major European currencies in 1958 which greatly facilitated the mobility of capital.

7. Foreign consumer preference for simplified models of various durable goods less expensive than those produced for sale within the United States.

8. Patent laws which, in some countries, require firms to manufacture locally in order to obtain patent protection and to achieve the legal status necessary to assert infringement claims.

9. Lower corporation income taxes and more generous depreciation allowances in certain countries; in some cases special tax and other financial inducements to stimulate the inflow of direct-investment capital.

10. A need to diversify product lines to avoid fluctuations in earnings.

11. The impact of antitrust laws on U.S. industry.[2]

The Eisenhower Administration also concluded that the fundamental forces impelling corporations to invest abroad were stability, security, and the quest for profit and the fear that their present or prospective market position would be lost to Western Europe and Japan. Therefore, every effort was made to make the climate favorable to investments abroad and to convince the investors of opportunities of an optimum return on their capital within a reasonable time period. Certain industries which by nature were international seized upon this opportunity and very quickly moved into areas where prospects were good and whose resources were essential to the development of industries in the United States and her allies.[3]

The effects of the direct investments abroad on the United States economy and their political impact do not lend themselves to facile or simple measurement. "The process established a vast complex of enterprises abroad; and producing with these facilities, new streams of goods and services," according to the U.S. Department of Commerce, "necessarily alters in many direct and indirect ways the existing structure of international transactions as well as that of domestic economics."[4]

The significant impact of the multinational corporations is in the internationalization of production and in the incipient development of a world economy. In this process the investment decisions and operations of companies are increasingly viewed in terms of world allocations of resources and of maximizing world welfare. The international corporations since the 1950's have become the most important vehicle for developing an economic system based on a more rational allocation of resources than has been the case in the past. It has also helped the development of resources in the developing nations. They have created a market for their raw materials, accelerated industrial growth, and helped in raising living standards in many countries. A good example is the development of the oil industry in the Middle East, Latin America, Africa, and Indonesia. The capital, technology, and market provided by the multinational corporations are responsible for the present extraordinary income, the affluence, and the industrial development of most of these nations.

"The internationalization of production brought about by the development of the multinational corporations is regarded by many analysts as the most important event to have occurred in many years and very likely its ultimate impact would be on a par with the industrial revolution of the 18th century. What is called into question by this development—which is likely to continue—is the whole concept of the traditional nation-state with its politics, sociology, and economics. In fact, the analytical implications of the development of the international company requires a rethinking and restructuring of our modes of thought."[5]

The traditional economic wisdom passed down to us by Adam Smith and David Ricardo taught us that commodities move internationally while production factors are very nation-minded. The Ricardian theory of comparative costs as developed by Hecksher and Ohlin[6] to apply to nation states concluded that a country tends to export those goods which use intensively the country's abundant production factors and import those goods which use intensively the country's scarce factors. Hecksher and Ohlin argued that trade tends to equalize the relative returns to land, labor, and capital throughout the world.

Empirical testing of traditional theory has led to increasing doubts of its relevance to actual developments in international trade and investment. For instance: 1) Leontief found that United States exports were heavily labor-intensive [7] (the U.S. scarce factor): 2) in some cases free trade has actually widened the margin between factor prices; and, 3) there has been a continually increasing mobility of the factors of production assumed immobile in classical theory. The patent inability of the traditional model to explain the pattern of trade in manufactured goods, or the diffusion of comparative advantages through the investment process, necessitates theoretical models more applicable to present reality.

The multinational corporation has caused international production to outstrip foreign trade as the main channel of international economic relations in terms of size, rate of growth, and future potential. Following World War II, Western Europe, and many nations in Latin America, Asia and Africa welcomed investments from abroad of almost any kind. The multinational corporation broke through the walls of the nation state. The International Monetary Fund, the International Bank of Reconstruction and Development, the General Agreement on Tariffs and Trade, the Organization for Economic Cooperation and Development, and the United Nations Conference for Trade and Development have all advocated the liberalization of capital. The United States Government, as covered *supra*, sought policies to increase private investment abroad.

Over the last two decades the concurrent growth of the multinational corporations and the rise of nationalism in many countries have brought to the fore conflicting schools of thought that rest on varying assumptions and conclusions as to what determines the massive growth of international investment and what course it is likely to follow.

Professor Robert Gilpin of Princeton University groups the theoretical work of several economists into three sets of contrasting dichotomies:

1. Those who are for the multinational corporation and those who are against it.
2. Those who consider the multinational corporations as naturally evolving from economic and technological developments and those who emphasize public policies' role in the development of the multinational corporation.
3. Those who believe the multinational corporations are essentially defensive or market-protecting and those who believe the multinational corporations are more agressive or using monopolistic advantage to exploit markets.[8]

The three categorizations are not mutually exclusive. The pro- and anti-multinational arguments, as they relate to labor, technology, taxes, and the balance of payments, are dealt with in subsequent chapters. Professor Gilpin, in presenting the dichotomy of natural economic developments leading to multinationalism vis-à-vis internationalism resulting from public policies, combines some of the diverse present theories of multinationalism.

The Economic Position

Starting with the assumption that the growth of multinational corporations and direct investment are the result of the economic perception of protected markets (e.g., Common Market) and technological advances in transportation and communication, the question arises: Why is there direct investment as opposed to exports and licencing? The problem is one of integrating trade patterns with the investment process.

Four theories are developed that may partially act in

concert: 1. The theory of international oligopoly; 2. The product life-cycle theory; 3. The organic theory of investment; and 4. The currency boundary theory.

The first theory, that of international oligopoly, has been developed by Charles Kindleberger and Stephen Hymer. Stephen Hymer in his M.I.T. thesis on "The International Operations of national firms"[9] viewed direct investment as belonging to the theory of monopolistic competition rather than that of international capital movements. The large, mainly American-based firms take advantage of advanced technology, patents, special access to large amounts of capital, advertising, or some other advantages such as superior management. The main condition stimulating the direct investment of firms is that a firm must be able to make a higher income stream abroad than it could at home, and it must be able to make a higher income stream abroad than other local firms can earn in their own markets.

> Until recently, most multinational corporations have been from the United States. Now European corporations, as a by-product of increased size, and as a reaction to the American invasion of Europe, are also shifting attention from national to global production and beginning to "see the world as their oyster." If the present trend continues multinationalization is likely to increase greatly in the next decade as giants from both sides of the Atlantic (though still mainly from the U.S.) strive to penetrate each other's markets and to establish bases in underdeveloped countries, where there are few indigenous concentrations of capital sufficiently large enough to operate on a world scale. This rivalry may be intense at first but will probably abate through time and turn into collusion as firms approach some kind of oligopolistic equilibrium. A new structure of international organization and a new international division of labor will have been born.[10]

Overlapping the oligopolistic theory is the "product-cycle" model as developed by Raymond Vernon[11] to further theoretically explain direct investment and market penetration on the part of large multinationals. The basic model identifies a number of phases beginning with the introduction of a product whereby market requirements outweigh profit maximization and labor costs. Exportation of a home-produced product develops a foreign demand but diffusion of technology may shift the advantage to potential foreign competition. Depending mainly on the size of the foreign market which develops and the tariff walls involved, direct foreign investment by multinationals will follow, and subsequently home exports will decline. As subsidiaries develop an efficiency of production, they in turn will be able to undersell the original home producers in their own country. Finally, the less developed countries with lower labor costs will become exporters of mature products. This last phase, as noted by Hirsch, will occur more likely where the product involved requires relatively little engineering, scientific, and managerial skill.[12]

The product-cycle model of investment behavior by multinationals is thus essentially defensive as the threatened loss of an export market and the rise of foreign competitors is the all-powerful stimulus for the establishment of foreign subsidiaries. Whereas, the oligopolistic theory of Kindleberger and Hymer is an aggressive theory of direct investment.

The third theory, the organic theory of investment, holds that a corporation invests abroad to maintain its position in a growing market. To maintain the profitability of existing investments, it is necessary to undertake new investments. To stop the outflow of investments not only cuts off future returns, but will undercut the present rate of return on investments. This position is one favored by the National Industrial Conference Board; that is, continued growth is a precondition to economic survival of the multinationals in an oligopolistic market. As the market expands, the firm operating abroad must also expand to maintain its position. In this view the creation of the Common Market necessitated the continued expansion of the American multinational, as a defensive strategy, to protect the home investments as well as foreign investments. As noted by Kindleberger, "the economist tends to be skeptical in the face of such an argument, but it is easy to understand how businessmen feel this way." [13]

The final theory as presented by Professor Gilpin is that multinationals cross national boundaries, taking advantage of secure currencies and exchange rates. Entrepreneurs from secure currency areas have an advantage over local enterprise and can, therefore, afford to pay more for real assets. Thus the international role of the U.S. dollar facilitated foreign investment, and may have been supplemented by an over-valued exchange rate, as was the case with the U.S. dollar in the late 1960's.

The Public Policy Position

On the other hand, whereas the above theories take into account economic and technological forces that motivate direct foreign investment, many have argued that the large movement of American capital to foreign-based subsidiaries is a result of governmental action or inaction. Thus the multinationals expand abroad to enhance their own growth and profits, minimizing their tax liabilities through deferral and foreign tax credit, and their culpability to U.S. antitrust laws.

The earnings of foreign subsidiaries of U.S. corporations generally are not subject to U.S. tax until repatriated as dividends. The basic concept, since 1913, has been that the United States has no jurisdiction to tax foreign corporations except on their income from sources within the United States or on income effectively connected with U.S. activities. Also since 1918, subject to certain limitations, a U.S. parent company may credit, against the U.S. corporate income tax imposed on foreign dividends from a subsidiary corporation, foreign income taxes attributable to the dividends distributed plus any foreign withholding taxes on them.[14]

Robert Gilpin argues that "a favorable tax policy is the critical factor in the high rate of American foreign investment abroad."[15] The high rate of foreign investment by American corporations is largely the consequence of an imperfect capital market abetted by present tax laws."[16]

The arguments for and against public policies designed to encourage or discourage direct investment abroad are included in subsequent chapters. Here the public policy question is raised very briefly as a theoretical explanation for the growth of U.S. foreign direct investment. It may be concluded that theories of direct investment are varied and largely in the formative state. Hopefully, the ever increasing interest in the growth of multinationals will generate a refinement of theories underlying their expansion.

There is no agreed definition of what constitutes a multinational corporation. Some authorities define it as a company whose foreign sales have reached a ratio of 25 percent of total sales. Others look to the distribution of ownership, the global products, and the mixed nationalities of management as the determining characteristics.

According to Professor Raymond Vernon of Harvard University, the definition of a multinational corporation is applied to any institution which tries "to carry out its activities on an international scale, as though there were no national boundaries, on the basis of a common strategy directed from a corporate center." Jacques Maisonrouge, President of IBM World Trade Corporation, defines the multinational corporation as one which: (a) operates in many countries; (b) carries out research, development and manufacturing in those countries; (c) has a multinational management; and (d) has multinational stock ownership.[17]

The Office of Foreign Direct Investment lists over 3,000 U.S. companies as multinational corporations.[18] *Fortune* Magazine's list of the 500 largest U.S. and the 200 largest foreign corporations includes the most important multinational corporations. In 1965 over 80 U.S. companies had over 25 percent or more of their assets, earnings, production, and employment overseas and 199 companies had 10 percent or more.[19] See Appendix B, Tables 1 and 2 for a detailed listing.

A study of multinational corporations' investments by the Organization for Economic Cooperation and Development (OECD) indicates that in terms of book value at the end of 1966, there was close to $90 billion in overseas direct investments by Belgium, Canada, France, Germany, Italy, Japan, the Netherlands, Sweden, Switzerland, the United Kingdom, and the United States. According to a study of the Senate Finance Committee there is roughly a two-to-one relationship between output and asset values. Applying this ratio to the $90 billion the total value of international production associated with this direct investment for 1966 would appear to be around $180 billion. If one adds to this portfolio investment in foreign countries, associated output rises to $240 billion. In comparison the $130 billion in exports from these countries is dwarfed by the output of their overseas holdings.[20]

Looking at the United States alone, direct investments in 1966 were $54.4 billion, approximately 60 percent of the total given by the OECD study. By 1973, preliminary figures indicate the book value of United States direct investment abroad has risen to $107 billion. Total private long-term investments including stocks and bonds in 1973 were $143 billion. If one uses the two-to-one ratio, here again United States exports of $70 billion in 1973 are dwarfed by four times as much output associated with United States output associated with production abroad.[21]

Another significance of the multinational corporation is the fact that since 1968, net foreign investment income has been much greater than net receipts from the trade account. This shift, as compared to the earlier 1960's has resulted from the decrease in our export surplus and continued increase in investment income. In 1960 there was a $4.9 billion net balance on the trade account and a $0.5 billion net balance on the direct foreign investment account. By 1970 the export surplus from trade was $2.1 billion while the net income from investments abroad reached $3.5 billion.[22]

In 1973 the net inflow of funds to the United States resulting from United States corporate transactions abroad, including additions to the direct investment, other capital account changes, and direct ownership benefits was $6.9 billion, down $0.9 from the 1972 record. Whereas export surplus in 1973 amounted to $0.8 billion and in 1972 there was a deficit of $6.9 billion.[23]

In 1973 net capital outflows from the United States came to $4.9 billion and reinvested earnings were $8.1 billion, while net earnings of foreign-incorporated affiliates plus foreign branches came to $17.5 billion. These figures represent an increase from 1972 in net capital outflows of $1.4 billion, in reinvested earnings of $3.4 billion and, adding to two together, the increase in direct investment is $4.8 billion, whereas net earnings increased $6 billion from 1972 to 1973. It should be noted, however, that the difference between the 1972 and 1973 figures reflect the influence of the dollar devaluation and that the rise in petroleum earnings was particularly steep due to restrictions in supply and concurrent growth in demand.[24]

In terms of location, United States private direct investments were spread throughout the world:

(In billions of dollars and percent of total)

	1960	1965	1973
Western Europe	6.7	14.0	37.2
percent	21.0	28.0	34.7
Canada	11.2	15.3	28.1
percent	35.0	31.0	26.2
Latin America	8.3	10.9	18.5
percent	26.0	22.0	17.2
Japan	0.3	0.7	2.7
percent	1.0	1.0	2.5
Other	5.4	8.6	20.8
percent	17.0	18.0	19.4
Total	31.9	49.5	107.3
percent	100.0	100.0	100.0

Source: Survey of Current Business, November 1972, Vol. 52, Number 11, pp. 21-34 and September, 1973, Vol. 53, Number 9, pp. 21-34 and August, 1974, Part II, p. 5.

The growth of private investments abroad since 1929 shows the largest proportionate increases going to Europe, the Middle East, Africa and Oceania, with smaller proportionate growth in Canada. The most dramatic percentage decrease was in United States direct investments to Latin America, which dropped from 46.7 percent in 1929 to 26 percent in 1960 and to 17.2 percent in 1973.

Canada still continues to be the largest single recipient of United States investment by a wide margin; but its share has decreased from 35 percent in 1960 to 26.2 percent in 1973. The concentration of United States investments in Canada has caused some resentment leading to the Gray Report, the creation of a government screening body, and to Prime Minister Trudeau's remark that "living next to the United States is like sleeping with an elephant."

The small and relatively unchanged amount of United States capital in Japan up until the 1970's is not a result of a lack of interest by the American corporations. Rather it reflects the restrictions imposed by the Japanese Government for fear of control of their business enterprises by outsiders, and the special problems foreign corporations would present in an economy with such a close interrelationship of labor, business and government.[25] These restrictions have been relaxed somewhat in 1972 and 1973.

United States direct investment by industry groupings was divided accordingly:

(In billions of dollars and percent of total)

	1971	1972	1973
Mining & smelting	6.7	7.1	7.5
percent	7.8	7.5	7.0
Petroleum	24.2	26.3	29.6
percent	28.1	27.9	27.6
Manufacturing	35.6	39.7	45.8
percent	41.3	42.1	42.7
Other industries	19.7	21.2	24.4
percent	22.8	22.5	22.7

Source: Survey of Current Business, September 1973, pp. 26-27 and August, 1974, Part II, pp. 16-17.

There were record increases in 1973 in each of the industry groups shown: petroleum, $3.3 billion, or 13 percent; in manufacturing, $6.1 billion, or 15 percent; and in "other industries" (mostly trade, finance, and insurance, public utilities and agriculture), $3.2 billion, or 15 percent.

Of the 1973 addition to petroleum direct investment, $2.2 billion was in developed countries, a 16 percent rise, resulting from the continuing response of United States petroleum companies to growing worldwide demand for energy and petrochemical feedstocks. Substantial expenditures were made to diversify sources of supply and accelerate development of new fields, also.

In terms of the rates of return by industrial grouping of United States direct investment petroleum earnings were up 87 percent in 1973 to $6.2 billion. Large gains were recorded in both developed countries, where the main markets are located, and in developing countries, where most of the production for export occurs.

The earnings ratio of the multinational corporations declined fairly steadily during the 1950's and 1960's from a high of 19 percent in 1951 to a low of 9.5 percent in 1967. Since that time, however, the trend has reversed in both developing and developed countries rates of return. In 1973 total earnings rose to $17.5 billion compared to a book value of $107.3 billion, giving an earnings ratio of 16.3 percent.[26]

The relaxation of the Interest Equalization Tax and the Office of Foreign Direct Investment controls[27] may well lead to the continued expansion of United States direct investment while at the same time permitting foreign investors to look to the United States markets as well, encouraged by the dollar devaluations and the potential expansion of American markets.

American corporations in 1970 invested more than six times as much on domestic operations than on foreign operations, but gradually that ratio is being reduced. And foreign corporations are increasing their foreign investment in the United States.

Foreign investments in the United States in 1973 were $163.1 billion of which $62.2 billion were in private long-term investments, $92.6 billion were in liquid assets, and the rest in nonliquid, short-term assets. Direct investments from abroad of $17.7 billion were only 28.5 percent of total private long-term investments, reflecting a preference in Europe for portfolio and other relatively liquid investments.[28] This preference, however, appears subject to change.

While foreign direct investment in the United States is still a small portion of private long-term investments as compared to U.S. direct investment (see Exhibit 1 and 2, p.56), in 1973 the value of foreign direct investment in the United States rose a record $3.5 billion, or 24 percent to $17.7 billion.

Foreign direct investment in the United States by country of origin is divided accordingly:

(In billions of dollars and percent of total)

	1971	1972	1973
United Kingdom	4.4	4.6	5.4
percent	32.1	32.2	30.6
Canada	3.3	3.4	4.0
percent	24.1	23.8	22.6
Netherlands	2.2	2.3	2.5
percent	16.1	16.1	14.1
Switzerland	1.5	1.6	1.8
percent	11.0	11.2	10.2
Germany	0.8	0.9	0.8
percent	5.8	6.3	4.5
Other Europe	1.1	1.1	1.6
percent	8.0	7.7	9.0
Other	0.4	0.4	1.6
percent	2.9	2.7	9.0
Total	13.7	14.3	17.7
percent	100.0	100.0	100.0

Source: derived from *Survey of Current Business*, August, 1974, Part II, p. 7.

The 1973 increase in foreign direct investment resulted from net capital inflows of $2.5 billion, reinvested earnings of nearly $1.0 billion, and valuation adjustments. Of the net capital inflow $1.3 billion reflects the net balance of payments effect of foreign parents' sales and liquidations of equity in their U.S. affiliates debt transactions between foreign parents and their U.S.-incorporated affiliates, and all transactions between foreign parents and their U.S. branches. The rest resulted from an increase of almost $0.8 billion in equity investments, which reflects a more than $500 million investment by a petroleum-producing country's participation payment to a major U.S. incorporated petroleum company and substantially higher more usual equity investments.[29]

By industrial grouping, of the $17.7 billion foreign direct investment in the United States, 47.4 percent was in manufacturing, 24.9 percent in petroleum and 15.3 percent was in finance and insurance.

Earnings on foreign direct investment totaled $1.8 billion in 1973, up 53 percent from 1972. The rise in earnings of foreign-owned U.S.-incorporated affiliates, coupled with a reduction in their overall dividend payout ratio, resulted in a 91 percent increase in reinvested earnings in 1973.

The dollar devaluations, the depressed stock market and healthy earnings will probably continue to attract foreign investment in the United States particularly if the stock market continues to show strong signs of recovery.

Sales of the United States multinational corporations have been growing almost twice as fast as exports during the past ten years. The Department of Commerce estimates of sales by majority-owned foreign affiliates of United States companies for 1966-1972 show that total sales more than doubled and reached $221 billion in 1972, an average annual rate of growth of 15 percent. Manufacturing was by far the largest dollar increase in sales, particularly in the developed countries.

Sales by United States foreign affiliates were divided by area accordingly:

(In billions of dollars and percent of total)

	1970	1971	1972
Europe	67.9	81.5	97.0
percent	44.0	42.8	43.9
Canada	34.8	42.9	48.7
percent	22.5	22.6	22.0
Latin America	20.7	23.9	26.3
percent	13.4	12.6	11.9
Other developing	12.1	15.2	18.4
percent	7.8	8.0	8.3
Other developed	15.1	20.7	25.1
percent	9.8	10.9	11.4
International	3.8	6.0	5.5
percent	2.5	3.1	2.5

And sales by United States foreign affiliates were divided by industry:

(In billions of dollars and percent of total)

	1970	1971	1972
Manufacturing	77.0	92.6	110.4
percent	49.9	48.7	50.0
Petroleum	42.3	54.9	61.1
percent	27.4	28.9	27.6
Trade	20.2	24.6	29.2
percent	13.1	12.9	13.2
Mining & Smelting	4.7	4.3	4.7
percent	3.0	2.3	2.1
Other	10.2	13.8	15.6
percent	6.6	7.2	7.1
Total	154.5	190.2	221.0
percent	100.0	100.0	100.0

Source: derived from Table I, *Survey of Current Business,* August, 1974, Part II, p. 26.

Local sales accounted for the largest portion of total affiliate sales — 72 percent — in 1972. Exports to the United States were only 7 percent, and exports to other foreign countries 22 percent of the total in 1972.

Several factors underlie this development. As foreign markets grow more sophisticated in their requirements it becomes necessary to tailor products to meet specific markets. This does not mean that these affiliates necessarily limit U.S. exports of that product. Quite the contrary, the presence of U.S. affiliates abroad to complete the final assembly often makes available an outlet for U.S. exports that otherwise would not have existed. The emergence of the multinational corporation has facilitated the development of worldwide markets and sources.[30]

In order to understand the nature of the multinational corporation which will increasingly affect our economy and our way of life during the 1970's and 1980's one must bear in mind some of its distinctive characteristics:

1. Multinational corporations depend heavily on overseas income. There are many U.S. corporations now earning from one-fourth to one-half of their income abroad. The MNC is

sensitive to policies affecting foreign investments which provide return flows of income that are a major positive factor in our balance of payments.

2. The multinational corporation is the only organization which has resources and scope to think, to plan, and to act with world-wide planning of markets and sources. Many international opportunities require capital and technology on a scale only large multinational corporations can effectively supply.

3. The multinational corporation operates across national boundaries; it provides capital, it speeds up the transfer of technology. It hastens changes, creates cooperation, introduces important benefits and, at the same time, accelerates adjustment problems.

4. The development of the multinational corporation has aroused some concern among labor unions. They claim these are major U.S. job losses resulting from these companies which are characterized as job exporters.

Other studies indicate that multinational corporations actually create more domestic jobs than they lose.

5. The multinational corporation is also a source of concern to some governments since, from its wide base, it is often able to influence politics and to circumvent national monetary and fiscal policy.

6. In the United States concern has been indicated about the possibility of distortions arising from price fixing and tax evasion by some of the multinational corporations.

7. Every study points out that multinational corporations tend to be companies that are growing at a much higher rate than any other manufacturing industries in the United States.

However, in spite of these pros and cons, it is clear that these corporations are a major force in expanding both world trade and the United States' role in the world economy. Also multinational corporations are an integral part of our technological and managerial expertise. To seriously restrict the activities of these corporations in their foreign operations would be a major step back from the relatively open and interdependent world the United States has tried to help build.[31]

Exhibit 2-1
United States Investment Abroad
(in billions of dollars
and percent of total)

	1960	1971	1972	1973
Direct				
investment	31.9	86.2	94.3	107.3
percent	71.7	74.4	73.1	74.7
Bonds	5.6	14.7	15.9	16.6
percent	12.6	12.6	12.3	11.6
Stocks	4.0	7.0	9.1	8.6
percent	9.0	6.1	7.1	6.0
Other	3.0	8.0	9.7	11.0
percent	6.8	6.9	7.5	7.7
Total	44.5	115.9	129.0	143.5
percent	100.0	100.0	100.0	100.0

Source: Survey of Current Business, August, 1974, Part II, p. 5.

Exhibit 2-2
Foreign Investment in the United States
(in billions of dollars
and percent of total)

	1960	1971	1972	1973
Direct				
investment	.6.9	13.7	14.3	17.8
percent	37.5	27.5	23.8	28.5
Bonds	0.6	8.6	10.9	11.9
percent	3.3	17.3	18.1	19.1
Stock	9.3	21.4	27.8	24.8
percent	50.5	43.0	46.2	39.9
Other	1.6	6.1	7.2	7.7
percent	8.7	12.2	11.9	12.4
Total	18.4	49.8	60.2	62.2
percent	100.0	100.0	100.0	100.0

Source: Survey of Current Business, August 1974, Part II, p. 5.

NOTES

1. Nasrollah Fatemi, Thibaut DeSaint Phalle, and Grace Keefe, *The Dollar Crisis.* Rutherford, N.J.: Fairleigh Dickinson Press, 1963, p. 163.

2. Ibid., p. 165, & U.S. Department of Commerce, *Policy Aspects of Foreign Investment by U.S. Multinational Corporations,* January, 1972, p. 14.

3. U.S. Department of Commerce, ibid., p. 14.

4. Fatemi, et als, *Dollar Crisis,* p. 166.

5. Office of International Investment, U.S. Department of Commerce, A report to the Secretary, January, 1972.

6. B. Ohlin, *Interregional and International Trade.* Cambridge, Mass.: Harvard University Press, 1935.

7. W. Leontief, "Domestic Production and Foreign Trade: The American Capital Position Reexamined," *Proceedings of the American Philosophical Society,* Vol. 97, Sept. 1953, pp. 332-349.

8. R. Gilpin, *The Multinational Corporation and the National Interest,* prepared for the Committee on Labor and Public Welfare. United States Senate, 93rd Congress, First Session, October, 1973, pp. 1-7.

9. S. H. Hymer, "International Operations of National Firms: A Study of Direct Investment" (doctoral dissertation, M.I.T., 1960).

10. S. H. Hymer, Prepared statement read before the Subcommittee on Foreign Economic Policy of the Joint Economic Committee, 91st Congress, Second Session, 1970, p. 907.

11. R. Vernon, "International Investment and International Trade in the Product Cycle," 80 *Q.J. Econ.* 190, 1966.

12. S. Hirsch, "The United States Electronics Industry in International Trade," in *The Product Life Cycle and International Trade,* L. Wells, ed., Harvard Business School, 1972, p. 50.

13. C. P. Kindleberger, *International Economics,* 4th ed., Richard D. Irwin, Inc., Homewood, Ill., 1968, p. 395.

14. "Multinationals: Perspectives on Trade and Taxes," Committee on Ways and Means, U.S. House of Representatives, 93rd Congress, First Session July, 1973, pp. 2, 6.

15. R. Gilpin, op. cit., p. 5.

16. Ibid., p. 51.

17. Ibid., p. 7.

18. The U.S. Government defines a U.S. multinational as having a U.S. ownership interest of at least 10%.

19. Ibid., p. 8.

20. U.S. Senate Committee on Finance, *Multinational Corporations* (file copy), February 21, 1973, pp. 44-45.

21. *Survey of Current Business,* Part II, August, 1974, p. 5.

22. U.S. Senate Committee on Finance, *Multinational Corporations* (file copy), February 21, 1973, pp. 44-45.

23. *Survey of Current Business,* Part II, August, 1974, p. 17 and Council of Economic Advisors, *International Economic Report of the President,* 1974, p. 96.

24. *Survey of Current Business,* August, 1974, Part II, pp. 11, 19-21.

25. Peter G. Peterson, *The United States in the Changing World Economy* (A report for the President), December 27, 1971, Vol. II, p. 44.

26. Derived from Table 9, *Survey of Current Business,* August, 1974, Part II, p. 16.

27. Presidential Documents, Title 3. The Presidential Executive Order 11766, Modifying Rates of Interest Equalization Tax, January 29, 1974, and Federal Register 74, 3305. Filed February 7, 1974.

28. *Survey of Current Business,* August, 1974, Part II, p. 5.

29. *Survey of Current Business,* August, 1974, Part II, pp. 7-8.

30. Peter G. Peterson, *The United States in the Changing World Economy* (A report for the President), December, 1971, Vol. II, p. 46.

31. Ibid., p. 48.

3.
The Impact of Multinational Corporations on Employment: Labor's View and Counter Views

The rapid growth of world economic integration and the emergence of the multinational corporation have evoked a not surprising response from organized labor, both domestic and international.

Trade unions at a national and international level are carefully considering their response to the new form of economic power represented by multinationals operating across national borders. As capital, managerial skill, and technology become increasingly internationalized, labor unions have developed an increasingly critical attitude of the effects of such flows on the level of domestic employment and other indicators of national economic well-being. The American labor unions are convinced that the activities of the multinational corporations result in the loss of jobs to American workers. "The international nature of these firms, moreover, puts them beyond the reach of collective bargaining and beyond regulatory powers of national government."[1]

American labor unions are not alone in their increasing

wariness. A resolution of the British Trade Union Congress in 1969 called attention to the transformations of British companies into multinationals "which, if not controlled by the extension of social ownership and/or a system of public accountability would create new problems of job security and economic difficulties both now and for the future of the British economy."[2]

Traditionally the labor unions have favored liberal free trade movements since the Reciprocal Trade Agreement of 1934. Little more than a decade ago George Meany, President of the AFL-CIO, appeared before the House Ways and Means Committee to lend his support to what became the Trade Expansion Act of 1962: "We can compete with anyone because we have the skill and know-how to do it."[3]

By contrast, in 1970 Andrew J. Biemiller, Director of the Department of Legislation of the AFL-CIO, stated before the House Ways and Means Committee: "The U.S. position in world trade deteriorated in the 1960's, with adverse impacts on American workers, communities, and industries. The deterioration continued in the 1970's with further job displacement of U.S. production and loss of American jobs. The basic causes are major changes in world economic relationships during the past 25 years, which accelerated in the 1960's. Among these changes are the Government-managed (sic) national economies, the internationalization of technology, the skyrocketing rise of investments of U.S. companies in foreign subsidiaries and the mushrooming growth of U.S.-based multinational corporations."[4]

In the view of the American labor unions, before the Second World War, imports embodying low-wage foreign labor were very small in volume and generally limited to goods not available in the United States. Over the last 25 years, however, and particularly in the latter 1960's, imports have risen faster than exports. The merchandise trade balance surplus averaging $5.4 billion from 1960 to 1964, and $3.3 billion from 1965 to 1968, dwindled and ran a deficit in 1971 of $2.9 billion. The deterioration in the U.S. merchandise trade balance resulted from strong foreign competition, particularly in areas such as home electronics, automobiles, textiles, pottery, and shoes. Labor further stresses that while high-technology items, such as computers and aircraft, still yield a trade balance, import of such items are rising more rapidly than exports.

Labor is particularly concerned about the impact that this rise in imports has on employment. Using Bureau of Labor Statistics estimates of employment related to exports, and the employment that would be required to produce imports that are most nearly comparable with domestic markets, labor cited potential job losses or job opportunities lost to be 527,000 between 1966 and 1969.[5]

(in thousands)

Employment related to	1969	2,651
merchandise exports	1966	2,464
Total		187
Employment required to	1969	2,538
produce imports	1966	1,824
Total		714
Employment required to produce imports		714
Less		
Employment related to merchandise exports		−187
Total		527[6]

The more recent labor estimates that close to a million jobs have been lost between 1966 and the present are generally based on projections of the Bureau of Labor Statistics study.

What has caused this trade deterioration? Nathaniel Goldfinger, Director of the AFL-CIO's Department of Research, cites the following reasons, here summarized:

1. The direct and indirect barriers to imports and export subsidies imposed by national governments.

2. The transfer of American technology and know-how reducing America's lead in this area.
3. The skyrocketing rise of U.S. foreign direct investment combined with licensing arrangements and patent agreements.
4. The increased sales by subsidiaries frequently in competition with U.S.-made products.
5. The growth of multinational corporations and banks juggling exports, imports, prices, dividends, and currencies internationally within the corporate structure.

He concludes:

> The major trouble, by far, is that American corporations and banks now have huge and increasing investments in foreign countries and they keep their American dollars there to expand their foreign holdings and often to avoid paying United States taxes on their foreign-earned profits.
>
> In the setting of the world economy of the early 1970's, there is an urgent need for the United States Government to face up to the realities of managed national economics, international technology transfers, American business investment in foreign manufacturing subsidiaries and the operations of multinational companies and international banks.
>
> ... The Foreign Trade and Investment Act of 1973, the Burke-Hartke bill provides a framework for dealing specifically and directly with the major causes of this country's deteriorating position in international economic relationships.[7]

Thus, as a concomitant of this assessment of the multinational corporations, labor has abandoned its traditional support for free trade and investment policies. Instead, the labor unions are pressing for restrictions on the movement of capital and overseas operations of the multinational corporations.

Labor is concerned not only with the transfer of entire production units overseas. They also point to the growing number of assembly plants established to assemble U.S.-made components which are then shipped back into the United States. The lower wage base of foreign manufacturing and the transportability of capital and technology relative to labor abetted this development.

In testimony before the Senate Committee on Finance, George Meany, President of the AFL-CIO, stated the following points:

1. The world economy has been changing considerably in the last 20 years. As part of that change, the American position in world trade has been deteriorating rapidly since the early 1960's. Imports shot up, while the rise of exports lagged far behind. Moreover, the U.S. position in world trade deteriorated in composition, as well as in total volume.

This deterioration has resulted in the net loss of about 900,000 job opportunities from 1966 to 1971. The situation was worsening in 1972. The industrial base of the American economy is being undermined and narrowed.

2. Some decline in America's economic position in the world was to be expected in the early years after World War II. This was the period in the late 1940's and 1950's when the war-ravaged economies of the other industrial nations were reviving, with the assistance of American aid. But this decline did not halt or taper off by the end of the 1950's when the other industrial nations were back on their feet. Instead, it accelerated in speed and widened in scope during the decade of the 1960's.

3. The major cause of this widespread deterioration could be found in the fact that other nations manage their economics carefully. They have direct and indirect subsidies for their exports and many restrictions and barriers to imports. The result is that foreign products have inundated the huge and still lucrative American market, while U.S. exports are often blocked or their expansion is retarded.

U.S. government policy, however, has not responded to these major changes in the world economy. Instead, government policy has been based on the 19th century theory of free trade and on world economic conditions of the late 1940's and 1950's which are hardly relevant in the 1970's.

4. The export of American technology has been reducing or eliminating America's technology and productivity leadership in many industries and product lines. U.S. firms have transferred American technology to their foreign branches and furthermore, there have been additional technology transfers through patent agreements and licensing arrangements of U.S. firms with foreign companies.

As a result, foreign plants operating with American technology probably are as efficient or nearly as efficient as similar factories in the U.S. But with wages and fringe benefits that frequently are 50 to 90 percent lower—and longer working hours—the unit-cost advantage can be substantial.

5. Sharply rising investments of U.S. companies in foreign subsidiaries have been key factors in the export of American technology, the displacement of U.S. production, and loss of American jobs.

Direct investments of U.S. firms in foreign facilities shot up from $3.8 billion in 1960 to $14.8 billion in 1971. The book value of such investments in foreign facilities rose from almost $32 billion in 1960 to more than $78 billion in 1971.

Although an estimated 25,000 foreign affiliates are controlled by about 3,500 U.S. corporations, the bulk of these foreign operations are highly concentrated among the corporate giants.

The sales of U.S. foreign affiliates in manufacturing, therefore, have been more than twice the volume of exports of manufactured goods from the U.S. in recent years. Some of these shipments have been to the U.S. where the goods and components are sold in direct competition with U.S. exports.

This process which displaces U.S. production and employment is encouraged and subsidized, according to George Meany, by the United States government. The deferral of Federal income taxes on earnings of foreign subsidiaries until the profits are repatriated and the full crediting of foreign tax payments against the U.S. income tax liability—both of these tax devices amount to about $3.3 billion per year.

6. The mushrooming growth of multinational corporations, most of them U.S. based, is a new factor in the accelerating deterioration of the American position in the world economy. Multinational corporations attempt to use a system approach to global production, distribution and sales, which are spread through plants, offices, warehouses, sales agencies and other facilities in as many as 40 or more countries. Such companies can and do juggle the production, distribution and sales of components and finished products across national boundaries and oceans, based on the decisions of the top executives for the companies' private advantage. They can and do transfer currencies across national boundaries, often beyond the reach of the central banks of the nations.

7. If the deterioration of the U.S. position in world trade is permitted to continue through the 1970's, the consequences could be widespread and far-reaching for American society.

"Unfortunately," concluded Mr. Meany, "international trade experts in government agencies, business and the universities usually show little interest and much less knowledge about the labor and social impacts of development in international trade and investment. As a result, so very little is known, in detail, about the employment impacts and other consequences for workers and communities.

"The rapid and widespread deterioration of the American position in the world economy is undermining and narrowing America's industrial base, with the potential of far-reaching adverse impacts, in the period ahead, if it is permitted to continue.

"The overdue action in late 1970 and early 1972, to bring about an increase in the value of major foreign currencies, such as the Japanese yen and German mark, in relation to the American dollar, can have only uncertain, uneven, and essentially temporary effects on the U.S. position in world trade."

In the setting of the world economy of the 1970's there is an urgent need for the U.S. Government to face up to the realities of managed national economies, technology transfers, American business investments in foreign manufacturing subsidiaries, and the operations of multinational companies and international banks.[8]

Mr. Meany's argument and his support of the Burke-Hartke Bill is based on the assumptions that foreign direct investment cuts exports and therefore reduces U.S. jobs. This new attitude proposes a radical change in United States policy; but to seek a change in governmental policies, however, implies that the effects of past policies are considered to be detrimental. It implies a causal connection between existing policies and the alleged undesirable impact on United States employment from foreign investment, which is worse than what the result would be if legislative changes in policy recommended by certain groups were put into effect.

For U.S. jobs to be increased by a reversal of existing policies toward the multinational corporations it would have to be shown that the drop in exports could be cured by such a policy reversal, and that other jobs would not be lost as a result of this new policy. Before this could be supported, however, it would have to be shown that the multinational corporations have been responsible for the drop in exports, increase in business and employment abroad, and the decrease in domestic employment. "And, even if these three statistical measures were in evidence, it would then have to be shown that the rise in investment caused the drop in exports which, in turn, caused a decrease in jobs."[9] It is easier to prove that a decline in exports causes a drop in employment than it could be shown that a rise in foreign investments caused a decline in exports. The complaints of labor have been intensified, since 1970, because of the poor policies of the administrations which have caused two recessions and a runaway inflation. If our economy were at the levels of full production and full employment, without a chronic inflation, labor could certainly continue its policy of free trade and international cooperation.

Labor's case is made difficult to prove statistically because, although investment abroad has risen, so also have exports and employment, both at home and abroad. There is practically no evidence that the multinationals have been responsible for the flight of capital and the drop in employment. But, to the contrary, domestic employment has risen in most companies that have also invested abroad. "Even in rare cases where a drop in exports and employment can be shown, it would have to be demonstrated further that in the absence of direct investment, foreign demand for the United States products would have remained the same as before, or could have been expanded."[10]

Given the facts that investment, exports, and jobs in most industry sectors investing abroad did rise before the recession of the 1970's, an alternative explanation has to be considered, namely, that exports will rise only with investment over the longer run, as growth occurs abroad. "This explanation is supported also by the location theory which indicates that with economic growth, production facilities tend to be located nearer the market. The shift in investment is needed to provide more marketing outlets; to permit local assembly, thus reducing transport costs and duties; to provide wider product selection through holding inventories close to the market; to get a prompt feedback on products from the market to production unit; to provide servicing and supply facilities; to reflect preferences for locally made goods, especially industrial purchases; and, very importantly, to gain markets which add to the demand for imports of sophisticated items in the lines produced only in the United States."[11]

This sequence of causation is reflected in a survey by the National Foreign Trade Council membership which gave the following reasons for investing abroad:

1. To jump tariff and import barriers and regulations.
2. To reduce or eliminate high transportation costs.
3. To obtain or use local raw materials.
4. To obtain incentives offered by host governments.
5. To maintain existing market positions.
6. To participate in the rapid expansion of a market abroad.
7. To control quality in the manufacture of specialized products.
8. To follow customs abroad.
9. To obtain foreign technical, design, and marketing skills.

The same reason is given by the European and Japanese multinational corporations investing in Latin America, the Middle East, and the United States. "But this list of location factors—as modified by governmental intervention—is not the same among different industrial sectors. The extractive industries have their own rationale for investing, and even the labor unions recognize that raw materials are necessary for U.S. production. Equally, it is virtually impossible for the American industries to export the wide range of services sought in growing economies such as banking, insurance, accounting, consulting, engineering, hotels and rentals, and food processing which have to be located in the market being served. Even in the case of the manufacturing sector and the high technology segments, which are the targets of labor criticism, the unions ignore the fact that hardly any country is prepared to let her market be inundated with American goods. With an elementary knowledge of international trade it is obvious that "to impose a broad range of controls and erect a new control mechanism for all, direct investment has to pay a heavy cost to correct a few situations which have produced undesirable effects. It would be much better from the standpoint of public policy and the national interest to identify the types of situations that are undesirable and to seek correctives that do not themselves produce still unwanted results."[1][2]

The labor unions must recognize the fact that as a market expands, the problem facing the companies in the investment decision-making process is one of where to locate production facilities. If the market could be served from the existing plants no businessman in his right mind would take his money and business to a foreign country. In many instances of foreign direct investment, the alternative to not investing would be to leave the market to another company which will invest. In a report to the Senate Committee on Finance, the National Foreign Trade Council takes issue with both the labor contentions and the Burke-Hartke Bill. It states that "it is clearly evident that not to invest in most instances would merely leave the market to others. Also what is often found is that despite decisions by one company to set up production facilities adequate to serve a given market, other companies have felt the need also to enter and protect their portion of the market."[1][3]

Therefore, to choose labor's plans to reach full employment through restrictive measures such as import quotas, slowing the flow of technology and putting an end to investments abroad is to destroy the economic progress of the last three decades and "to multiply several-fold the effects of the 'beggar-thy-neighbor' policies of the 1920's which no one should want to repeat."[14] Instead of the Burke-Hartke Bill we should pursue a policy of partnership with the developed and developing nations and cure the present economic maladies through cooperation and expansion and not contractions or economic isolationism.

The Foreign Trade and Investment Act of 1973 (Burke-Hartke) represents a major legislative challenge to the multinational corporations and economic expansion of the United States. It would set up a new regulatory body, the "United States Foreign Trade and Investment Commission," to administer quotas, dumping laws, escape-clause action, adjustment assistance, and countervailing duties. It would limit the multinationals and other trade generally by quantitative limits on certain imports. It would change the customs law aiding interaffiliated multinational imports. It would establish control over movements of capital and technology abroad and effect changes in the tax treatment of foreign businesses, eliminating deferral privileges.[15]

In the study commissioned by the Industrial Union Department of the AFL-CIO in 1971 the claim was made that about 500,000 job opportunities were lost betwee 1966 and 1969, according to Bureau of Labor statistics.[16] George Meany has since updated these figures to nearly a million.[17] As further evidence of job loss, the president of the International Union of Electrical, Radio and Machine Workers in the United States presented a paper to the Organization for Economic Cooperation and Development showing a U.S. job loss of about 38,000 workers in the radio and TV industry and about 56,500 workers in the electronic component and accessories industry between 1966 and 1971.[18] In accordance with this type of assessment a majority of workers' organizations in the United States have developed an increasingly hostile attitude toward the multinational corporation and have endorsed the Burke-Hartke Bill.

Businessmen have strongly objected to labor's position on several accounts. Gerald H. O'Brien, Executive Vice-President of the American Importers Association, states that the Burke-Hartke Bill would curtail imports by one-third, which in turn would lose jobs, not save them. "If we limit imports, we reduce income in other countries and thereby reduce their ability to buy our exports. Countries that suffer from our restrictions will, in turn, raise barriers against American exports. Import restrictions also eliminate jobs of Americans whose livelihood depends on imports."[19]

The difficulties involved in attempting to isolate and estimate the net effects of foreign trade on United States domestic employment, as noted in a study by the Department of Commerce, are widely recognized by analysts in this field. Imports that are competitive with U.S. products are difficult to qualify due to varying rates of substitution between imports and domestic production among industries, seasonal variation, and cyclical factors. Moreover, the estimating technique overlooks the American workers employed in producing exports that could have been made abroad. "While it is difficult enough to estimate the aggregate effects of foreign trade on U.S. employment, it is even more speculative to attribute a finite portion of the effect to the foreign affiliates of American multinational corporations. Accordingly, it is difficult to link increased U.S. foreign investment with import growth and then posit a causal, quantifiable relationship between these phenomena and domestic employment."[20]

Several studies have been prepared by various business groups, government, and other independent organizations which counter labor's position. Some have tried to answer labor's allegations with more complete data and analysis thereof. Others have concentrated on the necessity for the multinationals to expand abroad to maintain their competitive position, advocating domestic manpower adjustment.

Responses to labor charges include three major arguments:
1. American multinationals as a whole have created more new jobs domestically than American companies who do not have foreign affiliates.
2. Foreign investments generate more exports than the imports they may displace.
3. Imports from foreign affiliates help preserve American jobs that would not exist without available imports.

The Center for Multinational Studies of the International Economic Policy Association, in a detailed study for the Senate Committee on Finance, asserts that there is ample evidence that multinational corporations have increased their *domestic* U.S. employment at a substantially greater rate than total U.S. private employment. The extent to which some jobs have been displaced or exported, as some labor spokesmen allege, depends on how much of the expanded production abroad might have been carried on successfully in the United States, given foreign tariffs, import controls, transportation costs and other factors. Most studies point out that little, if any, of the production could have been performed in the United States on competitive terms. But even assuming that some could have been retained, the evidence is that U.S. multinational companies create even more jobs in this country, not only in production related to exports to overseas affiliates, but also in managerial, scientific, technical, and services positions—which tend to be higher paid with higher skills.[21]

The Emergency Committee for American Trade during the ten-year period covered by its survey found that "American multinationals have increased their domestic employment (exclusive of employment gains through acquisition) more rapidly than the average manufacturing firm. Their rate of new job creation was about 75 percent greater than that of all other manufacturing firms."[2][2]

Business International in its second survey of 133 foreign investment intensive U.S. companies found that their overall U.S. net employment rose by 29.6 percent from 1960 to 1972, whereas employment by all U.S. manufacturing companies rose by 14.3 percent over the same period. "The high-foreign-investment-oriented sample increased its employment rolls on a net basis—at more than twice the rate that the average U.S. manufacturer did."[2][3]

These figures were supported by the U.S. Department of Commerce findings that foreign direct investment does not result in a job position loss: A reasonable interpretation of available evidence leads to the conclusion that U.S. foreign direct investment is not contrary to the interests of U.S. workers but may, in fact, be a positive factor in stimulating U.S. employment and activity."[2][4]

Another allegation by labor is that multinational corporations displace domestic production. This may be true of particular products but on the whole is disputed by the Business International Study. This study, involving one-sixth of the international business of all U.S. manufacturing corporations, indicates that imports from foreign affiliates have indeed risen rapidly, but that the overwhelming portion of that increase results from the U.S.-Canadian auto agreement. If you exclude the transport and petroleum sectors, imports from affiliates increased 396 percent during 1960-1972, while comparable exports to affiliates increased 438 percent.

The study also found that exports to affiliates, which were one-third less than exports to unrelated customers in 1960, were 55.7 percent in 1972. Exports to affiliates increased over three times as fast as exports to unrelated customers during 1960-1972.[2][5]

The transfer of U.S. goods and services across U.S. national boundaries in the above analysis does not take into account the full range of international business activity which includes transportation, tourism, communications, private finance, and the sale of technology stimulated by multinational growth.

The major issue that the labor unions have concentrated on is that the multinational corporations are responsible for exporting U.S. job opportunities. The suggested means for curbing a job loss, they suggest, is to restrict the free movement of capital and technology and to impose restrictions on certain imports. In labor's view, American business has been attracted abroad by the low wage levels in many countries.

Studies by business groups, however, take issue with this appraisal. A survey by the Emergency Committee for American Trade of seventy-four U.S. corporations shows that "57 percent of the respondents considered market demands the most important reason for the foreign investment decision. By contrast, only 5 percent of this group considered labor cost advantages as the primary cause of investing abroad."[26]

In the middle 1960's the United States had on an average more than twice the productivity of a typical French or German manufacturer; the big U.S. companies also paid more than twice as much in wages. In comparison their unit labor costs were about the same as those in a French or German company. Thus, after freight charges and tariffs were added, many U.S. companies had trouble exporting to major European markets. Rising foreign competition threatened the U.S. export market. There seems little doubt that during this period U.S. companies saw cost advantages in moving from the U.S. wage structure. However, the Tariff Commission found that in 1966 and 1970 all-firm unit labor costs abroad (i.e., in the seven countries where the multinational corporations have taken most of their capital) were generally *higher* than in the United States, except for Mexico and Brazil.[27] But it also found that unit labor costs in the U.S. of the multinational corporations were approximately 35 percent higher than the average for U.S. manufacturing. The multinational corporations, in moving abroad to capture a cost advantage, did little more than the domestic "standard" for the United States, or foreign multinationals. But they did obtain a significant advantage over all foreign competition.[28]

Unit labor costs—or the costs of labor per unit of manufacturing output—hinge on two sets of forces that now tend to move in opposite directions: those that determine the hourly labor compensation, such as wage rates, fringe benefits, and other labor costs; and those that determine labor productivity, or the relationship between hours worked and the number of units produced.

More recently a study by the First National City Bank suggests that the U.S. competitive position, taking ratios of a country's unit labor costs to the "trade weighted" costs of six of its trading partners, has markedly improved after deteriorating until 1969. Between 1962 and the first half of 1973, foreign unit labor costs rose much faster than U.S. because large increases in foreign hourly compensation were not offset by sharp gains in productivity.[29]

Thus the wage motive behind American foreign investment becomes less and less persuasive. There is fairly conclusive evidence that in such areas as consumer electronics, footwear, toys, and textiles low labor costs are a major motive behind foreign investments.[30] However, these items are manufactured or assembled in the developing world, whereas the bulk of U.S. foreign investment is concentrated in the higher wage areas of Western Europe. Thus while unit labor costs account for a significant proportion of total costs, they appear increasingly less important relative to other considerations except in the low skill, high employment industries.

The most general defense of foreign investment, vis-à-vis job loss, made by the multinationals is that they had no choice. That is they invest overseas because they have no realistic alternatives. As is pointed out by Sanford Rose in *Fortune* magazine: "If Proctor & Gamble had not gone to Algeria, for example, Unilever would have preempted the soap business. If Caterpillar Tractor had not gone to Britain, Vickers might today be that country's leading producer of bulldozers. If Squibb had not gone to Italy, it would have surrendered the Italian market to Hoffman-LaRoche."[3][1] The only real choice, in this view, is between the establishment of an American affiliate abroad or the establishment by a foreign competitor of an export-displacing facility. In other words, markets, employment and domestic production might have been less had they not done so. While investment may displace a particular export which is being lost in any case, the investment generates additional exports.

In general the job loss argument due to lower wages abroad does not hold up when countered by such arguments as lower productivity tending to even out the wage differentials in many other industries and the defensive argument that there was no other choice against foreign competition. One must be wary of generalities, however, for in those industries where lower wages are in fact a major consideration, the United States needs effective, updated programs designated to alleviate potential as well as actual job loss.

Instead of disrupting world trade and foreign investments, we should find ways and means to remedy cases where U.S. industries are experiencing difficulties due to foreign competition. "Adjustment assistance to domestic firms and adequate compensation and retraining opportunities for labor, plus insistence on more equitable trade and investment rates from our trading partners, afford better alternatives to insuring high levels of income and employment in the United

States and abroad than to the inward-looking alternatives presently espoused by U.S. organized labor."[3][2]

Solutions through the Burke-Hartke Bill are found to be counterproductive, although the bill raises important issues about the relationship between foreign direct investment and trade. The restrictions recommended would cripple the multinational corporations' trade and resales in the United States. Capital and technology needed for efficiency by the corporations would be restricted and detrimental to the national interests of the United States. The trade provisions of the bill would severely limit U.S. imports in a generalized sense, provoking retaliation by other countries, which would result in lower levels of trade, investment and, ultimately in fewer jobs both here and abroad.

Since the national interest requires continued efforts to maintain maximum freedom of movement for goods, capital, people, ideas, and full employment at home, we must ask what can be done to overcome some of the justifiable objections of the labor unions. Labor is one of the least mobile of the factors of production. And while many studies indicate that the activities of the multinational corporations create more jobs than they displace—a "most relevant fact from a national policy standpoint—it is cold comfort to the worker whose job has been displaced."[3][3]

Prior to the Trade Expansion Act of 1962, the President of the United States could provide increased protection against imports where an industry needed time to adapt its products or methods to new conditions. The Trade Expansion Act made possible the provision of direct assistance to firms or groups of workers to enable them to make necessary adjustments.

Adjustment assistance for workers under the Act consists of:

1. Trade adjustment allowances which replace unemployment insurance with a ceiling of 65 percent of the average weekly wage in manufacturing payable for 52 weeks (with a possible extension of 26 weeks to complete a training program).

2. Full access to counselling, job referral, testing and training programs available in the worker's area.

3. Relocation allowances if there is no suitable job in the worker's field and there is a suitable job in another city. No worker can be compelled to move.

However, eligibility for adjustment assistance has depended on two criteria to be established: Increased imports must have been the major factor causing injury to the industry, firm, or group of workers; and increased imports causing the injury must have resulted in the main from concessions granted under trade agreements.[34]

In practice the two criteria were extremely difficult to meet and no affirmative findings of serious injury were made between 1962 and 1969. Since that time the Tariff Commission, charged with the responsibility of determining eligibility, has certified some petitions but the basic problems remain: 1) It is an *ex post facto* approach;[35] and 2) The criteria are too narrow in scope.

The theory of adjustment assistance is nonetheless sound. The government, in removing tariff barriers as a result of the Kennedy Round negotiations, may be held in part responsible for job dislocations. Current issues facing U.S. trade policy such as renegotiating tariff and non-tariff barriers, preferences to the less developed countries, and other trade negotiations will be aided by an effective adjustment assistance program. Moreover, it is to the United States' competitive advantage to improve the skills of the American worker.

A comprehensive bill proposing adjustment assistance for workers harmed by the multinational corporations has been introduced by Senator Ribicoff. Under the Ribicoff Bill, adjustment assistance would be made available to workers and companies when there are economic and unemployment problems caused by: 1) changes in government procurement and budgetary priorities; 2) the relocation of United States firms to other areas in or outside the United States; 3) economic dislocation resulting from increased imports; and 4) any other economic dislocation caused, in whole or in part, by governmental action.[36]

More in keeping with the direct problems created by the multinational corporations there are three basic elements to be considered in an effective adjustment assistance program:

1. The criterion that increased imports must have been the major factor causing injury to the industry, firm, or group of workers should be modified so that increased imports need only cause such injury "in whole or in part."
2. The criterion that increased imports causing the injury must have resulted in the main from concessions granted under trade agreements should be eliminated.
3. Relief should be anticipated as necessary before serious injury has already occurred.[37]

In a study for the Senate Committee on Finance in 1972, The Center for Multinational Studies suggested the following program of adjustment assistance to the industries and workers whose jobs are displaced:

1. The present limited program of adjustment assistance must be overhauled, upgraded, redefined, reorganized, and given Federal Government direction.

2. Eligibility of industries and workers must be redefined so as to eliminate the requirement that the unemployment rate stems from increased imports due to negotiated tariff concessions. Instead, the new program should apply to import-related employment adjustments and also expand and improve in level and duration benefits and incentives for retraining and relocation of the displaced employees.

3. Mechanisms must be devised for "effective government-business-labor collaboration in a joint system of forecasting, planning, relocating, and transferring of the workers who are displaced as a result of the relocation of the industry. At the same time, the best research center should be established to develop projections of skills likely to be in short supply; and finally, public and private resources must be mobilized to facilitate the transfer of skills from declining industries to new employment opportunities with the least possible human cost and with the economic cost transferred from the individual to the economy as a whole."

4. Some formula must be discovered to provide a terminal point in an expanded program so that its costs do not become an additional burden on the competitiveness of the American economy—whether through the inflationary effects of financing by borrowing, or the additional cost of production involved in financing by taxation. Adjustment assistance must be temporary and only for the purpose of facilitating transition but it will be self-defeating if this program—like foreign aid and other obsolescent programs—becomes an integral part of the bureaucratic waste of Washington. It should be cut off the moment that there are no good reasons for its continuance.

"How the cut-off point can be defined, and how the responsibility for determinations should be allocated among Congress, the Executive Branch, and the independent agencies, such as the Tariff Commission, are extremely complex questions *but very important*."[38] The experience of the last twenty years shows that every program devised by Congress in the future must have a provision for its termination; otherwise, the inefficient and incompetent Washington bureaucrats would continue it indefinitely.

The success and feasibility of this program depends on the willingness of industry to disclose, as much as a year ahead of time, probable plant closings or relocations.

"What about the forecasting of skill needs? This may depend upon investment and plant expansion plans, and here too, a better system of industry reporting could be used; but, over and above this, ways must be found to induce such expansion in labor surplus areas. This is by no means a problem unique to the United States. A recent UNCTAD Survey shows that many countries have programs for inducing location in depressed areas.[39]

Finally, we must face the reality that dislocation is the price we pay for industrial progress. The magnitude of adjustment requirements are much greater in domestic, technological, and regional shifts than any that can be attributed to the activities of the multinational corporations or imports from foreign countries. The present plans and programs of government and industry are inadequate and inefficient. It is important, therefore, for the Congress to view this problem in its total national scope. "Is there not a better way of utilizing the billion dollars expended every year for unemployment compensation, relief, rehabilitation and welfare than to pass out government handouts for not producing? Those concerned about redistribution of wealth often forget the primary fact that for everybody to have more to consume, we must all produce more. The starting point is to train unemployed workers for gainful employment."[40] If we develop a cohesive program to achieve this program on a national basis any displacement problem caused by foreign imports, relocation of industry or investments abroad could be easily solved.

One aspect of the multinational corporations' operation which has caused a great controversy is the provision of items 806.30 and 807 of the U.S. Tariff Schedule. These items permit certain duty-free exemptions for U.S.-originated goods reentering the United States.

Item 806.30 provides that "metals processed in the United States could be further processed abroad and sent back to the United States upon payment of duty on the value added abroad." This bill was introduced in 1956 as a means of facilitating the processing of metals between the United States and Canada—the measure was not specifically limited to a contiguous country. Item 807 was introduced in the new tariff schedules adopted in 1963. It provides essentially for duty exemption on U.S.-origin products when imported into the United States as identifiable parts of an assembled article.

Thus a Mexican affiliate could make a radio with certain American-made parts, and the duty paid upon re-entry into the United States would be the full value of the imported product less the value of the components fabricated in the United States.[41] Although this exemption is a boon to multinational corporations' imports into the United States, offshore production is really distinct from most foreign investment by multinational corporations.

United States imports under tariff items 807.00 and 806.30 increased from $1 billion in 1966 to about $2.8 billion in 1971. These imports came typically from U.S.-owned factories over the border in Mexico and other low-wage countries. The AFL-CIO has urged the deletion of these and similar provisions from the Tariff Schedules ever since 1967.[42] The labor union contends that these two provisions have encouraged the multinational corporations to establish firms in Mexico whose industrialization program permits materials and components intended for assembly and re-export to enter a 12.5-mile zone along the United States-Mexico border duty free. This program was introduced by the Government of Mexico in 1965 in order to provide work for Mexican farm workers whose jobs were terminated by cessation of a prior U.S. program which allowed a number of Mexican farmers to enter this country. According to a statement by the AFL-CIO, the number of American plants operating in the Mexican border zone has grown from 30 in 1967 to about 250 in 1972.

As a result of numerous protests by labor unions, in August, 1969, the Administration in Washington asked the U.S. Tariff Commission to study the economic effects of these firms on employment in the United States. In September, 1970, the Commission submitted a comprehensive report indicating the following important points:

1. It would be difficult to appraise with certainty the effect of tariff items 806.30 and 807 on unemployment in the United States "owing to many uncertainties."

2. The repeal of these tariff items will not increase any substantial job opportunities for U.S. workers but would result in a $150-200 million deterioration in the United States balance of trade.

3. Repeal of items 806.30 and 807 would not considerably reduce the volume of imports of goods that presently enter the United States. "Rather the products would continue," according to the Commission's Report, "to be supplied from abroad by the same concerns but in many cases with fewer or no U.S. components—or by other concerns producing like articles without the use of U.S. materials. The effects of repeal on U.S. employment can only be estimated. Foreign assembly operations utilizing these provisions now provide employment for about 121,000 workers in other countries. Only a small portion of these jobs would be returned to the United States if items 807 and 806.30 were repealed. On the other hand, these provisions now supply employment for about 37,000 people in the United States. Repeal would probably result in only a modest number of jobs returned to the United States which likely would be more than offset by the loss of jobs among workers now

producing components for exports, and those who further process the imported products."[4][3]

A comprehensive study by the U.S. Chamber of Commerce, presented to the Senate Committee on Finance, makes the following points about the impact of multinational corporations on employment in the United States.[4][4]

1. The employment issue is by far the most critical element of the national debate surrounding multinational corporations. The charge that international corporations have weakened the American employment base is the heart of the labor union critique and the basis for the AFL-CIO campaign to legislate controls over foreign investments.

A basic problem in dealing with the employment picture is that the union crusade has been mounted in the middle of economic trouble, unemployment, inflation, and trade deficits. The United States trade balance has seriously weakened over the past four years, with a $2 billion deficit in 1971, the first such excess of imports over exports in 83 years. The unions are trying to hold multinational corporations responsible for that trend as well.

2. The findings of the Chamber of Commerce based on surveys, facts, and figures show that the world-wide employment by multinational corporations has increased steadily. One hundred and twenty-one firms that answered the questionnaire of the Chamber of Commerce stated that their total jobs in 1960 were 2.3 million, rising to 3 million in 1965, and 3.7 million in 1970. While the actual gains were larger in the second five-year period (712,455) during 1965-70, vs. (688,593) during 1960-65, the rate of increase was slower (23.8 percent vs. 29.9 percent), largely reflecting the recession in the United States.

In examining trends in the U.S. job levels during 1960-70,

it was discovered that domestic employment for the same 121 firms indicates a higher rate of increase than the national average during the decade of the 1960's. The gain was from 2.5 million jobs in 1960 to 3.3 million in 1970, representing a 31.1 percent rise, accomplished in the face of serious unemployment.

3. Among the 121 multinational corporations surveyed, only nine reveal a decline in U.S. jobs during the ten years, 1960-1970. Of these, two are aircraft manufacturers whose operations were sharply curtailed during 1965-1970 due to shifts in military spending. Two others are in the automotive field operating under the Canadian Automobile Agreement, revision of which is now sought by the U.S. Government.

4. A study commissioned by the U.S. Department of Commerce estimates that roughly 600,000 U.S. jobs have been created by foreign investments of the companies involved. This study distinguished three kinds of domestic employment generated by multinational corporations through their overseas activities. First are jobs that are necessary to produce capital goods and intermediate goods (often assembled abroad) required in overseas plants. Secondly are those jobs in the main offices of U.S. multinational enterprises required to administer overseas operations. Thirdly are jobs for supporting workers.[4][5]

5. The Chamber Survey and the Department of Commerce Studies reach very similar conclusions on the trend in employment. While the growth of foreign-based jobs occurred at a rapid rate during the 1960's, from a relatively small base, there are no indications that this phenomenon had any negative impact in the aggregate on U.S. employment. In fact, the very opposite appears to be the case.

First, American multinational corporations' domestic employment did not diminish, but rather grew, and did so far more rapidly than was the case for other companies in the general manufacturing sector during these years.

Second, this healthy domestic employment picture would undoubtedly have been even more rigorous were it not for the presence of a serious recession during 1970. In fact, the multinational corporations surveyed represented the healthiest part of the manufacturing sector in the midst of serious unemployment. It can only be assumed that with a real recovery in the United States these corporations will show even livelier growth rates in their payrolls.

Third, U.S. employment has been helped directly by foreign investment through the generation of exports. An estimated 25 percent of American exports are normally sent to overseas subsidiaries. This activity, together with home office administrative operations and supporting functions, creates substantial and growing employment.

Fourth, many (possibly most) overseas operations have been established for defensive purposes, to retain markets that would otherwise be lost due to tariff and trade barriers or to aggressive moves by foreign business competition. The typical management choice was between retaining or losing a market, not between U.S. or foreign operations.

Fifth, financial return flows by foreign subsidiaries help to strengthen the profitability of the American parent companies thereby permitting them to expand at home and to sustain increases in domestic employment.[46]

Finally, the Department of Commerce, in a comprehensive study of "Policy Aspects of Foreign Investment" in January, 1972, states:

"Labor's advocacy of restrictions on U.S. international trade and investment is ill-founded. Rather a satisfactory level of employment in the United States depends basically on a vigorous domestic economy and the ability of U.S.

industry to be competitive and profitable in the world economy. The recently announced economic policies, aimed at improving domestic productivity, and international competitiveness, promise to move the United States speedily in this direction.

In addition to a healthy domestic economy, labor and business must be assured that they will be able to compete fairly in foreign markets. In this connection efforts to eliminate various non-tariff barriers and other non-market factors are being intensified. On the other side of the coin, *active* surveillance of possible cases of "foreign dumping" in the U.S. market is of considerable importance. Also, a U.S. commitment to a free international environment must be accompanied by a readiness to assist in the cases of legitimate job displacement from imports by providing flexible and responsible adjustment assistance for workers and firms."[47]

Exhibit 3-1
Employment of All U.S. Firms and of MNCs
in Sample by Industry

	United States Firms						Majority-Owned Foreign Affiliates of U.S. Reporters								
	All U.S. Firms			U.S. Reporters in 1970 Sample Survey			All Areas			Developed Areas			Developing Areas		
	1966	1970	AAR* 1966–70	1966	1970	AAR* 1966–70	1966	1970	AAR* 1966–70	1966	1970	AAR* 1966–70	1966	1970	AAR* 1966–70
	(Thousands)		(%)	(Thousands)		(%)	(Thousands)		(%)	(Thousands)		(%)	(Thousands)		(%)
All private industry	57,259	61,486	1.8	7,968	8,851	2.7	2,412	2,970	5.3	1,797	2,300	6.4	599	647	1.9
Manufacturing	19,095	19,224	.2	5,885	6,335	1.9	1,704	2,156	6.1	1,408	1,747	5.5	297	409	8.3
Food products	1,779	1,784	.1	235	260	2.6	119	141	4.3	82	102	5.6	37	39	1.4
Chemical & allied prod.	966	1,054	2.2	665	725	2.2	220	250	3.2	154	174	3.1	66	76	3.6
Primary & fabricated metals	2,702	2,698	.0	709	724	.5	86	103	4.6	67	79	4.2	20	23	3.6
Machinery	3,831	3,906	.5	1,617	1,860	3.6	555	731	7.1	486	615	6.1	69	116	13.9
Transportation equipment	2,210	2,063	–1.7	1,681	1,568	–1.7	421	546	6.7	382	474	5.5	39·	72	16.6
Other	7,607	7,719	.4	978	1,198	5.2	303	385	6.2	237	302	6.2	66	83	5.9
Petroleum	486	480	–.2	479	522	2.2	296	271	–2.2	159	158	0	124	98	–5.7
Other industries	37,678	41,782	2.6	1,604	1,904	5.6	411	542	7.2	229	395	14.6	179	140	–6.0
Mining	349	357	.6	†	91	†	79	74	–1.6	28	45	12.6	51	29	–13.2
Trade	13,320	15,108	3.2	516	589	3.4	169	308	16.2	122	252	19.9	46	54	4.1
Other	24,000	26,317	2.3	†	1,314	†	163	161		79	98	5.5	82	58	–8.3

*AAR = Average annual rate of growth 1966-1970.
†Suppressed to avoid disclosure of data for individual reporters.
Source: U.S. Department of Commerce, Bureau of Economic analysis, International Investment Division and National Income and Wealth Division.

Exhibit 3-2
Industry Distribution of Employment
of Sample MNCs
(percent)

	U.S. Reporters in 1970 Sample Survey		Majority Owned Foreign Affiliates of U.S. Reporters					
			All Areas		Developed Areas		Developing Areas	
	1966	1970	1966	1970	1966	1970	1966	1970
All private industry	100.0	100.0	100.0	100.0	100.0	100.0	100.0	100.0
Manufacturing	73.9	71.6	70.6	72.6	78.4	76.0	49.6	63.2
Food products	2.9	2.9	4.9	4.7	4.6	4.4	6.2	6.0
Chemical & allied prod.	8.3	8.2	9.1	8.4	8.6	7.6	11.0	11.7
Primary & fabricated metals	8.9	8.2	3.6	3.5	3.7	3.4	3.3	3.6
Machinery	20.3	21.0	23.0	24.6	27.0	26.7	11.5	17.9
Transportation equipment	21.1	17.7	17.5	18.4	21.3	20.6	6.5	11.1
Other	12.3	13.5	12.6	13.0	13.2	13.1	11.0	12.8
Petroleum	6.0	5.9	12.3	9.1	8.8	6.9	20.7	15.1
Other industries	20.1	22.5	17.0	18.2	12.7	17.2	30.0	21.6
Mining	*	1.0	3.3	2.5	1.6	2.0	8.5	4.5
Trade	6.5	6.6	7.0	10.4	6.8	11.0	7.7	8.3
Other	*	14.8	6.8	5.4	4.4	4.3	13.7	9.0

*Suppressed to avoid disclosure of data for individual reporters.
Note–Calculated from data in table 3-1. Details may not add to totals because of rounding.
Source: U.S. Department of Commerce, Bureau of Economic Analysis, International Investment Division.

Exhibit 3-3
Employment and Payroll Costs Per Employee
of MNCs in Sample, by Area

	Employment			Payroll Costs per Employee		
	1966 ($)	1970 ($)	AAR* 1966 –70 (%)	1966 ($)	1970 ($)	AAR* 1966 –70 (%)
ALL INDUSTRIES						
United States	7,968	8,851	2.7	7,750	9,620	5.5
All foreign areas	2,412	2,970	5.3	3,920	4,900	5.7
Developed areas	1,797	2,300	6.4	4,230	5,350	6.0
Canada	440	474	1.9	6,000	7,990	7.4
U.K.	420	587	8.7	3,460	3,760	2.2
E.E.C. 6†	593	770	6.7	4,030	5,440	7.8
Other Europe	134	214	12.4	3,610	4,460	5.4
Japan	39	49	5.9	2,690	4,290	12.3
Aust., N.Z., S. Africa	171	206	4.8	3,170	4,580	9.6
Developing areas	599	647	1.9	2,950	3,250	2.5
Latin America	423	452	1.7	3,080	3,630	4.2
Other	177	196	2.6	2,630	2,370	–2.6
MANUFACTURING						
United States	5,885	6,335	1.9	8,290	10,300	5.6
All foreign areas	1,704	2,156	6.1	3,820	4,820	6.0
Developed areas	1,408	1,747	5.5	4,120	5,290	6.5
Canada	329	319	–0.8	6,030	8,460	8.8
U.K.	367	444	4.9	3,410	3,940	3.7
E.E.C. 6†	475	651	8.2	3,950	5,320	7.7
Other Europe	79	145	16.4	3,030	3,680	5.0
Japan	33	37	2.9	2,520	4,160	13.4
Aust., N.Z., S. Africa	125	151	4.8	2,900	4,240	10.0
Developing areas	297	409	8.3	2,400	2,810	4.0
Latin America	249	319	6.4	2,600	3,240	5.6
Other	48	90	17.0	1,350	1,290	–1.2

*Average annual rate of growth, 1966-70.
†European Economic Community Six
Source: U.S. Department of Commerce, Bureau of Economic Analysis, International Investment Division.

Exhibit 3-4A
Percentage Distribution of Sales of Foreign Manufacturing Affiliates
of U.S. Firms by Industry and Destination
1965, 1967 and 1968

	Local Sales			Exported to United States			Exported to Other Countries		
	1965	1967	1968	1965	1967	1968	1965	1967	1968
All Manu-facturing	82.0	79.0	77.9	4.2	6.9	7.9	13.8	14.1	14.2
Food Products	86.7	86.8	85.6	3.0	3.7	3.9	10.3	9.6	10.5
Paper & allied products	52.4	54.9	56.0	35.7	32.1	29.4	12.0	13.0	14.6
Chemicals	84.3	83.6	83.2	2.5	1.9	1.9	13.2	14.5	15.0
Rubber products	91.8	91.1	91.6	0.4	1.5	1.4	7.8	7.5	7.0
Primary & fabricated metals	75.4	73.3	73.7	5.9	8.4	8.5	18.7	18.3	17.8
Machinery, excl. elect.	77.5	73.2	75.3	3.1	3.4	4.1	19.4	23.4	20.6
Electrical machinery	88.1	88.1	87.9	1.5	1.3	1.7	10.4	10.6	10.4
Transpor-tation equipment	83.5	75.9	71.6	2.6	13.6	17.1	13.8	10.5	11.3
Other products	83.0	80.9	79.1	3.4	3.4	3.8	13.6	15.7	17.1

Source: U.S. Department of Commerce *Survey of Current Business* Sales of Foreign Affiliates of U.S. Firms 1961-65, 1967 and 1968

Exhibit 3-4B
Percentage Distribution of Sales of Foreign Manufacturing Affiliates
of U.S. Firms in All Areas, Except Canada, by Industry and Destination
1965, 1967 and 1968

	Local Sales			Exported to United States			Exported to Other Countries		
	1965	1967	1968	1965	1967	1968	1965	1967	1968
All Manu-facturing	82.1	81.0	80.5	1.4	2.0	2.3	16.4	17.0	17.2
Food Products	85.1	84.3	82.3	3.2	4.3	4.8	11.7	11.3	12.8
Paper & allied products	91.4	90.4	91.2	1.1	0.7	0.7	7.5	8.8	8.1
Chemicals	82.9	81.0	80.7	1.6	1.2	1.3	15.5	17.8	18.0
Rubber products	89.3	89.1	90.0	0.0	1.0	0.8	10.6	9.9	9.1
Primary & fabricated metals	84.9	80.7	81.0	0.5	4.7	4.3	14.6	14.6	14.7
Machinery, excl. elect.	74.7	70.4	73.1	1.9	1.9	2.4	23.3	28.0	24.5
Electrical machinery	86.2	86.1	86.1	1.0	0.9	1.6	12.8	13.0	12.3
Transpor-tation equipment	81.3	84.2	81.8	1.0	2.0	2.7	17.7	13.8	15.5
Other products	81.1	78.7	76.4	1.2	1.5	1.5	17.7	19.8	22.1

Source: U.S. Department of Commerce *Survey of Current Business* Sales of Foreign Affiliates of U.S. Firms 1961-65, 1967 and 1968

Exhibit 3-5
Selected Multinational Manufacturing Corporations* of
Market Economies: A Profile of Foreign Content† of the
Corporation's Total Operations and Assets
(number)

Foreign Content	Sales	Assets	Production	Earnings	Employment	Total
More than 75 percent						
United Kingdom	2	1	–	3	2	8
Switzerland	3	–	–	–	3	6
United States	–	–	2	3	–	5
Sweden	3	–	–	–	–	3
Belgium	2	–	–	–	–	2
Netherlands-U.K.	1	–	–	–	1	2
50-74 percent						
United States	2	2	1	7	7	19
United Kingdom	–	–	–	1	–	1
Fed. Republic of Germany	4	–	–	–	–	4
Sweden	3	–	–	–	–	3
Japan	2	–	–	–	2	4
France	2	–	–	–	–	2
Italy	1	–	–	–	–	1
Netherlands	–	–	–	–	2	2
Belgium	1	–	–	–	–	1
Brazil	1	–	–	–	–	1
25-49 percent						
United States	14	5	3	7	11	40
Japan	15	–	–	–	1	16
Fed. Republic of Germany	13	–	–	–	1	14
France	8	–	–	–	–	8
United Kingdom	–	–	–	2	–	2
Italy	2	1	–	–	–	3
Sweden	3	–	–	–	–	3
Belgium	1	–	–	–	–	1
10-14 percent						
United States	6	4	–	2	1	13
Fed. Republic of Germany	7	–	–	–	–	7
France	6	–	–	–	–	6
Japan	2	–	–	–	–	2
United Kingdom	–	–	–	–	–	–
Less than 10 percent						
United States	1	5	2	–	2	10
Fed. Republic of Germany	3	–	–	–	–	3
Sweden	1	–	–	–	–	1
Total						193

* Selected from the 650 largest industrial corporations for which information on at least one measure of foreign content could be obtained. When information could be obtained on more than one measure, the highest figure was used to classify the corporation according to its percentage of foreign content.

† "Foreign content" refers to the ratio of the value of foreign sales, assets, production, earnings, or number of foreign employees with respect to the totals.

Source: Centre for Development Planning, Projections and Policies of the Department of Economic and Social Affairs of the United Nations Secretariat, based on table 1; *Belgium's 500 largest companies* (Brussels, 1969); *Entreprise*, No. 878, 6-12 July, 1972; Rolf Jungnickel, "Wie multinational sind die deutschen Unternehmen?" in *Wirtschafts dienst*, No. 4, 1972; Wilhelm Grotkopp and Ernst Schmacke, *Die Grossen 500* (Düsseldorf, 1971); Commerzbank, *Auslandsfertigung* (Frankfurt, 1971); Bank of Tokyo, *The President Directory 1973* (Tokyo, 1972); *Financial Times*, 30 March 1973; *Vision*, 15 December 1971; *Sveriges 500 Största Företag* (Stockholm, 1970); Max Iklé, *Die Schweiz als internationaler Bankund Finanzplatz* (Zürich, 1970); Schweizer Bankgesellschaft, *Die grössten Unternehmen der Schweiz* (1971); *Financial Times*, 15 May 1973; J.M. Stopford, "The foreign investments of United Kingdom firms", London Graduate School of Business Studies, 1973, (mimeo); *Multinational Corporations*, Hearings before the Subcommittee on International Trade of the Committee on Finance, United States Senate, 93rd Congress, First Session, February/March 1973; Nicholas K. Bruck and Francis A. Lees, "Foreign content of United States corporate activities", *Financial Analyst Journal*, September-October 1966; *Forbes*, 15 May 1973; *Chemical and Engineering News*, 20 December 1971; *Moody's Industrial Manual*, 1973; Sidney E. Rolfe, *The International Corporation* (Paris, 1969); Charles Levinson, *Capital, Inflation and the Multinationals* (London, 1971); *Yearbook of International Organizations*, 12th ed., 1968-1969, and 13th ed., 1970-1971; Institut für Marxistische Studien und Forschung, *Internationale Konzerne und Arbeiterklasse* (Frankfurt, 1971); Heinz Aszkenazy, *Les grandes sociétés européennes* (Brussels, 1971); *Mirovaja ekonomika i mezdunarodnyje otnosenija*, No. 9, 1970.

Exhibit 3-6
Growth in Trade, GNP, and Foreign Investment
of Industrial Countries, 1950 to 1970
(billions of dollars)

Economic Indicator	1950	1960	1970*	Aver. Annual Growth (%) 1950-1960	1960-1970
World exports	60.0	128.0	310.0	7.8	9.3
U.S. exports (f.o.b., merchandise)	10.3	20.6	43.2	7.2	7.6
U.S. imports (c.i.f., merchandise)†	9.6	16.4	42.5	5.5	10.0
Exports of other industrial countries**	26.5	54.4	156.2	7.7	11.1
Imports of other industrial countries**	29.9	58.1	157.2	6.8	10.5
U.S. foreign direct investment (book value)	11.8	32.0	78.1	10.5	9.4
−of which: U.S. direct investment in industrial countries**	5.2	17.7	46.4	13.2	10.2
Foreign direct investment in the United States (book value)	3.4	6.9	13.2	7.4	6.8
GNP of industrial countries† (including the United States)	449.0	873.0	1,923.0	6.8	8.2

*Preliminary.

†U.S. imports are reported c.i.f. to facilitate comparison with foreign import figures. The difference between f.o.b. and c.i.f. valuation is roughly 9% or 10% of f.o.b. values.

**The United Kingdom, Canada, Japan, France, Germany, Belgium, the Netherlands, Italy, Sweden, and Switzerland.

Source: Survey of Current Business, Sept. 1971, p. 42; Policy Aspects of Foreign Investment by U.S. Multinational Corporations, U.S. Department of Commerce, Jan. 1972, pp. 7-14; International Financial Statistics, International Monetary Fund (several issues); United Nations Monthly Bulletin of Statistics (several issues).

Notes

1. Department of Commerce, "Memorandum to the Secretary," February 21, 1972, p. 18.

2. This resolution was moved by the Chemical Workers' Union as noted by David Lea in J. H. Dunning, ed., *The Multinational Enterprise*. George Allen & Unwin, Ltd. 1971, p. 147.

3. *New York Times*, March 4, 1973, sec. 3, p. 2.

4. Hearings before the Committee on Ways and Means. House of Representatives, 91st Congress, Second Session, May, 1970, p. 1001.

5. This figure was cited by Biemiller as 700,000, ibid., p. 1008 and has been elsewhere quoted as 500,000 in many documents. one source of 527,000: *Needed: A Constructive Foreign Trade Policy*, Industrial Union Department, AFL-CIO.

6. *Source:* Derived from Bureau of Labor Statistics reported in *Tariff Commission Report*, 1973, p. 677.

7. *New York Times*, March 4, 1973, Section 3, p. 2, col. 6.

8. Subcommittee on International Trade, Committee on Finance, U.S. Senate. Statement by George Meany, May, 1971.

9. *National Foreign Trade Council's Report*, November, 1971, p. 5. Also see the U.S. Senate Committee on Finance (File Copy), November 1973, and the Report of the U.S. Department of Commerce, *Policy Aspects of Foreign Investment by U.S. Multinational Corporations*, January, 1972.

10. Ibid., p. 7.

11. Ibid., p. 8.

12. Ibid., p. 7.

13. Committee on Finance, United States Senate (File Copy), February 21, 1973, pp. 620-72.

14. Ibid.

15. Foreign Trade and Investment Act of 1973, S. 151 & H.R. 62, 93rd Congress, First Session, SS 301, 401, 402, and 501 (1973).

16. Supra, p. 72.

17. Supra, p. 74.

18. O.E.C.D., Social Affairs Division, Programme for Employers and Unions, Regional Trade Union Seminar on International Trade 7-10, Dec. 1971: Part III, (c) *A Case Study of the Electric Sub-Assemblies and Components Industry* by Paul Jennings, Paris, pp. 5-15.

19. *New York Times*, March 25, 1973, Business Section, p. 14.

20. U.S. Department of Commerce, *Policy Aspects of Foreign Investment by U.S. Multinational Corporations*, January, 1972, p. 21.

21. Robert G. Hawkins, *Job Displacement & Multinational Firms*, Center for Multinational Studies, Paper No. 3, June, 1972.

22. Emergency Committee for American Trade, *The Role of the Multinational Corporation in the United States and World Economies*. Based on an analysis of the International Economic Subcommittee for American Trade of E.C.A.T. of 74 U.S. Corporations, Washington, 1972, p. 5.

23. Business International, *The Effects of U.S. Corporate Foreign Investment 1960-1972*. New York, 1974, p. 56.

24. U.S. Department of Commerce, *The Multinational Corporation, Vol. I, Studies in Foreign Investment*, Washington, D.C. (A study undertaken by the Bureau of Economic Analysis on employment and payroll costs of 298 U.S. multinational companies and their 5,237 majority owned foreign affiliates indicates that the employment growth of U.S. parent companies employment growth exceeded that of all U.S. firms from 1966 to 1970). See exhibits at the of the Chapter.

25. Business International, op. cit., pp. 3, 4.

26. The Emergency Committee for American Trade, *The Role of the Multi-national Corporation in the United States and World Economies*, February, 1972, p. 11.

27. The seven countries are the United Kingdom, Belgium-Luxembourg, West

Germany, France, Canada, Mexico, and Brazil. See Tariff Commission, op. cit., 1973, p. 638.

28. Ibid., p. 638.

29. F.N.C.B. *Monthly Economic Letter*, January, 1974, p. 13. The six countries are: the United States, the United Kingdom, France, Germany, Italy, and Japan.

30. E.C.A.T., op. cit., p. 77.

31. Sanford Rose, "Multinational Corporation in a Tough New World," *Fortune*, August, 1973, p. 53.

32. *Policy Aspects of Foreign Investment by U.S. Multinational Corporations*, U.S. Department of Commerce, January, 1972, p. 24.

33. Committee on Finance, U.S. Senate, February 21, 1973, p. 125.

34. Department of Labor, *United States International Economic Policy in an Interdependent World* (the Williams Commission Report), U.S. Government Printing Office, Washington, D.C., Vol. 1 pp. 139-394.

35. National Planning Association, *U.S. Foreign Economic Policy for the 1970's: A New Approach to New Realities*, 1971, p. 208.

36. See S. 3739, 92nd Congress, Second Session, 1972.

37. See Bart S. Fisher, "The Multinationals and the Crisis in United States Trade and Investment Policy," 53 *Boston University Law Review*, 308 (1973); p. 360.

38. Senate Committee on Finance, *Multinational Corporations*, Feb. 21, 1973, pp. 125-128.

39. Ibid., pp. 128-129.

40. Ibid., p. 129.

41. Tariff Commission Report No. 332.61, 1970, p. 9.

42. Tariff Commission, 1973, op. cit., p. 130.

43. U.S. Tariff Commission, *A Report on Items 806.30 and 807*, September, 1970.

44. U.S. Chamber of Commerce, *United States Multinational Enterprise Survey*, (1960-1970), pp. 25-30.

45. Study of Professor Robert B. Stobaugh of Harvard Business School, for the Department of Commerce, January 1972.

46. Chamber of Commerce of the United States, *Multinational Enterprise Survey*, February 14, 1972.

47. U.S. Department of Commerce, *Policy Aspects of Foreign Investment by Multinational Corporations*, January, 1972, pp. 28-29.

4.
The Multinational Corporations and the Transfer of Technology

The transfer of technology, largely to other industrialized nations, by American multinational corporations has attracted considerable attention both here and abroad. During the 1960's widespread concern was growing in Europe over U.S. technological domination. It was feared that European countries were too small to support the large outlays on research and development necessary in those industries that are technology-intensive. But more recent findings show that throughout the 1960's Europe steadily improved its trading position in high-technology products.[1] By 1967 (with the exception of the aerospace industry, which was heavily aided by U.S. Government expenditures) industry-financed research and development and nuclear energy research was undertaken in European countries on a par with the United States. The European countries have not been able to achieve the cooperation amongst themselves necessary for integrating technological developments. However, individual European countries have done well on their own, facing the "American challenge" to indigenous industrial technology.[2]

The tables have turned. In the 1970's concern has been growing in the United States over the narrowing of the "technological gap," and Americans are expressing concern over the European and Japanese challenge. The erosion of the United States competitive advantage in industries that require high technology has motivated critics to take a protectionist stance. The Burke-Hartke Bill would delegate to the President the authority to prohibit any holder of a U.S. patent from either manufacturing a patented product or process outside the United States, when, in the President's judgment, such prohibition would contribute to increased employment in the United States.[3] Policies are advocated that would protect high-technology industries from foreign competition and give government subsidies to certain industries. However, it may be argued that just as European reactions to U.S. technological domination in the 1960's were often exaggerated, so the United States reactions to the closing of the technological gap may often be exaggerated, and the prospective challenge to the multinational corporations counterproductive.

It is difficult to define just what technology is, and, correspondingly, it is difficult to measure. Technology is the stock of knowledge of industrial arts. In the broad sense it includes a craftsman's know-how as well as industrial applications of scientific theories and laws. In this sense international direct investment flows may be its agent. The Bureau of Economic Analysis narrows the transfer of technology down by using data on U.S. receipts and payments of fees and royalties as a narrower measure. Most royalties and fees are payments for the use of technology. However, there are technological transfers not included in royalties and fees.

The transfer of technology by U.S. companies produces real benefits for the United States in the form of net royalties and fees—$2.8 billion in 1972, 75 percent of which came from U.S. affiliates abroad. Receipts have been expanding at a compound annual rate of 12.8 percent since 1960. Payments of royalties and fees to foreigners are relatively small by comparison—less than \$0.3 billion in 1972—yet their growth rate from 1960 to 1972 was 11.5 percent.[4]

Transactions in Royalties and Fees: Foreign Direct Investment-Related and with Unaffiliated Foreign Residents (millions of dollars)

Area	Receipts 1960	1965	1970	1971	1972*	Payments 1960	1965	1970	1971	1972*
Europe										
D.I.	131	381	700	828	957	16	28	42	50	93
Unaffil.	140	189	256	279	284	35	61	100	110	121
Canada										
D.I.	95	185	320	350	395	17	38	62	64	45
Unaffil.	23	27	35	33	41	2	3	4	5	7
Lat. Amer.										
D.I.	96	174	264	281	272	1	–	–	–	–
Unaffil.	20	24	47	46	48	1	2	5	3	4
Japan										
D.I.	7	20	66	80	101	–	1	4	1	–
Unaffil.	48	66	202	225	245	–	1	4	4	6
Other										
D.I.	74	165	270	325	366	1	–	2	2	–
Unaffil.	17	30	44	43	53	–	–	–	–	–
Total										
D.I.	403	924	1,620	1,865	2,090	35	68	111	118	138
Unaffil.	247	335	583	626	670	40	67	114	123	138

Source: Table derived from *Survey of Current Business*, December, 1973, pp. 16-17.
Note: Details may not add up to totals due to rounding.
* Preliminary figure
– Under one million

Receipts of royalties and fees from Japan grew especially rapidly, making up 6.8 percent of all receipts in 1965 and moving to 12.5 percent in 1972. This phenomenon reflects the multinational corporations' attempts to enter the Japanese market via licensing of technology and processes as an alternative to direct investment, which has not been allowed to any great extent by the Japanese authorities.

The leading industrialized countries outside the Western Hemisphere account for most of the growth in total receipts of royalties and fees. U.S. companies earn much more in royalties and fees through direct investment abroad than from unaffiliated foreigners, $2.1 billion, as compared to $0.7 billion in receipts from unaffiliated foreigners in 1972.[5]

These figures demonstrate that the multinational corporation is clearly an important channel for the transmission of technology abroad. However, they do not take into account the full range of services provided under contract to foreigners that may involve technological transfer. Moreover, figures on royalties and fees shed little light on the actual costs and benefits involved in technological transfer.

Studies by economists have shown that a significant proportion of the growth in productivity levels in the industrialized Western nations can be attributed to technological progress in addition to capital expenditure and the upgrading of labor skills. While this lends a difficult variable to growth model theory hence reluctantly considered by many economic theorists, technology nonetheless is an important concomitant of economic growth and has the greatest impact on employment, both in numbers employed and in skills required. Owing to its crucial role, a great deal of theoretical work has been done to integrate technology into growth and trade models to include its effects on employment.[6]

The growth in importance of industry-financed technology has led to greatly increased competition in research and development on the part of the major multinational corporations.[7] And it has led many of the industrialized nations to look for policy incentives that would increase research and development in their respective countries where it is assumed technological progress will increase output and employment. However, the multinational corporations themselves are the most successful in the management of technology. Research and development in American industry increased by 5 percent annually in real terms between 1966 and 1971—a period that included three years of economic recession, government cutbacks in funding, and growing public hostility toward science and technology.[8]

The success of the multinational corporation is often ascribed to its ability to manage technology. Having invested large sums of money in the development of a new product or process, it is in the interest of the corporation to maximize its returns on this investment by transferring the new technology into production in as many locations as possible. The "higher" the technology, the bigger the investment needed and hence the greater the incentive to establish production subsidiaries abroad.

Advocates of the multinational corporation consider this transfer of capital and technology as beneficial in raising the standard of living and improving the allocation of the world's resources. Critics abroad fear technological domination by the United States and are wary of what may be called "improved" standard of living. Critics in the United States argue that we are losing our competitive advantage in trade through the diffusion of technology and losing jobs in the process. The President of the A.F.L.-C.I.O., George Meany, has stated before the Senate Finance Committee that the most disturbing aspect of United States trade policy is that it allows the exporting of sophisticated technology that is used abroad to create jobs to manufacture products that will compete with American goods.[9]

There is no doubt that the comparative advantage gained from high technology innovation is decreased when the technology is transferred to foreign competitors. "However, research and technology, like other forms of ideas, cannot be imprisoned. The United States experience with government secrecy in both the atomic energy and missile technology areas since World War II shows that in the most sensitive areas, at most a delay factor can be introduced. The flow of basic scientific information now appears to be such that any advanced industrial nation can reproduce innovations." [10]

Moreover, efforts to control licensing and the transfer of technology may well lead to a further increase in research and development on the part of foreign firms eager to compete with United States products. Canada and the European countries are well aware of the benefits to be gained by stepping up their own research in those industries involving higher technology.[11] It should be added that these same countries are already concerned over the fact that almost all of the research and development of the American multinational corporations is done in the United States.[12]

The flow of technology is a two-way street and no country has a monopoly on innovations and inventiveness. Any limitations by the United States would invite retaliation by other countries which may limit or restrict foreign licensing of indigenous inventions. During the last twenty-five years the economic and political relations of the nations all over the world have been dramatically changed by events beyond the control of any power. Among these events have been the expansion of trade, the transfer of capital, the expanding operations of the multinational corporations, and the heightened economic importance of the ever-increasing pace of technological advance. The conjuncture of these dynamic forces has created many important issues and problems for business, labor, and national policy makers.

"The multinational corporation is clearly an important channel for the transmission of technology abroad. It overshadows, according to some observers, exports, licensing of technology, and the free exchange of scientific information as a means of transferring U.S. technology. Advocates of multinational corporations view it as a vehicle for raising living standards abroad—in part through the diffusion of technology—and improving the world allocation of resources. Critics in Europe, Canada, and labor unions, on the other hand, claim that it is undermining indigenous industry and leading to the control of key sectors of their industrial base by U.S. capital. To critics in the United States, technology transfers by multinational firms are closing the technological gap and eroding America's competitive advantage by combining U.S.-developed technology with efficient, low-cost foreign operations based on cheap labor." [13]

The National Commission on Technology, Automation, and Economic Progress in its report to the President and Congress stated:

> The vast majority of people quite rightly have accepted technological change as beneficial. They recognize that it has led to better working conditions by eliminating many, perhaps most, dirty, menial, and servile jobs; that it has made possible the shortening of working hours and the increase in leisure; that it has provided a growing abundance of goods and a continuous flow of improved and new experience for people and thus added to the zest for life.[14]

Similarly, the view that international exchange of technology is both necessary and beneficial is supported by another government-sponsored panel on the International Transfer of Technology reported to a Senate Committee:

"If we are going to solve the major problems facing humanity—overpopulation, air pollution, water pollution, and many others—we need a vast generation and exchange of new technology . . . practically all economists agree that a free flow of technology contributes in important ways to a rising standard of living both in this country and elsewhere. . . . The exchange of technology among economically developed nations and its application to research, production, and management are increasingly seen as vital elements in the development and maintenance of buoyant national economies."[1][5]

However, the optimistic views of economists concerning the benefits of technology transfer are not shared by everyone. There are many who dispute the surveys and argue that the "export" of the American technology has reduced the potential of expansion for United States trade, has contributed to intensified import competition in the U.S. market, and has caused the loss of many job opportunities in this country. Legislation has been proposed which would severely restrict the rights of multinational firms to engage in international technological transfer.

In order to get an impartial, clear answer to the questions raised by both sides, it is important to analyze the relationship between technology and trade so as to evaluate the effects of technology transfers on the American labor market and on trade. Before the Second World War, most economists and governments tended to focus their analysis of international trade on questions of "factor endowments, factor mobility, and the theory of comparative advantage." It is only over the last twenty years that concerted efforts have been made to integrate technological considerations into the theory of international trade in the Western world.

On the quantitative side, only limited information is available which can throw light on the subject in attempting to evaluate the influence of technology on trade. The well-known Danish economist, Professor Erik Hoffmeyer, in a thorough study of the pattern of trade in the United States, discovered that some corporations in this country "tended to specialize in research-intensive goods and, as a result, the exports of these corporations had increased twenty times in the period between World War I and the mid-fifties, while exports of traditional goods merely trebled."[1][6]

More recent research in this area by Professor Donald
Keesing indicates a high correlation between U.S. technological research and development expenditures "in relation to
sales and U.S. share of OECD countries' exports of manufacturers." The evidence discovered as a result of an industry-by-
industry survey leaves little doubt of a positive relationship
between export performance and technological advancement
in the United States.[17]

Another study by Dr. Michael Boretsky shows that the
progress and expansion of U.S. trade depends largely upon
the export of higher-technology products. Furthermore,
Boretsky states that "for the past several years the United
States has been losing its technological leadership in production and export of such products, and that if this trend is not
reversed, the United States will face a continually worsening
balance of payments position." This loss in competitiveness,
according to Boretsky, is the result of a number of factors
such as increased intensity of foreign firms' technological
research efforts, slower rates of productivity increase by U.S.
firms, and the ability of foreign countries to purchase and
assimilate relatively new technologies from innovator
countries.[18]

Professor Raymond Vernon has suggested the theory of
"product cycle." According to this theory he assumes that
the United States—in the future—will find its greatest export
competitiveness in the production and sale of technologically
advanced products. "Forces in the U.S. economy such as its
highly skilled and educated labor force, the high income
character of its demand market, the need for labor saving
devices and the availability of risk capital would encourage
the expenditure of a research and development fund and
would make it the natural development grounds for technological products."[19]

Once developed, according to the "product cycle" theory,
a new product would at first be created inefficiently; it

would embody a high degree of labor content and its price
would be very high. During the development stage production would be principally for the American market and any
foreign sales would be serviced from American firms. As the
product begins to improve in price and quality, the costs of
labor and materials would drop. During this stage of development exports will climb and the increasing foreign demand
might well cause the establishment of sales and service
facilities abroad. As the product improves and its production
becomes more standardized, the size of the foreign market
grows, the difficulties of providing the foreign market mount,
and the firm has no choice but to invest and establish
factories in foreign countries. At this time the multinational
corporation would continue to export machinery and components for sale to the subsidiary. As product standardization
becomes almost complete and the technology is spread
widely, trade competition in manufacturing at this stage
would be determined almost exclusively on the basis of costs,
productivity, and efficiency of firms.[20] Less developed countries in the final analysis become exporters of mature products to U.S. markets.

The United States Tariff Commission, in its exhaustive
study of the multinational corporations, found that the
multinational corporations in the high-technology industries
(based on R & D intensity) continue to generate a better
ratio of new exports to imports than do other firms in the
high-technology class. The direct erosion of U.S. comparative
advantage in trading high-technology goods is concentrated in
the performance of the non-multinational firms.[21]

The Commission found that the U.S. multinational corporations, while they are clearly the leaders in the large net flow
of technology to foreign countries in recent years, have not
had the expected effect of eroding the United States' trade
advantage in high-technology goods.

High-technology manufactured goods, and agricultural

products (which are also technology-intensive in the United States) have had very positive effects on the trade accounts for many years, while low-technology manufactured goods and raw materials have registered deficits.

(in billions of dollars)

	1960	1965	1970	1971
High-technology manufactured goods	+6.6	+9.1	+9.6	+8.3
Agricultural products	+1.0	+2.1	+1.5	+1.9
Low-technology manufactured goods	−0.9	−2.9	−6.2	−8.3
Raw materials	−1.7	−2.8	−2.5	−4.1[22]

Multinational corporations between 1966 and 1970 produced more than four times as much in new exports as in new imports in the high-technology category, easily outperforming the aggregate new U.S. exports of high-technology items, which were only about 1.2 times as large as aggregate new imports in this class. Further, new exports of high-technology goods to affiliates represented about half the aggregate new U.S. exports of such items, while imports from affiliates were only 13 percent of aggregate new imports. Thus the multinational corporations have had a directly favorable effect on the U.S. trade in high-technology goods.[23]

It is quite understandable that the multinational corporations do well in the trade balance of high-technology goods because the activities which generate and implement the technological innovative process—both the funding and the professional labor required in research and development—with few exceptions were overwhelmingly carried out by the multinational firms.

The evidence that multinational corporations play a significant role in the superior position which the United States still retains as an exporter of high-technology goods, however, still leaves open the question of the indirect trade effects. Foreign sales by multinational affiliates in high-technology items rose considerably faster than U.S. exports of these items, although the rise was much less steep than it was in medium- and low-technology items. How many of the new foreign markets found by multinational affiliates could have been obtained by U.S.-based corporations depends on the assumptions made. The Tariff Commission estimated the possible erosion of U.S. export markets for high-technology goods by new sales of the multinational affiliates between 1966 and 1970 to be a maximum of 18 percent of the affiliates' new foreign sales. This estimation assumed that U.S. exporters could have done at least as well as in 1966 against foreign competition in the markets for the high-technology goods.[24] Whether one attributes this 18 percent (or $1.6 billion) of new sales as an erosion caused by the multinationals depends on this assumption. In any case the indirect effects on U.S. trade produced by the U.S. multinational affiliates' foreign sales were probably relatively small compared to total new foreign sales by these affiliates.[25]

Hence, while many studies and theories indicate that the United States is losing its competitive edge in high technology goods, it is by no means clear that the U.S. multinational corporations are the responsible culprits. Many spokesmen for the corporations themselves have pointed out that the contrary may be the case; that if the multinational corporations had not moved ahead as vigorously as they have in areas of high technology, financed by increasing markets, and motivated by competition, the competitive edge in areas of high technology would have been foregone.

The Manufacturing Chemists Association, after surveying the chemical industry, on December 31, 1972, submitted the following statement to the Senate Committee on Finance:[26]

"The highly developed industry of the modern world is

based on publication and free exchange of scientific information and the competitive sale or licensing of technology. Any country which would attempt to isolate itself from this communication and exchange would rapidly find that obsolescence was shutting it out of world trade in technology-based products such as those of the chemical industry. The U.S.S.R. and Communist China have found themselves in that position. The U.S. is as vulnerable to that obsolescence as any country. It has no monopoly on science or technology. Even as far back as the 1930's and 1940's, six out of fifteen important product developments of E.I. DuPont de Nemours & Company were based on foreign inventions. This picture is not changing. Out of thirty great innovations of the past decade (nineteen of which are chemical), eleven of them were based on foreign discoveries or developments. Of the top ten chemical companies leading in research and development expenditures only three were in the U.S., and it is estimated that the $1.7 billion or so that was spent by the chemicals and related industries in the U.S. for their own research represents only about 40 percent of the free world effort."

Referring to technological innovations and gaps, a report by OECD in 1972 comments:

"A more open and liberalized world, together with growing research and development activities in a wider number of countries, and changing patterns in the relative sizes of member countries' R & D efforts, have meant greater opportunities for all countries to absorb and benefit from the results of foreign R & D, and—for many countries—the need to concentrate resources in sectors if they are to achieve international levels of excellence.

"Furthermore, there is some empirical evidence which shows that successful innovations have already in the past relied heavily on inputs of foreign knowledge. In a study of the history of successful innovations in the United Kingdom,

J. Langrish identified 158 important ideas used in 51 innovations. Of these ideas, approximately one-third were generated within the firms making the innovations, one-third came from outside the firm but within the United Kingdom, and one-third originated in foreign countries. Thus, even in a member country with a relatively large research and development effort, successful innovations have in the past relied to a considerable extent on imported knowledge."

Although there are many reasons for maintaining a healthy American research and development activity, as mentioned above, technological developments and exchange have a direct bearing on our balance of trade. Five U.S. companies with high research in chemical industries had a 5.2 percent increase in sales and exports. United States exports in eight technologically intensive industries, including the chemical industry, were 28.9 percent of the total exports of the industries; whereas, in sixteen other less technology-intensive industries, U.S. exports were only 17.3 percent of the world total.[27]

The IBM Corporation, in a letter to Senator Abraham Ribicoff on January 18, 1973, in defense of the role of the multinational corporations and the export of technology stated:

"The record shows clearly that the U.S. has benefited every bit as much as other nations. Protectionist legislation now before the Congress would authorize the President to prohibit the licensing of U.S. patents and know-how for foreign manufacture. The sponsors of this legislation claim that checking the flow of American ingenuity to foreign manufacturing operations would increase U.S. exports, protect U.S. jobs, and reestablish American dominance in several key industrial areas. The two-way flow of invention and innovation played a major role in the accelerated postwar recovery rate of many nations.

"For the U.S. in particular, technology transfer has had two benefits:

"First: The creation of new markets for technology-intensive U.S. products and techniques. These include heavy automotive equipment, atomic energy, data processing, chemicals, petroleum, and aircraft.

"Second: Foreign technology has led to the rapid expansion of many U.S. companies. These companies, with bases of research, development, and production throughout the world, have direct access to overseas technology.

"IBM, for example, has cross-licensing arrangements with dozens of European companies, including Phillips in The Netherlands, ICI in the United Kingdom, and Siemans in Germany. It has similar agreements with some fifteen Japanese companies. IBM's magnetic-tape-manufacturing facility in Boulder, Colorado, was set up under a cross-licensing agreement with the Sony Corporation of Japan. It uses Sony patents and a great deal of the technical know-how of the Japanese company.

"An important part of the development work on the IBM computer systems, IBM system, 360, and IBM system, 370, was done in the company's eight overseas development laboratories."[2 8]

However, the labor unions disagree with these surveys, research studies and theories and allege that the export of American technology has been reducing or eliminating America's technology and productivity leadership in many industries and product lines. American firms, according to labor spokesmen, have transferred American technology and know-how to their foreign subsidiary plants. And there have been additional technology transfers through patent agreements and licensing arrangements of U.S. firms with foreign companies.

As a result, labor unions contend that foreign plants,

created and operated efficiently with American capital and technology, with wages and costs 50 to 90 percent lower than in the United States (and additional advantages of lower taxes), can undersell and take away jobs from American labor.

So while the pace of productivity advance of the American economy during 1947-1971 shot up about 45 percent from the rate of advance during 1919-1947—a yearly rate of 5.2 percent per year during 1947-1971, as against 2.2 percent per year in the previous 28 years—the transfer of American technology and know-how contributed substantially to sharp advances of productivity in other countries.[29]

Floyd Smith, President of the International Machinists, in answer to the advocates of free trade and free investments, stated: "Perhaps protectionism is a dead end but it is just as likely that free trade, without any safeguards, is economic suicide."

The question is often asked, Why is labor getting so worried about multinational corporations, and why are labor unions abandoning their traditional support of free trade?

The labor unions' answer cites two fields in particular which have caused a major displacement and great unemployment in the United States. Three unions list 19 companies that have shut down or curtailed U.S. operations since the middle of 1969.

A Westinghouse color television plant in Edison, N.J., transferred production to Japan and Canada this year; a Sperry-Rand computer plant shifted assembly operations to Germany and Japan; and Emerson which has imported all its radios since 1966, arranged with the Admiral Corporation to have TV sets manufactured in Taiwan for sale in the United States.

The unions also charge that Taiwan's largest employer, with 12,000 workers, is now General Instrument Corporation, which has shut down operations in Massachusetts and

Rhode Island during the past two years. Other companies on the union list include Singer, IBM, General Electric, Ampex, Raytheon, Motorola, Sylvania, and Philco-Ford.

The Department of Commerce, while admitting some job displacement as a result of multinational investments abroad, states that labor's allegations are exaggerated and unfounded. "The charge that multinational corporations' foreign production displaces U.S. exports appears to arise from a small number of specific cases; the working assumption ought to be that the establishment of facilities abroad may displace particular exports, but not exports generally."

Even if the assumption of some displacement were true, the advantages of exchange of technology is so great that no country can progress without it.

"The magnitude of trade advantage resulting from innovation will depend not only on a continuing stream of new products but also on the intensity of that stream and on the rate at which the new knowledge becomes available for production outside of the innovating country. Of course, the intensity of the development stream will determine the amount of potentially exploitable technology available to the innovating country. The rate of diffusion will limit the time period within which the technology may be exploited by exporting the technology-embodying product, assuring the country of innovation that it will not also be the one in which the product may be most cheaply produced."[30]

The claim that exports of technology by firms within the innovating country are detrimental to the labor interest has not been supported by facts because of the following reasons:

1. Any immediate loss of jobs which might result from exports of technology would be substantially mitigated by exports of component parts to the subsidiary and by the return of royalties, fees and profits to the parent firm.

2. The subsidiary being the first firm with the innovation can increase its production and its demand for more machines and components from the United States.

3. The subsidiary will have advantages in building up an efficient industry to the extent that no local firm will be able to equal it for a considerable time after they have obtained the actual technology. All exports of machinery and components from the United States during this period represent more profits and jobs.

4. The multinational corporations taking technology abroad tend to create a market for their products by introducing foreign consumers to the products which the subsidiaries are not able to produce in sufficient quantities. The result would be additional demand not only for goods but for more high-technology U.S. products.[31]

Although there are few nations as primary sources of technological innovations, recent experience has shown that it is not difficult for any industrial country either to innovate or to imitate and improve upon the technology of other nations.

"Caution should be exercised so as not to place too much emphasis upon the United States as a generator of technology—it is the leading innovator, but the United States has also benefited from work done in foreign countries. A recent OECD study of the 'technology gap' investigated a selected group of 140 innovations and found that some 60 percent had originated in the United States. However, the study also noted several instances where U.S. innovations were based on foreign scientific breakthroughs, but few instances of the reverse process were discovered."[32]

As other industrialized nations become more like the United States in terms of their demand markets for high-technology goods, and as they increase their domestic ability to produce new technologies while retaining comparatively lower labor rates, American firms will feel strong pressures to export their technologies through foreign investment. Of course, any barriers to trade or national preferences given to domestic firms which act in such a way as to reduce the opportunities for the exploitation of technology through exporting will only add to the pressure for direct investment and the export of technology. In this respect the current strictures raised by the AFL-CIO against the activities of multinational firms should not be dismissed lightly, even though their proposals to curb and regulate the activities of multinational companies would probably serve to make more difficult improvements in our long-term balance of payments.

The multinational firm has become one of the principal vehicles for the exporting of capital, technical knowledge and management know-how from the United States. Although the percentage of U.S. investment in Europe compared to all European investment is relatively slight, the effect of the multinational firm has almost certainly been disproportionate to its size. By bringing technical knowledge and management know-how to Europe it has not only acquainted its potential customers with the benefits deriving from high-technology products, but it has also presented a competitive challenge to European firms to imitate American technology and to strive for new technological developments of their own. Through the direct and indirect effects of its technological exports, the multinational firm has assisted in narrowing the "technology gap." The OECD study previously mentioned studied this gap carefully and found that differences in technology did exist in some industries, but not in others. It also found that in some instances the availability of technology had not been a problem to European firms; in these cases a "gap" developed because European firms had not utilized available technology. One example of this lack of management perceptiveness is cited in a study of the electronic components industry.[33] It notes that although basic transistor technology became available for license from the Bell Laboratories in the

mid-1950's, many prominent European firms did not realize
the importance of this innovation until they were faced with
the competition of American subsidiaries in Europe some
time later. In the past several years, though, the "technology
gap" has narrowed, and probably remains in a broad sense
only with respect to the less developed countries, Eastern
Europe, and the U.S.S.R. With the industrialized nations it
continues only in a few industries.[34]

Although the multinational firm is the principal channel of
commercial technology diffusion, it is by no means the only
one. Substantial amounts of technology have also been
transferred to unaffiliated firms. In particular, Japan has
acquired vast amounts of foreign technology without allowing, until very recently, significant amounts of foreign investment. In Europe, also, significant transfers have occurred
between unaffiliated firms. The Japanese case is a special one,
because the Japanese were able to manipulate their investment and import regulations so as to make licensing agreements the only practical way in which technological advantages could be used to advantage in the Japanese market.[35]

The export of American technology has enabled multinational corporations, in a short period, to dominate faster
growing European industries such as transportation equipment, chemicals and synthetics, electronic components,
machinery, and food processing. By 1966 American multinational corporations controlled 33 percent of the petroleum
refining capacity, 25 percent of the European automotive
industry, 12 percent of the European chemical industry, 16
percent of electronic production, 80 percent of electronic
data processing, and 27 percent of new investments in the
machinery industry. These facts show that the technologically advanced American industries have been responsible
for the present hegemony of the multinational corporations.[36]

The results of our studies and research, so far, point out

the following conclusions:

A. A large portion of American **exports** is directly related to technological advantages enjoyed by U.S. industry. These technological advantages depend upon the continued research and exchange of ideas and technology with other nations.

B. Available evidence strongly indicates that the United States has not been a net supplier of new technologies to the world. It has, however, benefited substantially from the free international flow of technology by acquiring foreign scientific invention, foreign innovations, and an unqualifiable amount of technology through acquisition of foreign patents and the grantback of improvements made by foreign firms on licensed U.S. technology.

C. The extent of the technological gap between the United States and Western Europe has not been as wide as some writers have alleged. That gap has, however, now been narrowed in part by technology transfers by U.S. multinational corporations, and in part by the innovative capacities of the Europeans themselves.

D. The multinational companies have been responsible for the spread of American technology and the narrowing of the gap. But they have not been the sole cause of such a narrowing. The Western European and Japanese corporations have increased their research expenditures and investments in innovation and technological progress.

E. "To the extent that multinational firms have reduced the opportunities for exporting by diffusing technology before a foreign-owned company was capable of imitation, the United States might conceivably derive a short benefit from the regulation of such transfers. The potential benefit, of course, would be an extension of the time available for exploiting the technology by exporting."[37]

This short-term benefit might well prove illusory. The

multinational firm has frequently made its initial entry into foreign markets on the basis of its superior technology. By reason of its foreign investments, the multinational corporation has been able to extend the useful life of its technologies beyond the time when its exports—because of cost considerations—would no longer be competitive.[38]

However, it is extremely important to understand that the cost of research and development done in the United States can only be justified when it is spread over the largest available market. The very high cost of bringing a new product on the market includes an almost unbelievably complex amount of testing to meet expanding U.S. Government requirements. Therefore, the development of technology in any industry must be based on world-wide use of the new innovation and not restricted to use in the United States. Any American company would pare down its research and development effort if the resulting new technology was not usable in other countries. Shipments of goods to the United States from plants abroad, using U.S. technology, are minimal. A restriction on the use of this technology abroad would hurt the U.S. economy and the U.S. worker, and would in no way change the present level of imports or the level of U.S. employment.[39]

F. The economic recovery of Europe and Japan has allowed these countries to acquire the capital resources necessary to foster their own research and development and innovate their technological breakthroughs. Although the dollar expenditures for research and development in the United States still exceed that of any other nation ($14 billion annually in the United States; $5 billion in Japan, and $5 billion in West Germany), research expenditures in this country have been declining as a percentage of gross national product. As a result, several countries are now devoting a greater percentage of their income for technological research than the United States industries. Western Europe has more scientists and engineers working on industrial research than we have.

The effect of this increased emphasis on research and development abroad is indicated by the fact that 45 percent of U.S. patent applications are now of foreign origin. It is not surprising then that the Germans invented the rotary engine, which may be destined to revolutionize the automotive industry; that the Italians invented the radial tire; that the French developed and put into operation transfer machines to improve the manufacturing efficiency and quality of motor vehicle engines and other mechanical components; and that the Japanese have been leaders in the adaptation of computer technology to automobile production.[40]

G. Experience with past efforts of nations to control the international flows of capital and technology indicate that it would not be possible to control the exports of technology. Such a measure would be administratively difficult to manage and would not operate effectively. Apart from the technical difficulties inherent in operating a program to control the export of technology, there are other problems which the critics of the multinational corporations have ignored in their discussions: First, no nation would abandon its national interests to enforce an unrealistic program dictated by the United States. Second, such controls would tend to undermine a principal rationale for the acceptance of U.S. investments by other nations. This in itself would deprive U.S. corporations of access to new technology in foreign countries. Third, since technology is little more than knowledge in the minds of other individuals, restraint might have to be placed on the movement of individual inventors and innovators.[41]

H. Finally, every study points out the fact that U.S.

exports of manufactured goods depend upon product differentiation, whereas other industrial nations rely on price differences to export.

As a result, once a U.S. product reaches the height of its maturity, foreign firms start to imitate and modify that product to meet local needs and produce it more cheaply because of lower research and development costs. Today the competitive life of U.S. products (because of research progress in Europe and Japan), is about one-half the product life of goods produced prior to World War II.[4 2]

It is almost impossible to quantify the relationship between direct investment abroad and the transfer of U.S. technology for the following reasons:

The interrelationship which exists among employment, trade, technology, and foreign direct investment is highly complex.

The limited data available upon which we can base any conclusion show that the export of technology has helped both the U.S. economy and the labor market.

Despite all allegations, one thing is clear: The multinational corporations are among the most important vehicles for the transfer of commercial technology both to and from the United States. They not only export technology but through acquisitions and mergers of hundreds of foreign firms they have acquired billions of dollars' worth of foreign technology.

If the United States is to maintain its technology lead, policies must be adopted to encourage and stimulate research and development in the private sector as a means of strengthening the international competitive position of American industry as well as improving the standard of living and the quality of life in America and the world.

EXHIBIT 4-1
United States Multinational Corporations:
Research and Development Expenditures
in Manufacturing, Home Country and Abroad, 1966
(millions of dollars and percentage)

	Expenditures			
Item	Total	Home Country	Abroad	% of Total Spent Abroad
All manufacturing	8,124	7,598	526	6
Food products	154	136	18	12
Paper and allied products	67	64	3	4
Chemicals	1,332	1,258	74	6
Rubber products	·131	127	4	3
Primary and fabricated metals	322	312	10	3
Non-electrical machinery	833	743	90	11
Electrical machinery	1,917	1,814	103	5
Transportation equipment	2,671	2,537	134	5
Textiles and apparel	29	29	—	—
Lumber, wood and furniture	86	25	61	71
Printing and publishing	17	17	—	—
Stone, clay and glass	107	103	4	4
Instruments	393	372	21	5
Other	65	61	4	6

Source: Centre for Development Planning, Projections and Policies of the Department of Economic and Social Affairs of the United Nations Secretariat, based on United States Senate, Committee on Finance, *Implications of Multinational Firms for World Trade and Investment and for United States Trade and Labor* (Washington, D.C., 1973).

Notes

1. See Yvan Fabian, Alison Young. *R & D in OECD Member Countries: Trends and Objectives.* Paris, 1971.

2. Keith Pavitt. "Technology in Europe's Future" *Research Policy* I, August, 1972.

3. Foreign Trade and Investment Act of 1973, S 151 & H.R. 62, 93rd Congress, First Session, s 602 (a).

4. Mary Frances Teplin, "U.S. International Transactions in Royalties and Fees: Their Relationship to the Transfer of Technology," *Survey of Current Business*, Dec. 1973, p. 14.

5. Ibid., p. 16.

6. See Edward Dennison and Jean-Pierre Poullier, *Why Growth Rates Differ*, Washington, D.C., 1967.

7. Expenditures on research and development appear to be concentrated in a few firms. In 1964, out of 2,000 U.S. firms, 28 accounted for 63 percent of the total R & D. See O.E.C.D., *Gaps in Technology: General Report*, Paris, 1968, p. 15.

8. Keith Pavitt, "Technology, International Competition and Economic Growth," *World Politics*, January, 1973, p. 183.

9. *New York Times*, March 28, 1974, p. 67, col. 2.

10. Center of Multinational Studies, *The Benefits and Problems of Multinational Corporations*, December, 1972 (mimeographed copy).

11. See, for instance, O. M. Solandt, "Science, Policy and Canadian Manufacturing Industries," *The Canadian Forum*, Jan/Feb., 1972, p. 40.

12. According to Mansfield, estimated expenditures on R & D by American subsidiaries abroad amount to about only 4 percent of the corresponding expenditures made by parent companies at home. Edwin Mansfield, "The Multinational Firm and Technological Change" (mimeographed manuscript to be published in *The Multinational Enterprise and Economic Analysis*, ed. J. H. Dunning.)

13. *Policy Aspects of Foreign Investment by U.S. Multinational Corporations*, U.S. Department of Commerce, January, 1972, p. 30.

14. International Economic Sub-Committee of the Emergency Committee for American Trade, February, 1972, p. 42.

15. Senate Committee on Finance, February 21, 1973, p. 784.

16. U.S. Department of Commerce, op. cit., p. 31.

17. D. Keesing, "The Impact of Research and Development on United States' Trade," *Journal of Political Economy*, February, 1967, pp. 38-48.

18. M. Boretsky, "Concerns About the Present American Position in International Trade, *Technology and International Trade*, 1971, pp. 18-66.

19. R. Vernon, "International Investment and International Trade in the Product Cycle," *Quarterly Journal of Economics*, May, 1966, pp. 190-93.

20. Ibid., p. 200-205.

21. U.S. Tariff Commission, *Implications of Multinational Firms for World Trade and Investment and for U.S. Trade and Labor*, 93rd Congress, First Session, Washington, D.C., Feb., 1973, p. 604.

22. Ibid., p. 570.

23. Ibid., p. 578.

24. Ibid., p. 556.

25. Ibid., p. 557.

26. Manufacturing Chemists Association, *The Role of the Multinational Corporations in the Chemical Industry* (mimeograph), Dec. 31, 1972. Also reported in *Chemical Age*, Vol. 105, No. 2867, July 28, 1972.

27. William Gruber and Raymond Vernon, "The Technology Factor in a World Trade Matrix" *The Technology Factor in International Trade*, R. Vernon ed., New York, 1970, p. 235.

28. *IBM's Memorandum to Senator Abraham Ribicoff*, Chairman, Sub-Committee on International Trade, Committee on Finance, United States Senate, January 18, 1973.

29. American Federation of Labor, *An American Trade Union View of International Trade and Investment*, February 21, 1973, pp. 8-9.

30. U.S. Department of Commerce, op. cit., p. 33.

31. "Gaps in Technology: General Report," Organization for Economic Cooperation and Development, Paris, 1968.

32. U.S. Department of Commerce, op. cit., pp. 34-35.

33. J. Tilton, *International Diffusion of Technology: The Case of Semiconductors*, Brookings Institution, p. 66.

34. T. Ozawa, *Imitation, Innovation, and Japanese Exports in the Open Economy: Essays on International Trade and Finance* (Kenen and Lawrence, ed.) New York, Columbia University Press, 1968, p. 75.

35. U.S. Department of Commerce, op. cit., p. 34.

36. R. Hellmann, *The Challenge to U.S. Dominance of the International Corporation* New York, Dunellen, 1970, p. 60.

37. Memorandum for the Secretary of Commerce, by Assistant Secretary Harold B. Scot, January 10, 1972.

38. Ibid.

39. Statement to the International Trade Sub-Committee of the Senate Finance Committee by the Chairman of the Monsanto Company, December 31, 1972.

40. The National Association of Manufacturers, *U.S. Stake in World Trade: The Role of the Multinational Corporation*, New York, 1971, pp. 40-42.

41. The U.S. Department of Commerce, op. cit., p. 36.

42. R. B. Stobaugh, *The Product Life-Cycle of U.S. Exports and International Investment* (manuscript quoted by Senate Committee on Finance, February, 1973).

43. Ibid., p. 570.

5.
Multinationals
and the Tax Controversy

One of the more interesting questions raised by the rapid growth of the multinational corporations is the method by which income from foreign sources of these companies is taxed. The questions raised for economic policy by the functioning of the existing system of company taxation, or by the adoption of a new system, are complex and important. The interaction of the national systems of taxation have direct and indirect effects on the international flows of investment and trade.

The choice of a particular system of taxation in the past has, for the most part, been dictated by domestic policy considerations. Domestic policy considerations center on the issues of whether or not to tax retained profits, and how taxing retained profits more or less heavily than profits which are distributed as dividends will affect the level of capital formation and the allocation of funds for competing outlets of investment.

However, international considerations are playing an increasingly important role in influencing the systems of multinational taxation. International considerations center on the impact of the system of taxation upon the balance of capital transactions, upon the form taken by private direct and portfolio investment, and upon the government's share of revenue from international investment income.

The effective corporate tax rates of developed countries do not differ greatly, ranging from 35 percent for Japan to 50 percent for. France and Canada (with the United States at 50 percent).[1] The system of taxation, however, varies from country to country with further differences in their practical application due to technicalities of law and administrative practices. The basic differences in the systems center on the distinction between retained and distributed profits and the degree of alleviation of economic double taxation.[2]

Foreign direct investment subjects the multinational corporation to taxation in the parent (home) country, and also in the host (source) country. Without some form of relief this potential of double taxation can prove a barrier to foreign investment. Therefore, many of the developed countries, such as the United States, provide relief from double taxation in the form of credits against domestic taxes for foreign taxes paid. The general U.S. policy has been to give credit up to the amount of the effective U.S. tax (50 percent) for foreign taxes paid on earnings from overseas subsidiaries to prevent the inequity of double taxation.

United States tax policies relating to foreign source income are the outgrowth of decades of experience and study. Many of the prior loopholes were corrected in the Revenue Act of 1962. The present application of the Revenue Code to U.S. multinational corporations' operations abroad has been coordinated with the tax systems through 23 effective tax treaties with various nations. (see Infra p. 160.)[3]

The basic concept behind U.S. taxation of foreign source

income is, with certain exceptions, that the United States has no jurisdiction to tax foreign corporations except on their income from sources within the United States or otherwise connected with United States activities. Multinational affiliates can operate abroad as branches or as subsidiaries. The principal advantage of operating in the form of a subsidiary is that its income from sources outside the United States generally is not subject to current U.S. taxation. This income becomes subject to U.S. tax only when, and if, it is paid to the parent U.S. corporation as a dividend, interest, or service charge, or is repatriated to the United States as the result of liquidation. Tax on income not repatriated is "deferred" until the income is returned to the parent corporation. Thus, retained earnings of a foreign subsidiary generally may be reinvested without diminution by reason of the imposition of U.S. tax.

The principal exception to the basic concept of deferral of subsidiary income is the "Subpart F" base company income of certain U.S.-controlled foreign base corporations which is taxed currently as the income of the United States shareholders as if it had been paid as a dividend. Subpart F, which came into the tax laws in the 1962 Revenue Act,[4] imposes this exception that, when a corporation is a "controlled foreign corporation" (C.F.C., at least 50 percent owned by U.S. shareholders with "deemed distributed foreign income") a pro rata portion of the undistributed earnings of the foreign base company is taxable to those of its U.S. shareholders owning 10 percent or more of its stock.[5] The purpose of Subpart F was to eliminate double taxation. Also, if the controlled foreign corporation has certain types of "tainted" income, the U.S. shareholders are taxed currently regardless of repatriation.[6]

The purpose of Subpart F was to eliminate "tax haven" abuse. Before 1962 it was alleged that foreign subsidiaries abused their deferral privileges by using the foreign company, in a low tax country, as a "base company" for the accumulation of profits that should have rightfully been taxed to the domestic parent.

The other main tax advantage of operating abroad in the form of a subsidiary as opposed to a branch only affects subsidiaries located in less developed countries. The parents of subsidiaries are entitled to a "deemed" credit for foreign tax against repatriated dividends. The formula for estimating this credit differs according to whether the corporation is in a less developed country, in which case the tax rate can be reduced to a maximum of 6 percent. This results from the calculation of the deemed paid foreign tax credit whereby subsidiaries in developed countries are required to "gross up" and subsidiaries in less developed countries are not. The latter are not required, under the United States Code, to include in their income the portion of foreign corporations' income required to pay foreign income tax, but are allowed an indirect foreign tax credit for such income taxes.[7]

Branches, on the other hand, are taxed in the same manner as domestic corporations but are allowed a "direct" tax credit for foreign taxes. The tax credit operates so that when the foreign tax is lower than the U.S. tax, the United States collects the difference. The principal advantage of operating abroad in the form of a branch is that losses incurred by the foreign operations can be offset against U.S. source income for purposes of determining tax liability. Operating losses of subsidiaries can only reduce U.S. income tax liability of the parent corporation when the subsidiary is liquidated or sold.

It is possible for U.S. multinational affiliates to take advantage of the tax benefits afforded to both branches and subsidiaries by opening as a branch which in the initial stages incurs a loss, and then once operating becomes profitable, incorporating.

It should be noted that those U.S. corporations which qualify under the Domestic International Sales Corporations (DISC) legislation of 1971 are not subject to the same U.S. taxation on earnings and profit as are other subsidiaries. To qualify as a DISC 95 percent of a corporation's gross receipts must consist of sales of U.S. export property and 95 percent of its assets must be qualified as export sales. DISCs may defer tax on half of their income, as compared to overseas subsidiaries producing the same goods abroad, which can defer U.S. tax on all their income. However, the reduction of the extent of deferral is offset by their being taxed at a 24 percent rate rather than 48 percent. They are also not subject to foreign taxes to the same extent as foreign operating subsidiaries.

The Burke-Hartke Bill, reintroduced on January 3, 1973, proposes five amendments to the present Internal Revenue Code concerning multinational corporations.[8] The purpose of this bill, according to Senator Hartke, "is to stem the outflow of U.S. capital, jobs, technology and production." The bill would amend the Subpart F provisions to apply generally so that the undistributed earnings of all U.S.-controlled foreign subsidiary corporations would be taxed currently as income to their U. S. shareholders. It would legislate deferral privileges for foreign subsidiaries out of existence. In the case of corporate stockholders, both forms of foreign tax credit would be replaced by deduction for foreign taxes paid. The net result would be that shareholders of all multinational affiliates would be taxed currently, and would only be allowed to take foreign taxes as a deduction.

The Treasury Department, representing the Administration's point of view, issued a memorandum on June 11, 1973, that opposed the Burke-Hartke amendments and generally supported the present law. The Administration believes that the tax system is generally fair, proposing tax changes relating to "foreign tax haven manufacturing corporations." The proposals attempt to supply some objective standards to support a grant of Treasury discretion in the proposed legislation relative to "tax holidays" and "runaway plants."[9]

The Administration would expand Subpart F in a limited way. United States shareholders would be taxed on undistributed foreign earnings if the controlled foreign corporation engaged in manufacturing or processing makes new or additional investment in countries allowing a "tax holiday" or if it is a "runaway plant." There has been an increasing tendency for countries to attract investment in manufacturing by providing tax "holidays" from their income tax. To the extent that this influences investment decisions, it causes tax distortions that the Administration believes should be neutralized.[10]

The Administration also believes that the United States should tax currently the income of a corporation that is taking advantage of lower tax rates on manufactured goods destined for the U.S. market. The "runaway plant" provision would apply to a U.S.-controlled foreign corporation that has more than 25 percent of its receipts from manufacture of goods destined for the United States and that is subject to a significantly lower tax rate.[11]

There are many objections to the Burke-Hartke proposal that eliminates deferral altogether. The multinational corporations contend that taxation of undistributed earnings of foreign subsidiaries would place an undue burden on the U.S. shareholders of foreign corporations as opposed to domestic corporations. Domestic corporations are taxed on their dividend income and not on their undistributed earnings. Elimination of deferral abridges the fundamental principle of taxing income only when it is realized by U.S. stockholders.

It is also argued that the foreign affiliate in a low-tax

country without deferral would be paying more net taxes than his foreign counterpart. This would clearly give the foreign counterpart a competitive advantage. The after-tax profit of the American-owned subsidiary would be lower than a foreign-owned firm, assuming the same sales and costs. As a result, U.S. common stock values would deteriorate as foreign stocks would stand to gain in preference.

The case against deferral also revolves around the principle of tax neutrality. Proponents of the Burke-Hartke Amendment which would eliminate deferral argue that deferral violates the principle of tax neutrality by favoring American investors who place their investments in a low tax country. The American investor who invests in a low tax rate country is privileged to the extent that more is available for reinvestment purposes than for domestic corporations.[12] The present law, according to Senator Hartke, amounts to an interest-free government loan which—because profits are not repatriated—amounts to an outright tax exemption. The tax laws should not artificially encourage or discourage foreign investments.[13]

It is argued by proponents of the Burke-Hartke Bill that deferral also violates tax neutrality in differentiating between a subsidiary and a branch. Multinational corporations can open branches in order to be able to deduct losses from domestic incomes. Then in later years branches incorporate to take advantage of deferral. Also, if a U.S. corporation conducts exploration and production activities for oil and minerals through a branch operating abroad, it can deduct intangible drilling expenditures or mine development expenses against its U.S. income and can also claim a percentage depletion on its income from production abroad.

In addition to the questions raised regarding domestic and international tax neutrality there are other important considerations brought to bear on the elimination of deferral as opposed to retaining or expanding the present law. The National Foreign Trade Council has estimated that were deferral privileges and tax credits abolished, multinational corporations in developed countries would be effectively taxed in the range of 71-77 percent, an average increase of nearly 50 percent.[14] The much higher rates of effective taxation would probably result in a substantial amount of disinvestment by multinational corporations presently operating abroad. Investment by American firms in developing countries, with their lower tax rates, would decline since the lower rate would no longer offer an advantage, and those countries might then increase their tax rates to United States levels. These changes would come precisely at a time when the multinational corporations have to expand in order to provide the country with much needed oil and raw materials.

Some constitutional lawyers believe that the amendments not only violate certain long-accepted principles, but they may be subject to constitutional objections based on *Eisner v. Macomber*[15] since they involve the taxing of one entity based upon the undistributed profits of the other. Furthermore, they abridge the fundamentally sound principle of taxing income only when it is realized. Undistributed earnings of controlled foreign corporations are not realized by the U.S. taxholders. The philosophy behind tax deferral law is that the country in which the income is earned has the primary right to tax it. Violation of this principle will play into the hands of the host countries and give them an excuse to levy more taxes on the foreign firms.[16]

To measure the aggregate national effects of tax change is admittedly a complex and controversial calculation, but the effects on individual corporations could be very easily calculated. They will be undoubtedly adverse; and this in itself would harm the economy as a whole.

The study on this subject by the American Cyanamid

Company indicates that the tax provisions of the Burke-Hartke Amendment would force it to withdraw from many foreign markets and to decrease exports by about 50 percent with a proportionate loss in domestic employment. The Bendix Corporation has declared that adoption of the Burke-Hartke amendments "would be extremely serious for the company, and that a significant share of their direct exports would not have been possible in the absence of their foreign investment base." Goodyear believes that "the tax provision alone of the Burke-Hartke Bill could seriously impair not only our foreign operations but also our domestic operations."[17]

On the other hand, additional arguments presented by the advocates of the Burke-Hartke amendments include:

A. The tax deferral provision in the present law is inconsistent with our national policies to discourage the flow of capital abroad. Examples of such policies are: controls on foreign direct investment, the interest equalization tax, the Federal Reserve limits on foreign loans by U.S. commercial banks. The rate of U.S. investment abroad is so large as to be a major concern. Direct foreign investment has averaged about $8 billion a year recently and now aggregates near $90 billion. Profits are close to $42 billion from output produced abroad of about $200 billion. U.S. taxes paid on foreign profits have been about 5 percent, or about $1 billion. These compare with domestic corporate investment in the United States of about $30 billion annually, domestic profits considerably under $100 billion, and U.S. manufactured exports of some $50 billion. Corporation taxes paid on domestic profits are in the magnitude of 40 percent or more even after the reduction for foreign tax credit.

B. The opponents of the Arabs and the multinational oil corporations allege that speculation against U.S. dollars comes from oil-rich countries and multinational corporations.

Time and the oil crisis proved that there was very little truth to this allegation.

C. The Administration's proposals, according to Senator Hartke, do virtually nothing to close lucrative tax loopholes for the American-based multinational corporations. Despite the President's assertion in his trade message that tax changes will not solve our trade problems, taxation is a major part of the problem.

D. Finally, advocates of the Burke-Hartke Bill argue that substantial revenues could be raised by taxing earnings of subsidiaries currently. Peggy Musgrave has estimated that the privilege of deferral permits affiliates an annual tax saving of about $900 million.[18]

It is submitted that tax considerations in the past have been an important factor in corporate decisions to allocate resources. However, they are seldom the dominant consideration. The elimination of deferral would alter this. The elimination of deferral would place a very harsh tax burden on the multinational corporations' investment decisions precisely at a time when the United States stands to gain from international movements of trade and capital and is facing the fast growing competition of foreign multinational corporations.

The Administration's proposals to extend Subpart F in a limited way is also open to question. Subpart F was enacted as a revenue measure and as a means of preventing tax avoidance. However, as is noted by the Tariff Commission, "it has not generated any significant revenue and its complex provisions have produced a fruitless expenditure of business and accounting time."[19] The Administration's position on "tax holiday" incentives overlooks the fact that many foreign countries grant incentives because they consider them appropriate. The proposal would penalize American investors in those countries and encourage them to invest in high-tax countries.[20] There are numerous political and technical problems regarding "tax havens" of the multinational corporations. They are caught in the web of labor union politics, Middle Eastern affairs, and multinational lobbying.

The tax incentives are defined too broadly. Once an American-owned enterprise is "tainted," its future earnings are taxed punitively.

The runaway plant proposal is also unrealistic because the proportion of United States' imports from U.S.-controlled foreign corporations has been estimated to be "quite nominal." The proposal would help insure that the control of foreign operations producing for the U.S. market would be under foreign ownership. If tax holidays and incentives distort economic decisions, the appropriate remedy would appear to be bilateral negotiations under GATT rules or treaty negotiations. The United States should not give up economic benefits available to U.S. investors without securing other inducements in the bargain.[21]

The second tax issue raised by the Burke-Hartke Bill is whether the foreign tax credit should be eliminated and be replaced by deductions. An important aspect of tax reform which the bill does not consider, as it eliminates the tax credit altogether, is that multinational corporations may use either a per-country or overall foreign tax credit. Specifically, the taxpayer may elect the "overall" or the "per country" limitation subject to the requirement of consistency once a choice of method is made. The overall limitation permits advantageous averaging of foreign tax rates. It permits tax credits that could not be used under the per-country limitation, encouraging multinational corporations into low-tax jurisdictions in order to spread foreign tax credits. Peggy Musgrave has estimated that the overall limitation constitutes a revenue loss of approximately $230 million.[22]

Senator Hartke has indicated that the amendment that would abolish the foreign tax credit system is open to compromise on the basis of double taxation. He has added, however, that credits should not be permitted for "tax havens" or low-tax foreign jurisdiction.[23]

The credit against U.S. taxes for foreign taxes paid in the source country where income is earned developed out of Congressional recognition of the unfairness and discrimination involved in double taxation of income. The Revenue Act of 1918[24] provided for a credit against U.S. taxes in the case of any "income, war profits and excess profits taxes." The 1921 Revenue Act[25] narrowed the scope of the tax credit by providing that the tax credit allowed could not exceed the total U.S. tax on all of the taxpayer's foreign income. The taxpayer could not use his foreign tax credits to offset income from U.S. operations. In 1932[26] the limitation was tightened to provide that the amount allowed as a credit for taxes paid to any one country could not exceed U.S. tax on income derived from that country.

In 1958 it was recognized that the per-country limitation could lead to double taxation. Accordingly there was established a two-year carryback and a five-year carryover of foreign taxes which cannot be used as a credit in a particular year.[27] In the 1962 Revenue Act it was provided that a domestic parent corporation must "gross up" the foreign tax paid by the subsidiary with respect to dividends repatriated, as well as the amount of the dividend itself.[28] This has the effect of increasing the amount of income taxed and was directed to reducing foreign direct investment.[29]

The Administration proposal would modify the present system under which the United States bears the cost during the loss years but receives none of the revenue during the profitable years. Where a U.S. taxpayer has deducted foreign losses against U.S. income, such losses would be taken into account to reduce the amount of foreign tax credit claimed by such a taxpayer on foreign earnings in later years.[30]

The proponents of the present law argue that foreign direct investment is beneficial to the United States. The Burke-Hartke proposal would substantially increase the tax cost of foreign investment, with the increase being proportional to the foreign tax rate. Consequently, U.S. corporations would be forced to reduce, and perhaps eliminate, their foreign direct investments. We do not know the repercussions of reduced foreign direct investment. Would domestic investments be increased? Would foreign tax systems be changed in recognition of the abolition of the foreign tax credit by the United States? Would other countries adopt similar measures resulting in reduced investments by their companies in the United States? Consequently it would be very unwise to take any action which hurts the American economic interests in the United States, Western Europe, and the developing nations.

The foreign tax credit serves a very important purpose. It prevents confiscatory taxation of foreign source income, as compared with the taxation of other kinds of income, and assures effective competition with foreign industry both at home and abroad. As mentioned above, replacement of the credit by a deduction, and elimination of deferral privileges, would increase the effective total tax rate on foreign earnings to over 70 percent.

Repeal of the credit, according to witnesses before the Ways and Means Committee of the House of Representatives, would curtail domestic employment, have an adverse effect on the balance of payments by decreasing foreign investments, invite possible retaliation, and require negotiations of treaties. It would defeat the principle of double taxation of foreign source income. Moreover, it would destroy a stable tax system which people have relied on for fifty years, the existence of which has contributed so much to the expansion of the American economy.

Those who compare foreign taxes to state taxes, and use the state tax system as an example, ignore important facts.

The state taxes are small; foreign taxes are high. Giving a credit for state income taxes would result in a state takeover of federal revenues. The credit for foreign income tax recognizes the proposition that the taxing jurisdiction of the taxpayer's nationality should forego its tax, where necessary, to avoid double tax on the same income. This is because the source country provides the primary governmental benefits required to earn the income; whereas, in the case of domestic companies, such benefits are jointly supplied by the state, local, and federal government. The state gives a credit for taxes paid in other states. This is a more comparable analogy than the federal allowance of a deduction for taxes paid to states.

The two limitations on foreign tax credit, according to the multinational corporations and some economic analysts, are essential to the survival of American investments abroad: the "overall" to assure that the host countries do not increase their tax rates; and the "per country" to prevent losses in one country from spilling over to reduce the credit for taxes actually paid to another.

"The tax credit mechanism is nearly universal. The few countries which don't use it, as France and The Netherlands, levy no taxes on income earned abroad by their nationals."[31]

Senator Hartke and Congressman Burke, in support of their bill, present the following arguments:

A. Foreign investments export jobs from the United States and should therefore be discouraged. The tax credit has been responsible for the loss of jobs. Foreign tax credits in 1970 amounted to about $4 billion and represent a substantial concession to foreign investments.

B. The tax credit for foreign taxes contrasts with a deduction for state and local taxes. Why should a dollar in state taxes save the corporation 48 cents in U.S. taxes while a dollar in foreign taxes saves a full dollar of U.S. taxes?

C. The full credit has encouraged foreign governments to increase the tax rate on U.S. corporations, thus transferring revenues from the U.S. Treasury to their own.

D. "A practical tax credit," contends Senator Hartke, "would recognize that in many ways the United States does provide benefits to the foreign investments of its nationals. It would prevent preemptions by foreign governments of the U.S. ability to tax the profits of nationals from foreign investment. It would also give U.S. corporations, which are parents of foreign subsidiaries, a stake in keeping foreign income taxes down to reasonable levels."[32]

The third major tax provision of the Burke-Hartke Bill is the imposition of straight-line depreciation on subsidiaries. Under the present law, accelerated methods of depreciation such as double declining balance or sum of the years' digits may be used for property outside the United States. Branches and subsidiaries are permitted to take the depreciation allowance they are entitled to in the source country. Burke-Hartke would limit "any property which either is located outside the United States or is used predominantly outside the United States (to) an allowance computed under the straight line method on the basis of the useful life of the property in the hands of the taxpayer" in the case of a branch and would limit the depreciation allowance to straight-line in calculating earnings and profits of a subsidiary.[33]

Senator Hartke argues that rapid depreciation has been a significant factor in the imbalance of the current economic expansion. Its use for foreign investment adds to inflationary pressures encouraging a boom in business investment in machinery. It also is an excessive incentive toward foreign direct investment.[34]

The multinational corporations argue that the present system should be continued because foreign investments tend to carry more risk than domestic investments and should be written off before they are nationalized or confiscated. Furthermore, the laws of many countries permit faster write-offs than the United States. For instance, in the United Kingdom approximately 94 percent of a capital investment may be recovered in the first year as compared with only approximately 19 percent in the United States. In five years 99 percent can be recovered in the United Kingdom, whereas only 58 percent can be recovered in the United States. West Germany, France, Italy, and Canada also have comparably high capital recovery rates.[35]

It is submitted that the imposition of a straight-line depreciation would be very damaging to multinational subsidiaries placing them at a severe disadvantage in high-tax countries. Foreign multinational corporations already have a significant advantage over U.S. multinational corporations in their present respective depreciation allowances. Imposition of the straight-line depreciation would be punitive to U.S. foreign direct investors and would weaken the U.S. position in international trade.

The fourth tax amendment of the Burke-Hartke is the technology control provision. The proposal would recognize as ordinary income the transfer of technology in reorganizations by corporations. This "runs counter to the very idea of corporate reorganization which is that there is not more than a formal change in the original investment involved."[36]

Finally the Burke-Hartke Bill would repeal the law which permits a tax exemption to individual American citizens who work and earn incomes outside the United States. Under the present law, any U.S. citizen who is a bona fide resident of, or present for 17 of 18 months in foreign countries may be excluded from U.S. income tax. This exclusion is limited to $25,00 after three years of bona fide residence, and $20,000 in other cases.[37]

Senator Hartke would like to terminate this foreign earned income exclusion clause.

The Administration and opponents of the Hartke amendment believe that termination of the present law is against the national interests. The reasons cited are:

A. This law is an incentive for Americans to work abroad and transfer their savings to the United States.
B. It helps the job market in this country.
C. The United States benefits, both politically and economically, from having trained American citizens stationed abroad.
D. Individual income tax rates are often high abroad and little U.S. revenue would be realized with or without the exclusion.
E. Employees abroad often face high living costs, high indirect foreign taxes, additional costs of schooling, housing, and travel. The earned income exclusion can be justified as compensation for these factors and hardships which they endure.
F. Because of inflation adjustments in the exclusion limits should be raised and not lowered.
G. Elimination of the exclusion would force the industry to hire foreign nationals.[38]

The Burke-Hartke Bill received some attention especially from the labor unions. There have been long hearings on the bill both at the Senate Committee on Finance and the Ways and Means Committee of the House of Representatives. But so far, because of strong opposition by members of Congress, the press, and the business community, no action has been taken. The reason given by analysts and the Congressional Research Service is that the bill's approach is not realistic. It ignores the fact that a host of reasons influence any particular firm to invest abroad.

One major reason for foreign investment is the unavailability of certain natural resources and agricultural products in the United States. Investments abroad in petroleum, woodpulp, bauxite, iron ore, nickel, copper, uranium, and tropical fruits are essential to the well-being of this country and hardly anybody has expressed opposition to this kind of investment.

However, there is some controversy over the non-manufacturing or service sectors. The multinational corporations contend that services such as banking, advertising, packaging, and engineering can neither be exported from the United States nor imported back to this country and, therefore, should be excluded from the debate.

Labor is not in total agreement and contends that tax privileges encourage the transfer of American technology to a foreign manufacturing plant and thus help to erode the U.S. position in foreign trade. Furthermore, labor asserts that any investment abroad is a drain on domestic capital in the United States.

A survey of multinational firms by business study groups refutes both Senator Hartke's claims and labor's contentions. Tax incentives, according to the surveys, have never been a major factor. In most developed countries tax rates are roughly equivalent of the U.S. corporate rate. Special tax incentives for the initial investment exist only in a few countries, such as Luxembourg and Ireland, which do not, however, attract the bulk of U.S. investment in manufacturing.

In a statement before the Senate Finance Committee, the chairman of the Xerox Corporation presented the following arguments in opposition to the Burke-Hartke Bill:

"Protectionists assert that a principal reason for multinational corporation is the avoidance of taxes. Indeed, the tax provisions of the Burke-Hartke Bill are premised upon this assertion. This premise is simply not true."

A thorough study shows that in order to avoid the double taxation of income earned abroad most industrial nations have adopted one of two systems. One is to exempt foreign income from home country taxes while the other is to allow a credit for foreign taxes paid. The United States along with Canada, Germany, Japan, Mexico, and the United Kingdom have adopted the latter system. The credit is limited to the U.S. income tax liability associated with the foreign source income thereby insuring that the total tax burden will be the higher of either the U.S. or foreign tax on income.

In the case of Xerox this system has resulted in a total tax burden on its overseas earnings of 50.2 percent which is substantially equivalent to the U.S. tax rate upon purely domestic operations.

Under the Burke-Hartke amendment Xerox's tax would have been 75 percent or 50 percent more than the burden upon domestic operations. "This result would not only make it virtually impossible for U.S.-based corporations to compete in foreign markets, it would make it economically unattractive for them to even attempt to do so."[39]

The Emergency Committee for American Trade in a statement declared: "The notion that foreign investment is motivated by tax loopholes and foreign tax shelters is as erroneous as the notion that U.S. firms locate overseas to take advantage of lower labor rates."[40]

"Sufficient detailed analysis of the adverse consequence of the tax provisions of legislation along the lines of the 1972 Foreign Trade and Investment Bill has been made by knowledgeable authorities to establish that U.S. firms are not motivated by tax advantage—under either U.S. or foreign law—in making foreign investment, that U.S. tax revenues from foreign subsidiaries would be lost, in whole or part, rather than re-derived from substitute domestic operations; and that repatriated foreign earnings pay their full share of the tax bill of U.S. multinational corporations on a tax neutral basis."[41]

Thus, the proposed imposition of current tax on overseas earnings would cripple corporate operations by compelling the payment of dividends, thereby depriving the subsidiary of the multinationals abroad of capital for expansion and competition.

Similarly the proposal by Senator Hartke to repeal the foreign credit would involve a return to double taxation. Not only would this place American multinational corporations at a disadvantage with respect to their foreign competitors, it would constitute the abandonment of reciprocal tax agreements with other countries. "To prohibit U.S. citizens and corporations by domestic law from benefitting from these provisions would constitute a unique example of unilateral yielding of equitable U.S. tax treatment for individuals and firms while maintaining those advantages for foreign firms and individuals investing in the United States."[42]

An international comparison of total tax burden on foreign investment answers the question whether foreign direct investment provides U.S. multinational corporations with gaping tax loopholes. Such a comparison has been made by the National Trade Council and refutes the notion that foreign investment is motivated by the desire to avoid high domestic taxes.

The following figures show the current effective tax rates on income earned by wholly-owned manufacturing subsidiaries operating in selected countries with substantial U.S. investment.

The National Foreign Trade Council's comparison shows that the heaviest tax burden of all—56.2 percent vs. 50.9 percent in the United States, results from investment in

Canada where the book value of U.S. manufacturing investment is more than twice as high as in any other country and
almost as much as total investments in Western Europe. The

United States	50.9%
Canada	56.2%
France	51.2%
Germany	48.8%
Italy	53.9%
Japan	47.8%
Mexico	48.5%
Netherlands	48.6%
United Kingdom	50% in 1973
Brazil	30% plus other taxes on earnings
Columbia	40% plus other taxes on earnings
Venezuela	Progressive to 50%
Saudi Arabia	50%
Belgium	40%
Iran	50%[43]

average of total tax burdens of U.S.-owned foreign subsidiaries in the above countries compared, weighted by book
value of United States manufacturing investments in 1970, is
51.1 percent, which is slightly higher than the U.S. corporate
tax, counting both Federal and average state income taxes as
reduced by the Federal income tax deduction. Even where
the tax is lower, as in Germany and Japan, the differences are
too small to constitute significant motivation for foreign
investment.[44]

Furthermore, the small differences are offset by the
general inclination of other countries to apply higher indirect
taxes than prevail in the United States. This is an element of
taxation not included in the above comparison. The following comparison shows the percentage of indirect tax revenue
levied in different countries:

United States	30.4%	Japan	39.6%
Canada	48.4%	Mexico	N/A
France	42.9%	Netherlands	29.6%
Germany	39.4%	United Kingdom	47.2%[45]
Italy	41.3%		

Of the eight foreign countries mentioned above, and of 43 countries ranked according to the percentage of tax revenues from indirect taxes, only the Netherlands has a lower percentage than the United States. These fact comparisons of income tax rates hardly support the claim that the multinational corporations invest abroad because of low tax rates.

Even though U.S. Federal tax liabilities are reduced by the foreign tax credit, multinational corporations, both American and foreign-owned, pay billions of dollars to state and local authorities in the United States as well as abroad. A survey by the National Association of Manufacturers indicates that 83 multinational companies, which earned $18.3 billion before taxes, on sales of $152 billion, paid $8.5 billion or about 46 percent of their income in taxes.[4 6]

Finally, the Burke-Hartke tax proposals to eliminate the present system create a new situation by abrogating double taxation treaties signed by the United States with the following nations:[4 7]

Australia	1953	Luxembourg	1964
Austria	1957	Netherlands	1947
Belgium	1953	New Zealand	1951
Canada	1941	Norway	1951
Denmark	1948	Pakistan	1959
Finland	1971	South Africa	1946
France	1945	Sweden	1940
West Germany	1954	Switzerland	1951
Greece	1953	Trinidad&	1970
Ireland	1951	Tabago	
Italy	1956	United Kingdom	1945
Japan	1955		

The present U.S. tax, according to many impartial studies, reflects a very complex and complicated situation and it is in the best interest of the United States to continue the present arrangement and allow American industry to compete successfully in foreign markets by foreign investments as well as by exports. Congress in 1961 and 1962 held lengthy hearings on taxation of foreign source income and concluded then that the United States must continue to encourage U.S. direct foreign investments. This is even more true today as foreign competition has greatly increased.

The issue is not one of merely closing "tax loopholes." Many that may have existed were closed in 1962. Rather, at stake are tax issues of fundamental importance to both the United States and the international economy.

The possibility, submitted by the proponents of change, that up to $3.5 billion in additional tax revenue could be gained cannot be supported and documented on the basis of the data and models now available; the proponents of the change clearly have the burden of proof that substantial losses would not outweigh the gains sought. "The revenue gain might, as suggested above, prove illusory in the long run, as the income being taxed dried up under competitive pressure." [48]

Notes

1. Report of the President's Task Force on Business Taxation, September, 1970, p. 41.

2. For a concise exposition of the corporate tax systems of the OECD countries see *Company Tax Systems in OECD Member Countries*, Organization for Economic Cooperation and Development, Paris, 1973.

3. Tariff Commission, 1973, p. 896.

4. Internal Revenue Code, Section 952.

5. Exceptions to Subpart F occur in the case of certain corporations in less developed countries, corporations involved in exporting, and where a C.F.C. has agreed to repatriate as dividends an amount sufficient to bring its foreign and domestic tax up to 90 percent of the taxes that would have been paid were it a domestic corporation. See I.R.C. of 1954, Section 5.

6. "Tainted" income includes income from the sale of goods which are either purchased from or sold to a related party; income from services performed by the foreign corporation for or on behalf of a related party; and "foreign personal

holding company income"—income from the sale or exchange of stock or securities, or income from dividends, interest, rents, or royalties. See I.R.C., 1954, Section 954 (c), (d), (e).

7. The deemed credit is calculated by multiplying the foreign income taxes paid by a fraction: The numerator is the dividend paid to the parent; the denominator in developed countries is the amount of accumulated earnings after the payment of foreign taxes; the denominator in less developed countries is the amount of total accumulated earnings prior to payment of foreign taxes. The credit is then grossed up (added to the dividend actually sent back) in developed countries, and not grossed up for less developed countries. The credit (and the dividend actually repatriated) is then multiplied by the prevailing U.S. tax rate. The credit is then subtracted from the resulting figure, giving the final tax liability of the parent. See I.R.C. of 1954, Sections 901, 902.

8. Burke-Hartke (H.R. 62 and S. 151), Sections 102-105. The Burke-Hartke amendments would legislate: (1) the deferral privilege out of existence, (2) the repeal of the foreign tax credit, (3) affiliates to use the straight line method of depreciation only, (4) recognition of all gains realized by a parent from the transfer of patents and copyrights to affiliates, and (5) the repeal of Section 911 of the Internal Revenue Code which permits American citizens—residents abroad for at least 17 months—to be exempt from federal tax up to $20,000 of foreign earned income.

9. Committee on Ways and Means, U.S. House of Representatives, *Multinationals: Perspectives on Trade and Taxes*; 93rd Congress, First Session, July, 1973, p. 2.

10. Ibid., p. 3.

11. Ibid., p. 3.

12. See L. Krause and K. Dam, *Federal Tax Treatment of Foreign Income*, Brookings, 1964, pp. 56-62.

13. Committee on Ways and Means, op. cit., p. 6.

14. Derived from *Economic Implications of Proposed Changes in the Taxation of U.S. Investments Abroad*, National Foreign Trade Council, June, 1972, p. 12.

15. 252 U.S., 189.

16. Committee on Ways and Means, op. cit., pp. 4, 5.

17. Center for Multinational Studies *The Benefits and Problems of Multinational Corporations*, December 26, 1972. (Manuscript submitted to the Senate Committee on Finance.)

18. Musgrave, "Tax Preferences to Foreign Investment," in *The Economics of Federal Subsidy Programs*, Joint Economic Committee, 92nd Congress, Second Session, 1972.

19. Committee on Finance, United States Senate, "Implications of Multinational Firms for World Trade and Investment and for U.S. Trade and Labor," 93rd Congress, First Session, February, 1973, p. 905.

20. Committee on Ways and Means, July, 1973, op. cit., p. 5.

21. Ibid., p. 5.

22. Op. cit., p. 188.

23. Stated in a speech to the Board of Governors, Electronic Industries Association, January 26, 1973.

24. 40 Stat. 1057, ch. 18, sections 222, 238.

25. 43 Stat. 227, ch. 136, sections 222 (a) (5) and 228 (a).

26. 47 Stat. 169, ch. 209, section 131 (b) (1).

27. Internal Revenue Code of 1954, section 904 (e).

28. 76 Stat. 960, amending Internal Revenue Code of 1958, sections 78, 902.

29. Tariff Commission, 1973, op. cit., pp. 874, 875.

30. Committee on Ways and Means, op. cit., p. 7.

31. Ibid., pp. 8-9.

32. Statement by Senator Hartke before the Ways and Means Committee, July, 1973.

33. Burke-Hartke, Section 104. See B. Fisher, "The Multinationals and the Crisis in United States Trade and Investment Policy," 53 *Boston University Law Review* 308, 1973, p. 352.

34. House Ways and Means Committee, op. cit., p. 11.

35. Derived from Supporting Testimony by Dr. Pierre Rinfret, Rinfret-Boston Associates, Inc. offered to the House Committee on Ways and Means, Hearings on Tax Reform, Feb. 7, 1973.

36. B. Fisher, op. cit., p. 353.

37. Committee on Ways and Means, op. cit., p. 12.

38. Ibid.

39. "The Multinational Corporations," statement before Subcommittee on International Trade Committee on Finance, U.S. Senate (file copy, manuscript), February 21, 1973.

40. The Emergency Committee for American Trade, 1972.

41. New Proposals for Taxing Foreign Income, National Association of Manufacturers, December, 1972.

42. Ibid.

43. "Economic Implications of proposed change in the taxation of U.S. Investment Abroad," National Foreign Trade Council publication, June 1972, as quoted in the Report of the Committee on Finance, U.S. Senate, February, 1973.

44. Ibid.

45. Financial Times, London, April 13, 1972.

46. National Association of Manufacturers, New Proposals for Taxing Foreign Income, New York, 1972.

47. Tariff Commission 1973, op. cit., p. 896.

48. For further information, see Peggy Musgrave, Tax Preferences to Foreign Investment, Joint Economic Committee: The Economic of Federal Subsidy Program, Part II, International Subsidies, Government Printing Office, Washington, D.C., June 1972. Also statements by Dr. N. R. Danielian, before the Joint Economic Committee, July 31, 1972.

6.
The Impact of the Multinational Corporations on the United States Balance of Payments

The United States balance of payments has registered a deficit in almost every year since 1950 regardless of the type of measurement used. This fact has occasioned a great deal of analysis and research. Some experts focus on the trade account, others on the world monetary problems, inflation, the government sector, or the capital account. In this past year the balance of payments problem has taken on added dimension due to the world energy shortage and rising costs of raw materials.

Multinational corporations, prime movers of private capital, have concurrently come under closer scrutiny. The multinational corporations are the main agents of foreign direct investment. This capital outflow, for accounting purposes, is a debit item in the balance of payments, that includes money spent on corporate capital stock, bond purchases, plant purchases, and similar investment.

In the early 1960s the United States direct investment abroad was increasing rapidly, and more than doubled between 1962 and 1965. The deteriorating balance of payments at that time led to voluntary investment controls, which, it was assumed, would have a favorable impact on the United States' payment position. In 1968 controls on such capital outflows were made mandatory and continued to be mandatory until February 1974. Investment controls have encouraged affiliates abroad to reinvest their earnings without repatriation and have greatly increased foreign borrowing. This, of course, is not reflected in the balance of payments.

A cursory glance at foreign direct investment as a debit item on the balance of payments (see Exhibit 6-1) fails to take into account many positive and negative effects ascribed to this capital outlay. In a broad sense foreign direct investment has been a major factor in the economic growth of the world, making available not only capital but also technology and managerial skills. The United States, in turn, receives raw materials, remitted earnings, and an increased export demand. However, opinions vary greatly in the weighing of the costs and benefits of multinational direct investment.

Direct investment by the United States multinational corporations abroad affects the balance of payments in the following manner.

1. There are a variety of trade flows generated by U.S. direct investment abroad. There may be exports of capital equipment, raw materials or semiprocessed goods, and finished goods. The presence of U.S.-based affiliates may also indirectly stimulate demand for American products. On the other hand, U.S. exports may be displaced and imports from affiliates into the United States may replace formerly U.S.-produced goods.
2. There is usually an initial outflow of capital from the parent company, although in recent years funds have been increasingly obtained abroad. The direct investment then generates a stream of earnings in subsequent years in the form of dividends, interest, and branch profits. There may be other remittances such as royalties and fees for the use of patents and managerial services.
3. Other items on the balance of payments may be affected, such as

travel, transportation, interest payments on foreign borrowings, and other services related to foreign investment. These items are relatively small compared to the above trade and capital flows.

It is often overlooked that foreign multinational corporations have direct investments in the United States that also affect the balance of payments. This will be discussed subsequently in this chapter.

One other potential impact of the multinational corporations on the balance of payments is the short-term capital funds that multinational corporations move across international boundaries. Varying interest rates and exchange rates have made international monetary management a source of potential profit or loss in itself. Unfortunately, the balance of payments impact of multinational short-term capital movements have largely resisted quantification.

The Effect of Direct Investment on the Trade Account

On the positive side, it is submitted that direct investment stimulates the demand for exports of capital goods, exports for further processing, and the resale of finished products. The demand for exports of capital goods appears to be the least tenable benefit. Initially an affiliate may purchase capital goods from the parent corporation, but once it becomes established, it usually either purchases such equipment from third countries or manufactures it locally.[1] Exports for further processing are a more convincing benefit, particularly in the automotive industry. The most significant demand for exports by affiliates is for resales without further manufacture.

A study by Business International of 133 United States corporations found that between 1960 and 1972 exports to affiliates increased 484 percent as compared to a 154 percent increase in total U.S. exports of nonagricultural goods. Exports for further processing rose to $2.7 billion in 1972 while exports of finished products to affiliates rose to $4.4 billion.[2]

In the aggregate U.S. merchandise exports shipped to majority-owned affiliates of U.S. multinational corporations increased from $7.8 billion in 1966 to $13.0 billion, in 1970, an average annual gain of 13.5 percent. U.S. imports from such affiliates rose from $5.8 billion in 1966 to $10.9 in 1970, an average annual gain of 17.2 percent. In 1966 exports to U.S. affiliates accounted for 26.7 percent of all U.S. merchandise exports, rising to 31.0 percent in 1970 (see Exhibit 6-4 at end of chapter).

On the other hand, the overall effect of U.S. corporate foreign direct investment, it may be argued, is negative in terms of the balance of trade. Negative factors to be considered include U.S. imports from United States affiliates abroad, exports of affiliates to third countries, the affiliates' sales in local markets abroad that displace U.S. exports and the narrowing of the U.S. comparative advantage through the diffusion of managerial and technical know-how.

A complete assessment of the multinational corporations' effect on U.S. exports and imports would entail estimating trade flows that would have occurred if the multinationals' foreign affiliates did not exist. The principal difficulty facing all analysts is that it is impossible to know exactly what would happen if the United States firms did not make direct investments abroad. It is an open question subject to somewhat futile theorizing. It can be assumed at one extreme that the United States would export all the goods that the multinational affiliates now provide the world markets. At the other extreme, it can be assumed that foreign competitors closer to markets and with a cheaper supply of labor would have preempted the markets. The truth probably lies somewhere in the middle.

The Effect of Direct Investment on the Capital Account

Initially, when a United States parent company is setting up a branch or a subsidiary abroad, there is usually a large outlay of capital from the parent. Later on the investment in different countries is financed in large part out of funds obtained abroad or from revenues of the affiliates. In subsequent years there is a return flow of income to the parent company in the form of dividends or remitted earnings. And there may also be other types of income payments, such as dividends, royalties, and fees. Thus, the multinational affiliate, even if it were a negative factor on the balance of trade, may be a positive factor on the balance of payments if it repatriates enough earnings from abroad.

According to Professor Jack N. Behrman, a former Assistant Secretary of Commerce, the receipts of the multinational corporations normally pay for the initial capital outflow in the balance of payments within about two years.[3] It is estimated that more than $6 billion was returned to parent corporations in the United States in the forms of interest, dividends, and branch earnings in 1970, and that such earnings may amount to over $17 billion by 1975.[4] In 1970 the long-term capital outflows that go toward setting up and financing affiliates were $4.4 billion, and was down to $3.3 billion in 1972.[5] The multinational corporations, by repatriating their earnings, and by fairly paying taxes, thus can generate a positive effect on the balance of payments.

The question asked by many analysts is how long a period of time elapses between the initial outflow of capital and a positive return on capital investment registers on the balance of payments. Again this depends on the assumptions made. That is, whether the investment abroad supplements or substitutes for investment by foreign firms, and whether investment abroad does or does not reduce domestic investment. A study by Professors G. C. Hufbauer and F. M. Adler for the Department of the Treasury present the following assumptions:

1. U.S. investment abroad adds to capital formation in the host country—that is, it supplements rival foreign investment—while at home it adds to some capital formation.
2. U.S. investment abroad does not change total capital formation either in the host country or in the United States. It then substitutes rival foreign investment and leaves domestic investment unchanged.
3. U.S. investment abroad adds to capital formation abroad, but leaves domestic investment unchanged.[6]

The results depend considerably upon the initial assumptions made. However, in general, it may be stated that time is the essential factor. In the short run, direct investment is a negative factor in the balance of payments. In the longer run, the results of direct investment will have a positive effect on the balance of payments.[7]

The deterioration in the United States balance of payments since 1950 has raised the question of whether the capital outflow caused by multinational corporations has contributed to the deterioration, or whether it has helped save it from complete collapse. Particularly since the Foreign Direct Investment Regulations (FDIR) affected mandatory controls in 1968 extensive theoretical and empirical research has been directed toward this issue.

However, intensive analysis of this nature overlooks the major causes of the United States balance of payments deficits. Although the United States' balance of payments had been slowly losing ground through the 1950s, much of the deficit at that time was attributed to the dollar becoming a reserve currency. By 1960 the deficit was significant enough to call into question international confidence in the dollar. As was concisely stated in a Fairleigh Dickinson

University study in 1963, the new dimension added to the balance of payments difficulties was the heavy unilateral transfers by the government of the United States "composed largely of military expenditures abroad and economic and military grant assistance to foreign countries."[8]

Basically, the situation was brought about by a belief on the part of the policy makers in Washington that the economic and financial resources of the United States were inexhaustible. This belief has been shared and encouraged by successive administrations, regardless of political affiliation. Half-hearted attempts have been made by different administrations to remedy the chronic deficit with few long-term results.

There is also the temptation on the part of many to look to the private sector of the economy to solve the problem, while it is the government itself which must bear the primary responsibility. Initially the United States provided aid to rebuild the war-torn nations of World War II on a grant basis rather than in repayable loans. Even when the foreign aid program was on a loan basis currency devaluations could circumvent genuine repayment.[9] Secondly, the United States undertook the maintenance of troops and the dispatching of military equipment to foreign countries, which became an automatic guarantee to financial prosperity to those countries providing a surplus in their balance of payments and a deficit in the United States account. Finally, the growing cost of the Vietnam War, compounded by the inflationary spiral, assured the United States its present problems in balancing the accounts.

The United States "basic" balance of payments, which includes long-term capital in addition to the current account, indicates that the private sector has been in surplus in every year since 1950. Merchandise trade was in surplus from 1950 until 1970, registered a deficit in 1971 and 1972, and again was in surplus in 1973. Private services have been in surplus since 1950 increasing to over a $6 billion surplus in 1973, reflecting the substantially higher profits of the U.S. firms abroad. The government sector, on the other hand, has been running a deficit of around $7 billion every year since 1967 and has continuously been in deficit since 1950.[10]

Even the "liquidity" balance of payments, which includes U.S. monetary reserve assets and liquid liabilities, shows that the private sector has been in near balance from 1960 until 1969 and again in 1973. In a very real sense, then, the United States has a continuing balance of payments deficit because administrations have chosen to continue the mistakes of their predecessors.

Beginning in 1968, however, the deteriorating situation began to reach crisis proportions and in the first two quarters of 1971 it was in large part responsible for the destruction of the Bretton Woods monetary system. The causes of collapse were many and the roots can be traced to the many years of unlimited spending for foreign aid, the Vietnam War, inflation, the structural decline in the relative position of U.S. agricultural commodities and industrial goods, other military expenditures overseas, and, finally, the loss of confidence in the managers of the United States economy in Washington.

The unstable condition of the economy and the Administration's blundering and muddling encouraged the rapid outflow of capital. Many Europeans who hoped that the Nixon Administration would curb inflation and would create an environment favorable to investment in the United States (after 1970) started to withdraw their funds from U.S. security markets in response to the Nixon recession and sharp decline in stock prices. They were followed by many Americans who exported their capital in search of more attractive rates of return abroad and repayment of Euro-dollar debts.

Offsetting the rise in capital-outflow and government

spending overseas since 1969, has been the rapid increase in remitted earnings from multinational corporations as well as fees and royalties. The remitted earnings, fees, dividends, and royalties grew rapidly from $2.9 billion in 1960 to over $10.3 billion in 1971 and to $12.4 billion in 1972. As a result, the capital generated from our foreign direct investments abroad has now replaced the balance of trade as the single most important positive contributor to our balance of payments.

American direct investments abroad rose from a book value of a $31.9 billion at the end of 1960 to $94.3 billion by the end of 1972, spread throughout the world but concentrated most heavily in Canada and Western Europe (see Supra p. 61). This enormous expansion was financed by $25.2 billion of reinvestment of foreign earnings and $36.9 billion of direct investment capital outflows by U.S. multinational corporations from 1961 to 1972 inclusive.[11]

These capital outflows, however, were more than counter-balanced by the income on U.S. direct investments and the acquisition of more than $3 billion by sales of securities abroad. From 1961 through 1972 U.S. direct investors received $61.5 billion in interest, dividends, and branch earnings, and further $14.6 billion in direct investment fees and royalties. This amounted to balance of payments receipts of $76.1 billion in the same period compared with $33.9 billion of capital outflows for a net balance of payments advantage to the United States of $42.2 billion.

In 1972 net capital outflows were only $3.4 billion and earnings returned to the United States amounted to $12.4 billion. Thus, in 1972, while the country had a deficit of balance of payments in almost every account, the multinational corporations produced a surplus of $9 billion.

"Beyond the income and capital outflow statistics there is

the important contribution of direct investment to the merchandise trade balance of multinational firms." The U.S. Department of Commerce conducted a survey of direct investment of 3,000 multinational corporations for the year 1966. The results indicated that 23,000 affiliates of multinational corporations in 1966 sold $5.9 billion in the United States but at the same time bought $7.8 billion from their parents in this country. More significantly as the total figures include imports of petroleum and minerals from affiliates, U.S. sales by manufacturing affiliates totaled "$2.7 billion and U.S. exports to them $5.3 billion, for a $2.6 billion surplus in 1966." [12]

The 1973 Tariff Commission Report indicates that for the years 1966 and 1970 the multinational corporations were highly important in maintaining a merchandise trade surplus (especially in 1970), and a large and growing surplus on the private services account (principally from income on U.S. direct investment abroad) (see Exhibits, pp. 198-99). The surplus on the current account generated by the multinational corporations more than compensated for the net outflow of long-term and nonliquid short-term capital in both years. Of the $4.1 billion surplus on identifiable private transactions in 1966, almost $3.2 billion resulted from the operations of the multinational corporations. In 1970 the multinational corporations generated surplus on identifiable transactions had grown to $5.8 billion, while the balance for the aggregate private sector declined to $3.4 billion, indicating a steep decline and a negative balance for the nonmultinational portion of the private sector. [13]

Another factor distorts the quantitative measurement of the manufacturing affiliates' trade balance; the United States-Canadian Automobile Agreement of 1966 has resulted in an excess of U.S. imports of automotive supplies and automobiles from Canada over exports. This, of course, is included in the special survey in the accounts of the U.S. auto manufacturers. The "free trade" in automobile and parts between the United States and Canada is a special case, since the agreement was reached with the accord of both industry and labor in the two countries. "Removing exports and imports to and from Canadian transportation industry manufacturing affiliates, 1970 United States' sales by affiliates were $2.4 billion; U.S. exports to affiliates in Canada were $6.2 billion, and the adjusted multinational corporations trade balance was a surplus of $3.8 billion for the special survey MNC surplus including the remaining, smaller direct investors, the total trade surplus of multinational corporations in 1970 was well over $4 billion." [14]

The direct investment of the United States corporations overseas often takes the form of export of capital equipment needed in the new productive facilities. It also includes export of capital equipment for replacement purposes. A Department of Commerce report shows that, in some cases, the foreign affiliates purchase United States equipment because it is supplied directly by the parent company, but more often it is purchased from other U.S. suppliers for reasons of cost, quality, or familiarity. [15]

The practice of U.S. affiliates to buy U.S. capital equipment varies by region, being particularly low in Europe, where alternative sources of supply are usually available, and much higher in Latin America and other less-developed countries, where the equipment is often not produced locally. There is also variation by industry, with affiliates needing advanced technology equipment more likely to buy in the United States than those using simpler equipment that is widely produced. Where the purchases are made also depends at times on the source of financing. Capital equipment is commonly bought on medium- and long-term credit, and when such credit is obtained abroad it is likely to be tied to sales of local products. Since the adoption early in 1965 of Commerce's voluntary restraint program covering foreign direct investments, U.S. firms have resorted to large-scale foreign borrowing, long-term as well as short-term, to finance their operations abroad.[16]

A large part of multinational corporations' exports to foreign affiliates consists of raw materials or semimanufactured goods, such as parts and components, intended for further processing or assembly. In 1965, such exports alone amounted to $1,728 million or about one-third of total United States exports to the affiliates. Of this amount, $1,497 million went to manufacturing plants abroad and $231 million to non-manufacturing affiliates.[17]

Unlike capital equipment, parts and components are often produced by the parent companies, who therefore have direct interest in selling them to their foreign affiliates. Indeed, such sales are one of the factors considered in setting up production facilities abroad.

Exports of goods for further processing are highly concentrated. Nearly half of the reported total went to automotive plants abroad, mainly in Canada, and most of the rest went to affiliates in the machinery, chemicals, and rubber products industries. Four U.S. firms accounted for half of the total, whereas 105 parents did not report any such exports. Goods for further processing are more likely to be bought from the parent companies by affiliates located in areas where the United States has a dominant or long-established trading position such as Latin America and Canada and by affiliates in less-developed areas than by affiliates located in Western Europe where parts and components are more readily available. There are also differences between industries, some requiring highly specialized parts and components available only from the parents and others using more standardized goods that are widely available.

In general, according to a study by the Department of Commerce, U.S. affiliates abroad are more likely to obtain from the United States the goods they need for further processing than are their counterpart local firms. To this extent, foreign direct investment increases U.S. exports. However, it seems likely that this advantage diminishes with the passage of time and that the buying practices of U.S. affiliates generally tend to become more like those of local firms, particularly where cost considerations favor purchase outside of the United States.[18]

Foreign affiliates also act as sales agents for the parent corporations. United States exports of finished manufactured goods intended for resale amounted to $2,247 million in 1965, and about 44 percent of total exports to foreign affiliates. It is rather interesting that more than 50 percent of the exports went to affiliates engaged solely in manufacturing than in trade or distribution. Another $273 million in finished manufactured exports were sold through the affiliates on a commission basis.[19]

The above facts and figures are the convincing evidence that multinational corporations and their affiliates play a great role not only in selling American products all over the world but also contribute annually billions of dollars to the deteriorating balance of payments.

Multinational corporations also serve U.S. exports indirectly. The presence of the American corporations abroad creates foreign interest and awareness of American products, thereby leading to greater demand for goods made in the United States as well as for goods made abroad by the U.S. affiliates. Such awareness and interest may affect sales of products quite unrelated to those handled by the multinational corporations.

While it is very difficult to assess the impact of the indirect influence of the multinationals, businessmen generally attribute considerable importance to it and economists have often stressed the income effects of foreign direct investment. Such investment it is held, expands directly and indirectly the economic base and increases local incomes, thereby creating a greater demand for products from other countries, including the United States. This argument has much validity for investment in developing nations. Investments in these areas usually increase national product, employment, income, purchasing power and imports of goods from the parent countries. With respect to investments in developed areas like Canada, Japan, and Western Europe, the consequences may have been different, if there were enough local funds to provide for needed investments. However, in view of the enormous amounts of the multinational corporations' capital, and technology available, and the dire need in Western Europe, Japan and Canada for all the investments and technology which they used to help build up the industrial sector, direct investment was essential to their development. "It is probable, therefore that, U.S. investment in these areas has significantly raised their national incomes and thereby led to increased purchases from the United States. The effects on the United States exports cannot be estimated with any precision although they are probably substantial." [20]

Contrary to the above analysis the opponents argue that production abroad by affiliates of the multinational corporations may displace similar goods that would otherwise have been exported directly from the United States. Much foreign investment is undertaken because lower wage rates abroad promise higher profit margins. The result is an export of capital, jobs, and technology at the expense of U.S. economy and trade balance.

The Department of Commerce disagrees with the displacement theory and states that the extent to which such export displacement actually occurs is a controversial matter. "On one hand, it is asserted that there is little displacement of U.S. exports by the output of foreign affiliates. U.S. companies set up production facilities abroad, in this view, only when they are on the verge of losing their export market anyway. If they do not produce the goods abroad, non-U.S. firms would do so and the United States would lose both the exports and the income. Foreign direct investment is regarded as 'defensive' in the sense of being aimed at the retention of foreign markets."[2][1]

An intermediate position taken by some analysts is that there is no doubt that some displacement of U.S. exports takes place as a result of certain types of investment abroad but only for a limited period of time. Hence, while U.S. investment abroad may displace U.S. exports for a time, it will in the end preserve foreign markets for U.S. goods, and exports lost will be more than offset in the long run by earnings from the investments and by U.S. exports that are stimulated by such investment.

Judgment on these matters depends largely on the assumptions made about substitution possibilities. The proponents of the classical theory of Hufbauer and Adler argue that American investment abroad increases capital in the foreign countries and decreases funds for investment at home. Because of the additional production abroad, the United States exports decline and unemployment increases.

The followers of the reverse classical theory minimize the export displacement argument and contend that investment abroad merely substitutes for investment that would otherwise be undertaken by foreign corporations, and that net capital formation is not changed either at home or abroad. On these assumptions, U.S. exports will be equally displaced by investment of non-U.S. firms if U.S. corporations do not undertake such investment abroad. The most realistic assumptions undoubtedly lie somewhere between the two extremes but opinions differ as to precisely where.

Both groups, however, agree that the assumption concerning displacement of exports applies only to investment in manufacturing. Foreign direct investment of other types, such as mining, petroleum, utilities, or trade, is not likely to displace U.S. exports significantly.

It is surprising that in all the debates regarding multinational corporations no mention has been made of foreign direct investment in the United States. The rapid growth in the international operations of U.S. multinational corporations has been paralleled by growth in foreign direct investment in the United States. Such investment increased from $6.9 billion in 1960 to $14.4 billion in 1972 (Exhibits 2-3, 2-4). Foreign investment in U.S. manufacturing industries rose from $2.6 billion in 1960 to $7.2 billion in 1972.

Responding to the attractiveness of U.S. stock prices, the two devaluations of the dollar, the relatively lower rate of inflation here than in the other major industrial countries, less U.S. dependence on outside oil than in Western Europe and Japan, foreign direct and portfolio investment in the United States has increased substantially in 1972 and 1973.

The developed countries of Western Europe and Canada were responsible for virtually all of the $14.4 billion in direct investment in the United States at year's end 1972. The breakdown of foreign investment in the United States by nationality of ownership has remained almost static since 1962, with United Kingdom investors holding 32 to 33 percent of the total, followed by Canadians with 25 to 27 percent, Dutch with 14 to 16 percent, Swiss with around 11 percent, other Europeans with 11 to 14 percent, and all other investors with 2 to 4 percent. Although the total book value of Japanese foreign investment in the United States still is insignificant, the Japanese invested almost $100 million in the United States in 1972, 14 percent of the 1972 increase.

The sectoral pattern of foreign investment in the United States has shown a significant shift away from insurance and finance to greater emphasis on manufacturing and petroleum. The manufacturing share increased from 38 percent at the end of 1962 to 50 percent at the end of 1972, while petroleum showed smaller growth, increasing from 18 percent to 23 percent.[22]

The direct investment in the insurance and finance sector fell from 25 percent a decade ago to 17 percent by the close of 1972, with the other sector dropping from 18 percent to 10 percent during this period. Sectoral investment patterns vary significantly among countries. The Swiss, Canadians, and other Europeans tend to invest heavily in manufacturing, while Dutch investments are largest in the petroleum sector. The United Kingdom has a more balanced investment posture, with holdings divided more evenly among the manufacturing, finance and insurance, and petroleum sectors.

During the last five years, stocks have been the preferred portfolio instrument of foreign investors. Although stocks still account for the majority of foreign investment in the United States, their relative importance declined from 50 percent of the total foreign investment at the close of 1960 to 46 percent at year's end 1972.

Another popular investment by foreigners has been in bonds, whose shares increased from 3 percent in 1960 to 18 percent in 1972. Two-thirds of the portfolio investment in the United States has been undertaken by Europeans, with Canadians responsible for an additional 9 to 12 percent, Latin Americans 9 to 11 percent, and Middle Eastern investors for the remaining 8 to 17 percent.

In the case of stocks, Europeans were responsible for 70 percent, Canadians for 14 percent, Latin Americans for 11 percent, and Middle Easterners for 7 percent at the end of 1972.

The energy crisis makes it very difficult to forecast the near term future for foreign investments in the United States. However, in the absence of major changes in the factors attracting foreign investments to the United States in 1973, it is likely that both direct and portfolio investment in the United States will continue to grow. The dollar devaluation and inflation in Western Europe and Japan will continue to make both direct and portfolio investment in the United States attractive.[2 3]

The growth in the United States activities of foreign controlled multinational corporations offers further confirmation of the following two points:

1. The flow of capital, technology, and other resources associated with foreign direct investment is a two-way street. U.S. firms, for example, control only about 60 percent of the total foreign assets of all multinational corporations.[2 4]

2. Low wage rates are not a major factor in the majority of foreign investment decisions. In this connection, it is interesting to note that some Japanese corporations are now building manufacturing plants in the U.S. market to produce products previously exported to the United States.

Finally, the pattern of growing foreign direct investment in the United States dramatizes the constantly changing character of the market place and overriding importance of market demands in foreign investment decision.[2 5]

A survey of several American multinational corporations concerning the balance of payments, reveals the following facts:

1. IBM's balance of trade in manufactured goods—exports minus imports—rose from $52 million in 1960 to $277 million in 1970.

In a period of ten years between 1962 to 1971, IBM's contribution to the United States balance of payments exceeded $3.7 billion. In 1971 alone, IBM contributed $765 million to the U.S. balance of payments. Approximately two-thirds of this amount represented the return on IBM's overseas investments in the form of dividends and royalty payments; most of the remainder was accounted for by IBM's export trade.[26]

2. The American tire industry's contribution to the balance of payments of the United States between 1964 and 1971 amounted to $2.6 billion. Fifty percent of this sum came from the royalties, dividends and fees of the investments in the foreign countries.[27]

3. The automobile industry's record of the balance of payments has not been as favorable as other industries. The value of the exports of cars from the United States to other countries has changed very little in the past two decades while other car-producing countries such as Japan and Germany have increased their exports to the United States tenfold. The result has been a decline from a $1 billion surplus in 1951 to $2 billion deficit in 1971. The only favorable market for American automobile industry is Canada. This is a special relationship resulting from the 1965 Automotive Products Trade Act. The Act provides for duty-free trade by manufacturers between the two nations in vehicles and components. U.S. motor vehicle manufacturers have been able to integrate the operations of their Canadian subsidiaries with their own U.S. operations in order to achieve production specialization.[28]

4. Xerox's contribution to the U.S. balance of payments between 1967-71 was $370.5 million. The 1971 contribution alone amounted to $109.4 million. Export sales to Xerox foreign affiliates constituted the major single portion of Xerox's positive balance of payments contribution with

export revenues during the 1967-71 period totaling $223 million, or 48 percent of the total inflow. Dividends from foreign affiliates amounted to $134.4 million, or 29 percent for the period 1967-71. Income from interest, royalties, and fees exceeded $111 million, or 23 percent of the total.

Xerox's capital outflows during 1967-71, totaled $98.2 million, or less than 21 percent of the total receipts from the affiliates and other customers.

The compound growth of Xerox's international activities has been very fast. Net income from international operations has grown from 18 percent of consolidated corporate income in 1967 to 43 percent in 1971 and 47 percent for 1972.

This performance has enabled Xerox to finance a major portion of its overseas activities from overseas income. As a result, only 14 percent of Xerox's current total permanent overseas investment represents capital transferred from this country. At the same time Xerox has repatriated over one-half its earnings from its international affiliates.

Xerox also claims that overseas investment has not been at the expense of domestic investment. Domestic manufacturing comprised two-thirds of the Xerox worldwide total in both 1967 and 1972, even though, during that period, domestic and foreign expansion experienced a compound growth rate of approximately 11 percent per year.

"What Xerox has experienced is, in effect, an accelerating growth spiral; that is, foreign investment raises foreign demand, which raises exports, which increases both domestic jobs, and foreign earnings which raises foreign investments."[29]

5. The Kennecott Corporation in response to an inquiry of the Subcommittee on International Trade, stated that a narrow spirit of isolationism in regard to multinational corporations seems unwise in view of the realities that this country depends so much on the outside world for raw

materials. Multinational corporations have not only increased world production and trade but they "give the United States an assured flow of critical materials in time of war or crisis which might not be the case if development were left to others."

The multinational corporations, according to the Kennecott Corporation, also have furnished the strongest element in this country's foreign accounts, whether we look at the performance of individual industries, or at the awesome statistics as recorded for the entire economy by the Department of Commerce. In the decade 1961-70, net capital outflows of the mining and smelting industry ran to about $2 billion. But receipts from abroad, including dividends, interest and branch profits, ran to $4.8 billion. Net contribution of the mining and smelting industry to the balance of payments was, therefore, close to $3 billion.

This contribution is the more impressive when we consider where mining investments are made. The chief threat to the dollar of recent years has come from Western Europe. But little mining investment is made in Europe for the good reason that nature has deposited useful minerals in Canada, South America, the Middle East, Africa, Asia, and Australia.[30]

6. The case of Clark Equipment Company merits special study and scrutiny. It shows very clearly how multinational corporations can serve both the exports and the balance of payments of the United States.

In 1950 total export sales of the Clark Equipment Company amounted to $5 million. Export sales from the U.S. plants in 1971 surpassed $85 million, but total consolidated sales of the parent company to its foreign affiliates in that year reached $741.5 million. Consolidated overseas sales of the subsidiaries accounted for 29 percent of the total sales, or $218 million. For 1972 the total sales both inside and outside the United States amounted to $900 million, of which $267 million, or 30 percent, came from the overseas sales.

As to the contribution of Clark's operations overseas to the balance of payments funds flowing from these operations, they totaled $629 million in the ten-year period 1962-71, while funds flowing from the United States totaled $122 million, a net inflow of $507 million. Almost $250 million of this total inflow was recorded during the last three years. "Not only have these funds helped the overall U.S. trade balance, but they have helped support Clark's domestic growth, contributed to the new product development programs, expanded production, and created jobs in Clark's domestic plants as well as overseas."

Between the years 1962 and 1971, Clark has invested some $68 million overseas, or an average of just over $6 million per year. Domestic investment during the same period totaled $208 million.[31]

7. The chemical industry's contribution to the United States balance of payments has been very positive. According to the Bureau of Census of the Department of Commerce, the 1972 foreign trade surplus of the industry approximated $2 billion, and the industry has provided a trade surplus of $19 billion over the past ten years.[32]

Overall investment income from U.S. direct investment abroad increased from $5.4 billion in 1966 to $9.46 billion in 1971.[33]

Furthermore, this investment income has exceeded U.S. capital outflows associated with chemical investment abroad. In 1966, U.S. direct investments abroad in chemicals and related products amounted to $3.7 billion.[34] This amount increased to $4.5 billion in 1971. In 1971, when U.S. recorded a trade deficit of over $2 billion, investment income far exceeded direct investment outflow and contributed a positive $4.7 billion to the balance of payments.

A special survey of international economic activities of some 298 U.S. multinational companies includes forty-one companies that manufacture and sell chemicals and allied products show that in 1970 investment in foreign affiliates approximated $2.6 billion. The resulting data are believed to be representative of the U.S. chemical industry.

According to the Department of Commerce Survey, U.S. merchandise exports of these chemical companies rose from over $1.5 billion in 1966 to over $2 billion in 1970.[35] During the same period, U.S. merchandise imports of these companies rose from $664 million to only $788 million. Thus, the trade surplus of these chemical companies increased from about $800 million to about $1.2 billion during this five-year period, a margin of about $400 million.[36]

The multinational chemical companies, according to the Manufacturing Chemists Association, in 1966 exported $1,560 million in merchandise, 41 percent of which went to majority owned affiliates.

Of the $633 million of merchandise shipped to foreign affiliates in 1966, $316 million was intended for resale (which can be attributable in part to the establishment of a stronger marketing effort resulting from the existence of the affiliates), $53 million of which was in the nature of capital equipment for use by the affiliates and $265 million of which was in the nature of products which required further processing. The comparable 1970 figures were $749 million worth of merchandise shipped to majority-owned foreign affiliates, $440 million of which was for resale and $283 million of which was intended for further processing.[37]

Imports into the United States of products made by foreign affiliates is relatively small and is hardly indicative of any desire to supply the U.S. market from abroad. In 1966, the net sales of goods and services of these majority-owned affiliates of U.S. chemical companies was $5,143 million, of which $123 million came from sales to the U.S. In 1970, the comparable figures were $7,875 million in net sales, of which only $169 million was derived from sales to the United States.

Net returns from the chemical industry from overseas, after taxes, each year have always exceeded capital outflow. From 1966 to 1970, the income received by U.S. chemical companies from their foreign affiliations increased from $312 million to $462 million. In 1966 the chemical industry's contribution to balance of payments was $604 million, but in 1971 it was close to $1.7 billion.[38]

8. The Eaton Corporation, responding to some questions concerning its international activities, has submitted the following summary of its activities for the twelve-year period commencing 1960:

In 1960, Eaton's worldwide net sales totaled $391 million. Of this amount, $21.5 million represented export sales from the United States. Approximately 1,500 men in the United States were responsible for the production of $21.5 million in exports. In 1961, Eaton decided to expand its world trade and establish affiliates abroad.

By 1966 net worldwide sales were up 124 percent to $878 million, of which $42 million represented export sales from the United States. At that time, in spite of a significant increase in direct foreign investments of some $30 million, Eaton was maintaining reasonable job parity as between domestic and foreign employments.

Eaton has, moreover, made a significant contribution to the U.S. balance of payments. Since 1960, Eaton has spent or invested $130 million in overseas business operations, from which it has recovered $544 million in trade dollars, dividends, royalties, and other payments.

On a flow-of-funds basis, Eaton's outflow has thus been

$130 million compared with an inflow of $544 million, resulting in a net favorable contribution of $414 million to the U.S. balance of payments. These funds have played an important role in expansion of Eaton's production, supplying of capital and equipment to support the competitiveness of domestic jobs.[39]

Eaton's overseas operations import $17 million in goods each year from U.S. corporations. This is in addition to Eaton's own 1971 exports of $74 million. On the import side of Eaton's total $11.6 million in imports to the United States in 1971, only $646,000 were from its own affiliates abroad.

9. Monsanto Corporation, in answer to the question why the U.S. needs strong multinational companies, stated:

The world chemical industry includes a large number of multinational corporations with only three of the first ten located in the United States:

U.S.	Foreign	1971 Sales ($ millions)
Dupont		3,848
	I.C.I. (United Kingdom	3,733
	Hoechst (Germany)	3,665
	Montedison (Italy)	3,460
Union Carbide		3,038
	BASF (Germany)	2,948
	Bayer (Germany)	2,928
	AKZO (Netherlands)	2,314
	Rhone-Poulenc (France)	2,191
Monsanto		2,087

All the foreign firms are strongly competitive, and have foreign operations which make them truly multinational. Most of them are owned or controlled to a major degree by the national governments and in all cases are an integral part of the planned economies which are common to all major industrial countries except the United States.

Multinational corporations are now being charged with causing the problems that a number of them warned about and worked hard to avoid. Many of those who opposed multinationals in the public forums helped create the very conditions about which they are concerned. While agreeing for the most part with the analysis of U.S. trade problems, it is wrong to blame the multinational corporations for the nation's woes. Destruction of the multinational corporations would not solve any problem, but would damage American exports and create more trade and balance of payments deficit.[40]

The U.S. Chamber of Commerce, in a survey of sixty-four multinational corporations, recently reported the following points:

While U.S. multinational corporations have expanded both exports and imports rapidly and substantially, they are making a major contribution to export development, enjoy a growing balance of payments and trade surplus, and have, accordingly, increased their U.S. employment more rapidly than the national average.

First of all, multinational corporations have broadened their surplus of exports over imports in the face of serious weakness in the American trade position.

Second, this strong balance of payments and trade surplus has been accomplished despite the presence of severe inflationary trends which make U.S. products less competitive in the world market. It can only be assumed that with a reduction in the rate of inflation this multinational trade and balance of payments surplus will be further enlarged.

Third, the rate of expansion in exports and imports has been more rapid among smaller multinational corporations, strengthening the belief that larger companies underwent internationalization earlier and most of this longer-term shift has already occurred.

Fourth, even multinational corporations that have added most substantially to their imports have in the aggregate shown no decline in U.S. employment, but, quite the contrary, have added substantially to domestic job levels. In general U.S. multinational firms have been conspicuously absent from those industries that have experienced a weakening in international competitiveness, negative trade balances, and declining U.S. employment levels.

Fifth, American affiliates abroad sell 92 percent of their production in other countries and only 8 percent in the United States. When cars shipped from affiliates in Canada are excluded, affiliate exports to the United States are exceedingly modest (4.2 percent of total sales).

Sixth, while imports from affiliates have represented an enlarged part of total U.S. imports, all of this proportionate gain has been contributed by Canadian cars. If Canadian motor vehicles are excluded, U.S. imports from affiliates have actually declined slightly as a proportion of total imports.[41]

Exhibit 6-1

U.S. International Transactions: 1960 to 1972

[In millions of dollars. Minus sign (−) denotes debits]

Type of Transaction	1960	1965	1968	1969	1970	1971	1972*
Exports of goods and services[1]	**27,490**	**39,408**	**50,603**	**55,502**	**62,870**	**66,150**	**73,546**
Merchandise, adjusted, excluding military[2]	19,650	26,438	33,576	36,417	41,963	42,787	48,840
Transfers under U.S. military agency sales contracts	335	830	1,392	1,512	1,478	1,922	1,166
Travel and transportation	2,701	3,795	4,723	5,170	5,946	6,165	7,134
Miscellaneous services	865	1,253	1,679	1,864	2,057	2,378	2,614
Income on U.S. investments abroad[3]	3,939	7,092	9,233	10,539	11,426	12,898	13,792
Imports of goods and services	**−23,383**	**−32,310**	**−48,178**	**−53,591**	**−59,307**	**−65,400**	**−77,765**
Merchandise, adjusted, excluding military[2]	−14,744	−21,496	−32,964	−35,796	−39,799	−45,453	−55,656
Direct defense expenditures	−3,087	−2,952	−4,535	−4,856	−4,852	−4,816	−4,707
Travel and transportation	−3,665	−5,113	−6,288	−6,954	−8,007	−8,597	−9,717
Miscellaneous services	−789	−952	−1,377	−1,422	−1,484	−1,630	−1,796
Income on foreign investments in the U.S.[3]	−1,098	−1,797	−3,013	−4,564	−5,167	−4,903	−5,889
Unilateral transfers (excl. military grants), net	**−2,292**	**−2,835**	**−2,909**	**−2,946**	**−3,207**	**−3,574**	**−3,764**
U.S. Government capital flows, net	**−1,104**	**−1,598**	**−2,268**	**−2,193**	**−1,584**	**−1,892**	**−1,581**
Loans and other long-term assets	−1,213	−2,454	−3,714	−3,477	−3,287	−4,178	−3,815
Foreign currencies and other short-term assets, net	−528	−16	62	89	−16	182	163
Repayments on credit[4]	637	872	1,383	1,195	1,718	2,104	2,071
U.S. private capital flows, net	**−3,878**	**−3,793**	**−5,383**	**−5,424**	**−6,886**	**−9,781**	**−8,339**
Direct investments abroad[3]	−1,674	−3,468	−3,209	−3,254	−4,400	−4,765	−3,339
Foreign securities	−663	−759	−1,226	−1,494	−942	−909	−619
Claims reported by U.S. banks:							
Long-term	−153	−232	358	317	175	−565	−1,250
Short-term	−995	325	−105	−867	−1,122	−2,373	−2,263
Claims reported by U.S. nonbanking concerns:							
Long-term	−40	−88	−220	−424	−586	−109	−219
Short-term	−354	429	−982	298	−10	−1,061	−649

Type of Transaction	1960	1965	1968	1969	1970	1971	1972
Foreign capital flows, net	**2,120**	**383**	**9,414**	**12,309**	**5,945**	**22,485**	**20,967**
U.S. Government nonliquid liabilities to other than foreign official reserve agencies	215	66	110	267	-433	-486	214
Other foreign private capital:							
Direct investments in the United States [3]	141	57	319	832	1,030	-67	322
U.S. securities other than Treasury issues	282	-357	4,389	3,112	2,190	2,282	4,502
Other long-term, reported by U.S. banks and nonbanking concerns	7	270	787	861	1,135	303	562
Short-term, reported by U.S. nonbanking concerns	-91	149	759	91	902	-24	139
Long-term, reported by U.S. banks	–	–	–	–	–	-249	148
U.S. liquid liabilities to private foreigners	308	131	3,809	8,662	-6,240	-6,691	4,816
U.S. liquid liabilities to foreign official agencies	1,258	-18	-3,101	-517	7,637	27,615	9,676
Other readily marketable liabilities to foreign official agencies [5]	–	-38	534	-836	-810	-539	400
Nonliquid liabilities to foreign official reserve agencies reported by U.S. Government	–	123	1,806	-162	535	341	189
Transactions in U.S. official reserve assets, net	2,145	1,222	-880	-1,187	2,477	2,348	32
Allocations of special drawing rights (SDR)	–	–	–	–	867	717	710
Errors and omissions, net	-1,098	-477	-399	-2,470	-1,174	-11,054	-3,806

Source: U.S. Bureau of Economic Analysis, *Survey of Current Business*, June 1972 and March 1973.
* Preliminary.
– Represents normal zero.
1. Excludes transfers of goods and services under U.S. military grant programs.
2. Excludes exports of goods under U.S. military agency sales contracts identified in Census export documents, and imports of goods included under direct defense expenditures identified in Census import documents, and reflects various other balance-of-payments adjustments (for valuation, coverage, and timing) to Census statistics.
3. Excludes reinvested earnings of foreign incorporated affiliates of U.S. firms of U.S. incorporated affiliates of foreign firms.
4. Includes sales of foreign obligations to foreigners.
5. Includes changes in nonliquid liabilities reported by U.S. banks and in investments by foreign official agencies in debt securities of U.S. Government corporations and agencies, private corporations, and State and local governments.

Exhibit 6-2
U.S. Basic Balance by Area, 1972*
(in billions U.S. dollars)

	Global†	EC	Japan	Canada	Other Developed	Developing Countries	Communist Countries	International Organizations and Unallocated
Trade								
Exports	48.8	11.8	5.0	12.6	4.6	13.9	0.9	—
Imports	−55.7	−12.6	−9.1	−14.4	−4.4	−14.8	−0.4	—
Net Trade	−6.9	−0.8	−4.1	−1.8	0.3	−0.9	0.5	—
Services (non-Military)								
Investment Income Receipts	10.8	2.0	0.4	2.0	1.0	4.9	—	0.5
Investment Income Payments	−5.7	−2.7	−0.9	−0.6	−1.0	−0.3	—	−0.2
Net Investment Income	5.1	−0.7	−0.5	1.4	**	4.6	—	0.3
Travel Income	3.4	0.5	0.2	1.0	0.3	1.4	**	**
Travel Expenditures	−6.4	−1.8	−0.2	−1.0	−1.1	−2.2	**	**
Net Travel	−3.0	−1.3	—	—	−0.8	−0.8	—	—
Royalties and Fees Net	2.8	0.8	0.4	0.4	0.4	0.8	—	—
Other Services and Private Remittances								
Net	−0.6	−0.2	0.2	−0.3	−0.3	−0.1	0.1	−0.2
Net Non-Military Services Balance	4.3	−1.4	0.1	1.5	−0.7	4.5	0.1	0.1
Government (Military and Foreign Aid)								
Military Sales	1.2	0.3	**	**	0.2	0.6	—	—
Military Expenditures	−4.7	−1.9	−0.8	−0.2	−0.3	−1.5	—	—
Net Military	−3.5	−1.6	−0.7	−0.2	−0.1	−0.9	—	—
Government Grants (excluding military)	−2.2	—	**	—	—	−1.9	—	−0.3
Government Long-Term Capital Flows	−1.3	**	**	—	−0.1	−1.1	−0.1	−0.1
Net Foreign Aid	−3.5	**	**	—	−0.1	−3.0	−0.1	−0.4
Net Government	−7.0	−1.5	−0.6	−0.2	−0.2	−3.9	−0.1	−0.4

	Global†	EC	Japan	Canada	Other Developed	Developing Countries	Communist Countries	International Organizations and Unallocated
Private Long-Term Capital								
U.S. Direct Investment Abroad	-3.4	-1.0	-0.2	-0.4	-0.5	-0.9	**	-0.4
Foreign Direct Investment in U.S.	0.2	-0.1	**	0.1	0.1	**	**	**
Net Portfolio Investments	3.7	3.0	0.2	-0.7	1.3	-0.2	**	0.2
Other Long-Term Private Capital	-0.7	0.1	0.3	-0.2	**	-1.1	**	**
Net Long-Term Private Capital Flows.	-0.2	2.0	0.3	-1.1	1.0	-2.2	**	-0.1
Basic Balance	-9.8	-1.7	-4.3	-1.6	-0.3	-2.5	0.4	-0.4

Source: Council of Economic Advisors *International Economic Report of the President* 1974. p 96.
* May not add due to rounding.
† Global data are preliminary and other estimates.
** Less than $50,000,000.

Exhibit 6-3

U.S. Basic Balance by Area, 1973*

(in billions U.S. dollars)

	Global	EC	Japan	Canada	Other Developed	Developing Countries	Communist Countries	International Organizations and Unallocated
Trade								
Exports	69.9	16.7	8.4	15.4	6.7	20.0	2.7	—
Imports	-69.1	-15.4	-9.7	-17.2	-5.8	-20.4	-0.6	—
Net Trade	0.8	1.3	-1.3	-1.8	0.9	-0.4	2.1	—
Services (Non-Military)								
Investment Income Receipts	16.2	3.0	0.7	2.5	1.4	8.1	**	0.5
Investment Income Payments	-8.6	-4.2	-1.1	-0.8	-1.7	-0.6	**	-0.2
Net Investment Income	7.6	-1.2	-0.4	1.7	-0.3	7.5	**	0.3
Travel Income	4.2	0.7	0.4	1.1	0.4	1.6	**	**
Travel Expenditures	-7.0	-2.1	-0.2	-1.1	-1.1	-2.3	-0.1	-0.1
Net Travel	-2.8	-1.4	0.2	**	-0.7	-0.7	-0.1	-0.1
Royalties and Fees Net	3.2	1.2	0.5	0.4	0.4	0.7	**	—
Other Services and Private Remittances Net	-1.5	-0.2	0.1	-0.3	-0.2	-0.6	**	-0.3
Net Non-Military Services Balance	6.5	-1.6	0.4	1.8	-0.8	6.9	-0.1	-0.1
Government (Military and Foreign Aid)								
Military Sales	2.2	0.4	**	0.1	0.4	1.3	—	—
Military Expenditures	-4.6	-2.2	-0.8	-0.2	-0.3	-1.1	—	—
Net Military	-2.4	-1.8	-0.8	-0.1	0.1	0.2	—	—
Government Grants (excluding military)	-2.2	**	—	—	—	-2.0	—	-0.2
Government Long-Term Capital Flows	-1.5	**	0.6	—	-0.1	-1.6	-0.4	-0.1
Net Foreign Aid	-3.8	**	0.6	—	-0.1	-3.6	-0.4	-0.3
Net Government	-6.2	-1.8	-0.2	-0.1	—	-3.4	-0.4	-0.3

	Global	EC	Japan	Canada	Other Developed	Developing Countries	Communist Countries	International Organizations and Unallocated
Private Long-Term Capital								
U.S. Direct Investment Abroad	−4.0	−2.1	−0.1	−0.3	−0.5	−0.7	**	−0.3
Foreign Direct Investment in U.S.	1.9	0.8	0.2	0.1	0.2	0.6	**	**
Net Portfolio Investments	3.8	1.6	0.7	−0.2	1.3	**	**	0.4
Other Long-Term Private Capital	−0.8	**	0.3	−0.1	**	−0.7	−0.3	**
Net Long-Term Private Capital Flows	0.9	0.3	1.1	−0.5	1.0	−0.8	−0.3	0.1
Basic Balance	**2.0**	**−1.8**	**	**−0.6**	**1.1**	**2.4**	**1.3**	**−0.4**

Source: Council of Economic Advisors, *International Economic Report of the President, 1974* p. 97
* Estimated. May not add due to rounding.
** Less than $50,000,000.

Exhibit 6-4
U.S. private balance of payments summary
Aggregate, MNC-generated & non MNC-generated
1966 & 1970*
(In millions of dollars)

Item	1966			1970		
	Aggregate	MNC Generated	Non-MNC Generated	Aggregate	MNC Generated	Non-MNC Generated
Merchandise trade balance	**3,824**	**2,023**	**1,801**	**2,164**	**2,048**	**116**
Exports	29,287	7,826	21,461	41,963	12,988	28,975
Imports	−25,463	−5,803	−19,660	−39,799	−10,940	−28,859
Balance on services	**4,016**	**4,473**	**−457**	**4,453**	**6,400**	**−1,947**
Dividends, interest, & branch earnings, net	3,786	3,370	416	4,150	4,802	−652
Fees and royalties, net	1,285	1,192	93	1,902	1,747	155
Other services, net	−1,055	−89	−966	−1,599	−149	−1,450
Remittances & other transfers net	−613	–	−613	−1,012	–	−1,012
Balance on current account	**7,227**	**6,496**	**731**	**5,605**	**8,448**	**−2,843**
Long-term capital, net	−3,006	−3,252	246	−1,940	−2,422	482
Direct investment, net	−4,026	−4,026	0	−3,912	−3,912	–
Other long-term, net	1,020	774	246	1,972	1,490	482
Basic balance (Current Acct. plus long-term capital)	**4,221**	**3,244**	**977**	**3,665**	**6,026**	**−2,361**
Non-liquid short-term capital, net	−104	73	−177	−482	−531	49
Liquid short-term capital claims	−14	−150	136	252	351	−99
Balance on identifiable transactions	**4,103**	**3,167**	**936**	**3,435**	**5,846**	**−2,411**

Source: Principally from the Bureau of Economic Analysis, U.S. Department of Commerce; MNC data partly estimated by the Tariff Commission in consultation with the Bureau of Economic Analysis.
* Excludes all government transactions on current and capital accounts.

Exhibit 6-5
U.S. Merchandise Trade,
Aggregate and with Majority-Owned Affiliates
of U.S.-Based Multinational Corporations
1966 and 1970
(in millions of dollars)

Item	U.S. Total	With Majority-Owned Affiliates				
		Total	Manufac- turing	Petrol- eum	Mining & Smelting	Other
1966						
Exports	29,287	7,826	.5,293	527	105	1,901
Imports	−25,463	−5,803	−2,719	−1,523	−682	−879
Trade balance	3,824	2,023	2,574	−996	−577	1,022
1970						
Exports	41,963	12,988	9,042	733	105	3,108
Imports	−39,799	−10,940	−6,751	−2,657	−770	−762
Trade balance	2,162	2,048	2,291	−1,924	−665	2,346

Source: Bureau of Economic Analysis, U.S. Department of Commerce.

Exhibit 6-6
U.S. Private Services Accounts
Aggregate and MNC-Generated,
1966 and 1970
(millions of dollars)

Account	Aggregate Private Services	MNC- Generated Services
1966		
Dividends, interest, and branch profits, net	3,786	3,370
Fees and royalties, net	1,285	1,192
Other services, net	−1,055	−89
Balance on services	4,016	4,473
1970		
Dividends, interest, and branch, profits, net	4,150	4,802
Fees and royalties, net	1,902	1,747
Other services, net	−1,599	−149
Balance on services	4,453	6,400

Source: Principally from the Bureau of Economic Analysis, U.S. Department of Commerce; MNC data partly estimated by the Tariff Commission in consultation with the Bureau of Economic Analysis.

Exhibit 6-7
U.S. Private Current Account,
Aggregate and MNC-Generated
1966 and 1970
(millions of dollars)

Item	Aggregate			MNC-generated		
	Credits	Debits	Balance	Credits	Debits	Balance
1966						
Merchandise trade	29,287	−25,463	3,824	7,826	−5,803	2,023
Services	11,705	−7,689	4,016	6,424	−1,951	4,473
Net transfers	−	−613	−613	−	−	−
Current Account	40,992	−33,765	7,227	14,250	−7,754	6,496
1970						
Merchandise trade	41,963	−39,799	2,164	12,988	−10,940	2,048
Services	17,351	−12,898	4,453	9,600	−3,200	6,400
Net transfers	−	−1,012	−1,012	−	−	−
Current Account	59,314	−53,709	5,605	22,588	−14,140	8,448

Source: Principally from the Bureau of Economic Analysis, U.S. Department of Commerce; MNC data partly estimated by the Tariff Commission in consultation with the Bureau of Economic Analysis.

Exhibit 6-8
U.S. Private Capital Account,
Aggregate and MNC-Generated
1966 and 1970*
(millions of dollars)

	1966		1970	
Item	Aggregate	MNC-Generated	Aggregate	MNC-Generated
Long-term capital, net	**−3,006**	**−3,252**	**−1,940**	**−2,422**
Direct investment:				
Credit	86	86	1,030	1,030
Debit	−4,112	−4,112	−4,942	−4,942
Securities transactions:				
Credit	909	594	2,190	822
Debit	−482	0	−942	0
Other long-term:				
Credit	705	180	1,310	1,112
Debit	−112	0	−586	−444
Nonliquid short-term				
capital, net	**−104**	**73**	**−482**	**−531**
Credit	296	279	902	987
Debit	−400	−206	−1,384	−1,518
Balance on nonliquid				
capital	**−3,110**	**3,179**	**−2,422**	**−2,953**
Liquid short-term				
capital claims†	−14	−150	252	351
Balance on identifiable				
capital flows	**−3,124**	**−3,329**	**−2,170**	**−2,602**

Source: Principally from the Bureau of Economic Analysis, U.S. Department of Commerce; MNC data partly estimated by the Tariff Commission in consultation with the Bureau of Economic Analysis.

* Excludes all government transactions on capital account.

† Data on liquid liabilities to private foreigners generated by the MNCs are not available.

Exhibit 6-9
Contrasting U.S. Balance of Payments Performance
by the MNCs in Six Countries* and Japan
1966 and 1970
(millions of dollars)

	Current Account	Trade Balance	Services Balance	Long Term Capital	Basic Balance
Six Countries*					
Values					
1966	2,074	1,351	723	−1,088	986
1970	3,429	2,196	1,233	−893	2,536
Change (1966-70)					
Amount	1,355	845	510	195	1,550
% of					
1966 value	65	63	71	18	157
Japan					
Values					
1966	343	207	136	−56	287
1970	624	294	330	−110	514
Change (1966-70)					
Amount	281	87	194	−54	227
% of					
1966 value	82	42	143	−96	79

Source: Bureau of Economic Analysis, U.S. Department of Commerce.

* United Kingdom, West Germany, Belgium-Luxembourg, France, Brazil, and Mexico.

Exhibit 6-10
Balances of Payments of Seven Key Countries,
1966 and 1970
(in millions of U.S. Dollars)

| | 1966 | | | 1970 | | | Net change: 1966-70 | | |
| | | With United States | | | With United States | | | With United States | |
	Global	Aggregate	MNCs	Global	Aggregate	MNCs	Global	Aggregate	MNCs
Current account balance									
Canada	-933	-1,867	-1,453	1,208	-275	-329	2,141	1,592	1,124
United Kingdom	967	139	-666	2,916	520	-880	1,949	381	-214
Belgium-Luxembourg	-30	78	-272	914	-18	-460	944	-96	-188
France	172	-21	-328	310	-537	-812	138	-525	-484
West Germany	-286	-611	-446	322	-259	-665	608	352	-219
Brazil	74	-51	-116	-500	-308	-241	-574	-257	-125
Mexico	-310	-405	-246	-1,050	-421	-371	-740	-16	-125
Capital account balance*									
Canada	1,132†	961	1,052	601†	877	662	-531	-84	-390
United Kingdom	-79	378	215	-219	-1,195	-38	-140	-1,573	-253
Belgium-Luxembourg	34	N.A.	100	-372	N.A.	115	-406	N.A.	15
France	-68	176	89	1,590	590	452	1,522	414	363
West Germany	885	252	335	1,166	29	310	281	-223	-25
Brazil	51	224	279	445	447	403	394	223	124
Mexico	233	220	102	452	356	425	219	136	323
Basic balance**									
Canada	114	-756	-324	1,988	584	294	1,874	1,340	618
United Kingdom	1,138	549	-421	3,204	-117	-1,342	2,066	-666	-921
Belgium-Luxembourg	-18	154	-168	638	-46	-384	656	-200	-216
France	328	108	-244	916	-260	-396	588	-368	-152
West Germany	129	-436	-149	-276	-431	-463	-405	5	-314
Brazil	114	179	172	-168	100	95	-282	-79	-77
Mexico	-147	-285	-176	-596	-181	-46	-449	104	130

* Non-liquid capital, long and short term.   ** Balance on current and long-term capital accounts.
† Includes net errors and omissions.

Notes

1. See Wm. N. Hazen, "U.S. Foreign Trade in the Seventies," 6 *Columbia Journal of World Business*, Sept.-Oct., 1971, p. 47.

2. Business International. *The Effects of U.S. Corporate Foreign Investment*, 1960-1972. New York, N.Y., 1974, pp. 15-17.

3. J. N. Behrman, "Foreign Investment Muddle: The Perils of Ad Hoccery." Columbia Journal of World Business, Fall 1965, p. 54.

4. *Newsweek*, April 24, 1972, p. 66.

5. U.S. Department of Commerce, *Statistical Abstract*, 1973, p. 766.

6. G. C. Hufbauer, and F. M. Adler, *Overseas Manufacturing Investment, The Balance of Payments*, U.S. Department of Commerce, 1968.

7. See Tariff Commission Report, *Implication of Multinational Firms for World Trade*, 1973, p. 171.

8. N. S. Fatemi, T. de Saint-Phalle, and G. M. Keeffe, *The Dollar Crisis*. Fairleigh Dickinson University Press, 1963, p. 293.

9. C. J. Hynning, "Balance of Payments Controls by the United States," 2 International Lawyer 400, 1968, p. 412.

10. *International Economic Report of the President*, Feb. 1974, pp. 29-30. See Exhibits 6-2, 6-3.

11. Bureau of Economic Analysis, Department of Commerce, *Survey of Current Business*, September, 1973, pp. 20-29.

12. Center for Multinational Studies: *The Benefits and Problems of Multinational Corporations*, (a manuscript) Dec. 26, 1972.

13. Tariff Commission Report, *Implications of Multinational Firms for World Trade* Feb. 1973, pp. 173, 4.

14. Op. cit.

15. U.S. Department of Commerce, *Policy Aspects of Foreign Investment*, January, 1972, p. 67.

16. Ibid., p. 69.

17. Ibid., p. 69.

18. Ibid., pp. 68-69.

19. Ibid., p. 69.

20. Ibid., p. 70.

21. Ibid.

22. U.S. Department of State, "The U.S. Role in International Investment," December, 1973, pp. 9-10.

23. Ibid., p. 19.

24. Stefan H. Robock, and Kenneth Simmonds, "International Business: How Big Is It—The Missing Measurement," *Columbia Journal of World Business*, May-June, 1970.

25. "Emergency Committee for American Trade," Statement Before the Senate Subcommittee for Finance, February 24, 1972.

26. International Business Machine Corporation, Report to Congress, January 18, 1973.

27. The Report of the Rubber Manufacturing Association, February 21, 1973.

28. Report of the Motor Vehicle Manufacturers Association, December 29. 1972.

29. Xerox Corporation statement to the Senate Committee on Finance, February 21, 1973.

30. Kennecott Corporation, "Statement before Subcommittee on International Trade," December 29, 1972.

31. Clark Equipment Company, "Statement to Senate Committee on Finance," February 21, 1973.

32. "The Multinational Corporation," *Studies on U.S. Foreign Investment*, Vol. 1, Department of Commerce, Study 3.

33. *Survey of Current Business*, Department of Commerce.

34. Ibid.

35. Special Survey of U.S. Multinational Companies, 1970.

36. Ibid.

37. Ibid.

38. U.S. Direct Investment Abroad, Senate Finance Committee, pp. 403-04.

39. Statement by The Eaton Company, February, 1973.

40. Monsanto Company's statement to the International Trade Sub-committee of the Senate Finance Committee, December 31, 1972.

41. U.S. Chamber of Commerce, *United States Multinational Enterprise Survey*, January, 1973.

7.
The Multinational Corporation and National Sovereignty

The previous chapters have concentrated primarily on the major costs and benefits that the growth of the multinational corporations have incurred in the United States, and the policy implications thereof. However, an assessment of the multinational corporations' effect on employment, technology, taxation, and the balance of payments of the United States is only a part of the larger issue, the internationalization of investment and production.

In the future, the assets, sources of supply, production facilities, work force, and markets of the multinational corporation will be increasingly transnational. The nationality of corporations in all probability will be an increasingly fictitious appellation. One of the main agents of the contemporary internationalization of world affairs is the multinational corporation. Its objectives and interests to a degree already transcend national interests.

This internationalization by multinational corporations has been encouraged by both home and host nations who seek to develop sources of supply, production facilities, and markets. Nevertheless, in a fundamental sense multinational corporations are a challenge to the traditional concept of the

196

nation-state. Their economic power necessitates a rethinking of traditional economic theory and policy. Politically they have at times proved themselves too powerful a lobby—as in the ITT case—and legally they are often beyond the power of international courts.

The impact of the multinational corporation thus raises questions ranging from sovereignty over resources to collusion over distribution and disruption of national priorities. The desired concurrence of multinational corporations' objectives and the nation-states' objectives in areas such as trade and investment flows, technological and managerial transfers, repatriation of earnings, and termination of investments is not automatically guaranteed by an "invisible hand."

Multinational corporations have attained a more global strategy than has ever been evidenced by private business enterprise. Their emphasis on technology and skills has brought about major contributions to international economic development, making them highly desirable on the one hand, while at the same time presenting a host of debatable issues on a national and international scale. Their success in developing commercially viable products and processing technological knowledge is unique while at the same time their command of resources and markets raises crucial questions for national policy makers. The multinational corporations' growth incentive has encouraged them to invest in and develop areas of the world that are in great need of capital and increased labor demand. The freer exchange of commodities, technology and skills has enhanced international economic development. However, no scheme of world order can afford to ignore the enormous power wielded by these corporations who can operate increasingly independent of national authority, or the fact that at present no international authority exists which can effectively control them.[1]

The economic impact is only one aspect of the effect of

the multinational corporations. Their operations must also be viewed in a social, cultural, and political context. The perceived threat to a country's sovereignty has highlighted the need for regulation on a national level in both the capital exporting and the host countries.[2]

The enormous size, wealth, and mobility of the multinational corporations have caused many to allege that politically they have ceased to be ordinary corporation citizens of both home and host countries in any meaningful sense. It is alleged that multinationals operating in developing nations are states within states. In the developed nations the fear of United States domination is commonly voiced and the American policy makers themselves have been increasingly aware of their responsibility or lack thereof in regulating multinational corporations.

As early as 1952, in a statement before the Security Council of the United Nations, Dr. Musaddeq, then Prime Minister of Iran, stated that the Anglo-Persian Oil Company with a worldwide perspective of production and market planning, had interests that were often contrary to the interests of the Persian government, and that as a result for three decades it subverted governments which were not ready to accept all the dictates of the corporation.

Extensive hearings in 1973 before the Senate Foreign Relations Committee on International Telephone and Telegraph's involvement in the overthrow of President Allende in Chile are a more recent example of the concern about subversion on the part of the multinationals.

In most of the developing countries fears of the multinationals' involvement in issues of "sovereignty" or "accountability" are voiced loudly and clearly. The 1953 overthrow of the Musaddeq Government in Iran, the ITT interference in Chile, and President Nixon's threatening remarks to the government of Libya on the nationalization of some of the U.S. oil companies holdings are brief examples of the concern that U.S. affiliates serve their own interests, and potentially serve U.S. government interests to the detriment of host countries.

> The size of the United States economy and the subsequent pervasive power of the U.S. Government in the economic sphere far exceed the economic muscle of any other nation. Practically without exception the M.N.C.'s have a stake in the United States that precludes in practical terms any attempt to enter into a head-on confrontation with the U.S. Government on a matter of fundamental policy. Moreover, not many M.N.C.'s, in the final analysis, are "world" companies with a truly international outlook; most of them remain basically U.S. firms which merely have significant international operations. Therefore, they remain oriented to the U.S. economic system and basically are accountable to the U.S. Government.[3]

From a different perspective, Leonard Silk of the *New York Times* editorialized that:

> The danger is not that corporations will pursue their pecuniary interests, especially if they do so within the constraints of competition, but that they will corrupt and capture the powers of government and transfigure national values and institutions to serve their corporate interests.[4]

The Chairman of the United States Tariff Commission, in his report to the Senate Committee on Finance, mentions several major examples of foreign complaints about the multinationals:

1. *Size and economic power.* The leading multinationals are very large in relation to the economies of their host countries. If G.N.P. is considered in comparison to a company's annual revenues, then General Motors is about the size of Belgium, Standard Oil of New Jersey is as large as Denmark; General Electric is the equivalent of Greece; and I.B.M. is as large as Norway and Portugal. The sheer size

raises fears about the ability of the host government to continue to guide the national destiny and control the multinationals within its borders. "There are worries that a country could become economically and even politically subservient to the power of giant multinational enterprises."

2. *Trading with the Enemy Act of 1917 and the Export Control Act of 1949.* These acts forbid sales of many items to Cuba, North Korea, North Vietnam, Communist China, the U.S.S.R., and other countries. A United States corporation often finds itself in conflict with the host government which has either no such restrictions, or different laws. This situation occurred when France tried to sell French aircraft to China. Because they contained some United States' parts, the U.S. government blocked the sale. But recently, in the case of Canada and Argentina, the Nixon Administration— fearing nationalization of the American subsidiaries—agreed to the sales of cars and trucks to Cuba.

3. *Antitrust legislation* of the United States is intended to protect competition in domestic business and foreign trade without taking into consideration the domicile or nationality of the affected party. A European subsidiary that sells little or none of its output in the United States and does all of its business with other countries, may not escape United States' antitrust liability. The United States government intervened in Gillette's acquisition of Bran, and Litton's acquisition of Triumpf-Alder in Europe, because both companies were making similar products in the United States. With respect to European investments in the United States, the Europeans allege that the extra-territorial application of the antitrust laws will make European companies vulnerable even in operations outside the United States. The vagueness and uncertainty of the antitrust laws are the cause of real concern to foreign firms operating in the United States.

4. *Buy-American policy of multinationals.* Although this policy is not official, the foreign countries complain that the

multinational subsidiaries are under strong pressure from home offices sensitive to the domestic critics and government suasion to buy U.S. equipment and supplies. The critics do not realize that foreign nationals have policies and transfer laws and restrictions, and that no country's hands are clean in the field of the government procurement and "buy-local" policies.

5. *Complaints relative to ownership.* The U.S. multinational corporation always prefers wholly-owned subsidiaries. Full ownership permits flexibility and selective centralization of management and thus realization of the enhanced benefits of multinational operation. However, host countries usually prefer some equity participation by local residents, and laws sometimes are passed to enforce such preferences. One factor is the desire to share in the control, production, management, and profits of a multinational's local subsidiary; another factor stems from the suspicion that a management independent from local control will make decisions helpful to its own interests and harmful to the local political and economic interests.

6. *Acquisition of foreign corporations by multinationals.* Canadians and Western Europeans vociferously complain that when multinationals buy an industry they make a number of changes which cause disruption and dissatisfaction amongst the businessmen and employees of the firm. Furthermore, the charge is, that "national ownership of technology and know-how is renounced to the proprietary interest of the U.S. parent; the top manager is often a U.S. national; the firm becomes subject to U.S. laws; there is possible loss of meaningful annual financial reports for the acquired company; the parent company may decide to cut production or shut down the acquired company in favor of another operation in another country; and the research and development effort is likely to be concentrated in the United States." [5]

7. *Neocolonialism.* Another source of resentment of the host countries against the multinationals is that their presence has been responsible for cultural, political, and economic influence by the home government. "Beyond these popular and perhaps unconsequential factors, however, the magnitude of American investment abroad has aroused more serious resentment with both economic and political ramifications. In 1968 United States companies owned 43 percent of the capital of all Canadian industry, and along with a few other countries, controlled 60 percent of Canada's mining and manufacturing companies. In the United Kingdom, U.S.-owned firms supplied 10 percent of the output of British factories and 17 percent of Britain's visible imports. Penetrations of such proportions is perforce a matter for public policy concern." [6]

The most serious problem confronting multinationals in the future is how to establish partnership in host countries. At present most subsidiaries are wholly owned by the parent company and local investors are excluded from attractive investment areas. If they want to invest in the subsidiaries they must buy stocks of U.S. parent firms; yet foreign investors in such firms can have only a miniscule voice in determining the policies of these companies in their own countries.

The difficulty in weighing the costs and benefits of multinational corporations in the host countries in many ways parallels the home countries' diverse evaluations. Policy implications often depend on the assumptions made, and host countries often merely rely on generalizations that multinationals are a challenge, that foreign control is dangerous, or that multinational corporations' interests do not coincide with national interests.

Countries in need of capital and technology must weigh the balance of payments effect of foreign direct investments, which though initially favorable, may over time constitute a drain on currency reserves from repatriation of earnings, transfer pricing, royalties and fees and dividend payments to the home countries' stockholders. There is also the additional concern that the multinational will withdraw its investment, finding the local economic or political conditions unfavorable. While the U.S. multinational investor is to some degree protected by the Hickenlooper Amendment[7] which cuts off aid to expropriating countries, the host country has few guarantees that the multinational investor will continue to find its investment necessarily profitable.[8]

8. *Lack of reciprocity*. Foreign countries which generally have welcomed American investments complain that there is a lack of reciprocity for their multinationals to invest in the United States. Foreign corporations, according to federal and state laws, cannot invest in the United States in coastal shipping, domestic aviation, hydroelectric power generation, leasing or mining of federal lands, insurance, alcoholic beverages (in some states), many banking activities, and domestic radio communications. All officers of any firm that has defense contracts must be American citizens.[9]

The wealth, power, mobility, and aggressiveness of multinational corporations have caused fear and suspicion in host countries. They contend that their sovereignty is endangered, that their national companies have been pushed out of markets and weakened economically. "Although these threats may not materialize, or may be offset by the benefits to local industry, certain problems or negative effects have been noted. The entry and subsequent activity of a single, large multinational company is frequently beneficial to all and may not disrupt local markets, but the fact is that several multinational companies often enter all at once. This simultaneous entry into an area of market opportunity is characteristic of oligopolistic competition in the United States in which the competing large enterprises employ similar methods of analyzing and exploiting new investment opportunities." [10]

A study by the Senate Committee on Finance indicates that the operations of the multinational corporations, even in the developed areas of the world, are under very close scrutiny and suspicion. "Large U.S. firms operating in Europe and elsewhere are under constant suspicion, if only because of their sheer size in relation to the economies in which they have affiliates. It may be corporate policy at I.B.M. to be an exemplary corporate citizen in every country in which it operates—and that policy is carried out with reasonable faithfulness—but I.B.M.'s control of 60 to 70 percent of the European computer market still rankles in every major capital on the continent. To mention another example, Common Market officials admittedly raised no formal objection to Westinghouse's recent acquisition of A.C.E.C., a large Belgian electrical equipment manufacturer—but, privately, they opine that the deal was 'just a little too easy' for the American firm." [11]

The thinking of the officials of the European Community is that the arrival of the U.S. multinational corporations is not in itself detrimental to the interests of the host countries. In fact, the evidence put out by the European community shows that the multinationals have brought to Europe positive benefits in terms of employment, faster economic growth, more international trade, and higher levels of technology. However, the European economic leaders would like to see European-owned business develop on a multinational basis within the community as vigorously as the U.S. multinationals are penetrating the area. As barriers to such development they cite the superior financial muscle of the U.S.-owned firm and its access to better capital markets and banking facilities than smaller European competitors enjoy; the American M.N.C.'s larger home-based research and development effort, competitive national incentive programs to attract foreign investments; and the legal and tax barriers which still hinder cross-border mergers among European community firms. In the framing of community policy, therefore, the stress is on removing the obstacles to the development of the European firm rather than on throttling the opportunities available to Americans.[1,2]

If the worldwide integrative role of the multinational is controversial, its importance and usefulness to the interrelationship of developed market economies is beyond doubt. Most of the developed market economies serve both home and host countries.

"During the period 1968-1970, inward direct investment flows were on the average only 20 percent of the outward flows for the United States; 30 percent for Japan; 63 percent for the United Kingdom and the Federal Republic of Germany, and 90 percent for the Netherlands. The opposite is the case with most of the other countries. In France inward direct investment flows were almost twice as high as the outward flows; in Italy and Canada, a little more than twice; in New Zealand, three times higher; in Belgium, four times, and in Australia, Spain, Portugal, and South Africa, 7.5 to 12 times greater than outward flows."[13]

As far as the United States is concerned, according to a report of *Business International*, more than one-third of its manufacturing output is represented by the top 187 U.S. multinational manufacturing corporations with subsidiaries and trade all over the world. In certain industries, such as automotive, pharmaceutical, and fabricated metal products, the consolidated sales of these corporations account for more than three-fourths of the sales of all U.S. firms, and in petroleum refining, chemicals, rubber, and electric machinery, for more than half. A group of 264 multinationals is responsible for half of all U.S. exports of manufactured goods. In 1971 U.S. multinationals exported $4.8 billion for direct investment abroad and brought home approximately $9 billion in interest, dividends, royalties, and management fees. Furthermore, given the practice of extensive local borrowing, their control of overseas assets is substantially higher than the book value of long-term equity and debt held abroad.[13]

The foreign nations complain, without valid reasons, that their investment activities in the United States are very limited. Foreign investment in the United States is mainly portfolio investment. Whereas 80 percent of the American investment in Europe is direct investment, 70 percent of European investment in the United States is in portfolio form, almost equally divided between stocks and bonds. Thus the book values of U.S. investments in other developed countries, with the exception of the Netherlands, is several times higher than the book value of direct investments of those countries in the United States. The U.S. direct investment in Western Europe is 3.5 times higher than the Europeans' investment in the United States; it is seven times more in the case of Canada and 70 times more in the case of Latin America.[14]

Sixty percent of total direct investment in the United States belongs to the British, Dutch, and Swiss multinationals. Although recently the oil-producing governments of the Middle East and some European and Japanese corporations have penetrated the petroleum industry, manufacturing, and the service sector of the United States, there is no single industry in which they have assumed an important role.[15]

With the exception of Japan, the opposite is true in the case of the other developed economies, where foreign multinationals account for an important share of production, employment, exports, and investment. Multinationals in Japan are subject to most restrictive regulations. In 1968 only 2.3 percent of total fixed assets and 1.66 percent of total sales in manufacturing belonged to foreign corporations. The multinationals' share of the Japanese oil and rubber industries is much higher (60 percent in oil and 19 percent in rubber).

As a result of recent Japanese liberalization measures, the share of the multinationals in Japanese joint ventures has increased.[16]

In Canada, foreign multinationals represent one-third of total business activity. They account for 60 percent of manufacturing output and 65 percent of mining and smelting production. U.S. multinationals account for 80 percent of total direct foreign investment and the United Kingdom for most of the rest. In England, American multinationals represent almost 70 percent of the total stock of foreign direct investment. They are also responsible for 13 percent of total manufacturing production, employ 9.2 percent of the labor force, and account for one-fifth of all manufacturing exports. In Belgium multinationals are responsible for a quarter of the gross national product, one-third of total sales, 18 percent of employment, and 30 percent of exports. More than half of the total foreign direct investment is accounted for by U.S.-controlled affiliates.[17]

"In the Federal Republic of Germany, Italy, and France, foreign penetration is less pronounced, with the United States accounting for at least half of it, except in the case of France where its share is less than half."[18]

Based on an objective study of the United Nations, the multinationals are very important in a developed market economy. Their role varies in different industrial sectors. "There is a high concentration in a fairly small number of industrial sectors characterized by fast growth, export-orientation and high technology—sectors which are regarded as key sectors by host countries." Without multinationals' high technology, managerial skill, research and development, many industries would never have attained the present great achievements. Thus, there is a very high percentage of multinational investment in oil, chemicals, automotive industries, computers, and electronics. The U.S. multinationals control more than half of the petroleum industry in Belgium; three-fifths of the food, tobacco, refineries, metal manufacturing, instrument engineering, computer, and technical manufacturing industries in the United Kingdom; 80 percent of computers and electric data-processing equipment in the European community.

In the service sector, the multinationals' presence is considerable in the hotel and recreation industries, consulting, public relations, and banking.[19]

"If the role of the multinational corporation in the national allocation of resources on a world-wide basis is debatable, its importance in intertwining the economies of most developed countries is commendable."

"Through its capacity to move capital, technology, and entrepreneurship across national frontiers, the multinational corporation has become the main vehicle for the internationalization of production, which is acquiring growing importance in international economic relations."[20]

Any objective study of the multinational corporations shows that the issues raised by them are not only complex but their implications in international relations and economic development are far-reaching. On the surface the multinational corporations produce economic benefits for both the home and the host countries. For the host country, there is a net addition to output, which is always greater than the investing company's earnings, remitted or unremitted. But the question is always asked: "Does not the home country undermine its own export base, and actually lose balance of payments income?" The research of the Department of Commerce and the judgment of businessmen seems to be that they cannot hold markets by exports alone and that production abroad is a far better guarantee of foreign markets.[21]

The positive contributions of multinational corporations to the many facets of development have been recognized everywhere. At the same time the problems raised have become increasingly apparent. The generally welcome reception given to the multinationals in the host countries, as vehicles for scarce capital, modern technological know-how, skills, mobility, and as a link to the world market, recently has been tempered by suspicion and concern.

In the search for solutions, both the home and the host countries have failed to come out with acceptable solutions. Some radicals in host countries suggest nationalization. A few politicians in the United States have tried to blame the multinationals for all the ills of the country. Both approaches are unwise and harmful to the interests of both home and host countries.

"In the first place, most of the issues identified are interrelated, whether they pertain to sovereignty, size, concentration, competition, *dependencia*, development objectives, 'truncated' development, monetary and payments disequilibrium, labor relations, alternative means for the sale or transfer of technology, location of industries, or equitable distribution of benefits. Secondly, many key issues already identified do not lend themselves to frontal attack at the international level, given the present world realities. An untimely debate on solution on which no possible agreement can be reached may, in fact, block progress. Finally, while some issues can no doubt be singled out for special study, a concerted approach is still needed so that the essence of the problem is not missed and a basis is laid down for future evolution." [22]

So far both the home and the host governments have failed to come out with an acceptable plan. Therefore, the time has come for the United Nations to prepare a general guideline and then set up a flexible machinery capable of implementation. There is, of course, no unique solution whereby the interests of all parties can be reconciled. Nor is there a ready means of attaining "the accepted goal of greater distributive justice in the international context. Few can doubt, however, that the issues raised by multinationals have a direct bearing on the international community. All the governments and the corporations, at this point, agree that some measures to protect the multinationals against arbitrary confiscation and to provide for their accountability to the national and international community should be introduced."

A conference organized by the United Nations in 1973 on the "Problems and Prospects of the Multinational Corporations" discovered some disturbing trends both in the home and host countries.

Among the most evident trends affecting the operations of multinationals have been a number of recent cases of nationalization and expropriation. Furthermore, many restrictive measures aimed at multinationals have been introduced. In many countries, developing as well as developed, a substantial sector has been reserved for nationals only. "In addition to certain sectors, such as defense, in which most governments prohibit foreign ownership, a number of industries, such as transport, communications, banking and insurance, have increasingly come to be reserved for national ownership."

Recently there have been new trends in some countries to restrict foreign investments in the areas of electronics, computers, automotives, oil, and aeronautics.

Another very significant development is the recent attempt by many host countries to gain participation and control of policy-making, production, and pricing. The Organization of Petroleum Exporting Countries has adopted a plan to phase out the multinational corporations in ten years. Because of the very strong financial position, the O.P.E.C. members have suggested "joint venture" with multinationals in the home countries as well.[23]

Some countries have announced a selective investment policy and have established some form of machinery for screening foreign investors. In January, 1973, Canada proposed The Foreign Investment Review Act; in Australia there are many restrictions such as curbs on exports of minerals and surveillance of intra-company accounts. Mexico requires foreign investment to be registered with the National Foreign Investment Registry. It also requires a 60 percent domestic ownership of auto parts manufactured in the country.

Japan is an exception to this trend. In 1973, through a series of progressive measures, she liberalized foreign investment regulations.

At the regional level, the most significant foreign investment regulations were adopted by Bolivia, Chile, Colombia, Peru, Ecuador, and Venezuela.[24] Current multinationals are required to sell majority holdings to local investors, and new foreign investors must take minority positions, within a period of 15 to 20 years, in order to be eligible for the Andean Pact Trade Concessions. Several economic sectors are closed to direct foreign investment, and foreign investors in these sectors have been given three years to divest themselves of 80 percent of ownership.

In the European Community, a major recent development affecting multinationals is the rule of competition. A recent ruling by the European Court makes future restrictive agreements between multinationals very difficult. The expansion of the European Community from six to nine members is a prelude to new regulations, especially in areas of competition and direct taxation.

In the United States too, a coalition of labor, protectionists, and politicians, for different reasons, criticize multinationals and suggest stricter scrutiny of their activities. The numerous Congressional investigations, the long and comprehensive reports of the Tariff Commission, the Senate Committee on Finance, the Burke-Hartke Bill, are indicative of concern, misunderstanding, and of an emotional and simplistic approach to a very complex situation. Although the outcome of the investigations in the United States is as yet uncertain, the bargaining position of the multinationals all over the world has been eroded and as a result they have started to reevaluate their position. Fortunately, their response has not been limited to the defense of their activities but aimed at positive measures which attempt to deal with some fundamental causes of criticism.[25] On the whole many multinationals have taken steps to correct mistakes of the past and to negotiate directly with the host countries for new arrangements. Attempts by administrations and a few stubborn corporations to induce others to adopt common programs against certain host countries, such as Libya and Iraq, have been generally rejected. The policies, the guidelines, and the priorities of the host countries have been followed. New arrangements for joint venture and participation in the oil industry have been implemented in Iran, Saudi Arabia, Kuwait, Algeria, Libya, and Iraq. "Attempts have been made to increase the local contents of goods produced (e.g., the local contents of Sears products range from 80 to 90 percent) and foreign participation in decision-making and management (e.g., Xerox, Black and Decker Manufacturing, Texaco, Exxon, First National City Bank, Westinghouse, and I.M.A., among others, have foreign directors.)" Several multinationals have offered shares for local subscription in developing nations and fade-out agreements have been concluded in several recent investments abroad.[26]

Furthermore, the International Chamber of Commerce has produced a set of guidelines for the multinationals' investment abroad. These guidelines include local equity ownership, local participation in management, and promotion of local personnel to positions of responsibility, as well as suggestions for protection of the rights of the multinationals in the host countries. Multinationals are also asked to act as good citizens of the host country, promoting the social and economic welfare of the workers, respect for national laws, support of priorities, policies, and social objectives of the host country.[27]

While these self-imposed guidelines are great steps forward, their efficacy has been questioned and both the host countries and labor have labeled them mere window dressing. Thus a large part of the international trade union movement not only advocates measures on the part of the public authorities to control multinational corporations on a national and international basis, but is also concerned with organizing itself better to deal with these corporations on a bilateral basis.

At its Tenth World Congress, held in London in July, 1972, The International Confederation of Free Trade Unions adopted a resolution on multinational corporations in which it proposed a research program concerned with (a), the position and development trends in the process of multinational concentrations; and (b), the publication of information on the decision-making structures of multinational concerns, their internal organization, their accounting system and the basic features of their investment policy; and (c), the effects of the spread of multinational concerns on national economic policy and the carrying out of democratic reforms.[28] There have been several other resolutions passed by the I.C.F.T.U., World Conference of Labor, World Federation of Trade Unions, and Oil Workers' Anti-Monopolist World Conference calling for coordinated action by the workers to meet the threat of multinational corporations which are growing because of the increased internationalization of capital in the search for a maximization of profits.[29]

Another problem facing the multinationals, not through fault of their own, is the fear and suspicion expressed against the policies of their home governments. The host countries mention too many examples of gunboat and dollar diplomacy. For example, the United States Foreign Assistance Act of 1961, as amended by Senator Hickenlooper, states that "aid will be cut off for any country that expropriates and has not, within six months of such action, taken appropriate steps to discharge its obligations under international law." As late as October, 1973, President Nixon warned Colonel Gaddafi of Libya "to remember Dr. Musaddeq [sic] of Iran and what happened to him after nationalizing Iran's oil industry in 1953." The host countries now are saying that it would be helpful if the attitude of the home countries could be made explicit through the adoption of the Calvo Doctrine,[30] or some other declarations initiated by the United Nations. This would improve the atmosphere and allay the host countries' fears of foreign domination. Some screening and even auditing of the operations of the multinationals, and requirements for greater disclosures, would promote trust and mutual interests.[31]

During the last two years a number of host countries have introduced the Calvo Clause in their foreign investment laws. They threaten to penalize any corporation which appeals to its home government for help in cases of dispute. "Such unilateral application of the Calvo Doctrine by host countries, however, will tend to be largely ineffective unless it is also adhered to by home countries. Willingness on the part of home countries to accept such measures as the Calvo Doctrine will be increased if the host countries adopt policies such as 'national treatment'; i.e., non-discriminatory treatment, as compared with national enterprise." [32]

Moreover, the home countries should ask for reciprocity from the host governments by asking them to add to the Calvo Clause provisions guaranteeing security and economic rights to the multinationals, "such as procedures for compensation following nationalization and even the use of a specified formula determining the level of such compensation." [33] Although many host countries would regard these guarantees as a violation of their sovereignty, it would facilitate the acceptance of the Calvo Clause by home countries and give assurance to the multinationals that their rights would be protected. Disputes and tensions often arise out of suspicion, uncertainties, and vacillations of policies. Recently many multinationals have realized that their past policies of reliance on the power of the home governments and money must end and a new era of mutual interests and partnership should begin. [34]

This is demonstrated by the new policy implemented in the Middle East and Latin America where machinery for the screening or review of foreign investments has been established. This gesture of cooperation has removed an important source of uncertainty. Even in places where nationalization has taken place there may still be room for contributions by multinationals in the areas of service, technology, and marketing. Furthermore, the new tendency in Socialist countries to enter into joint ventures demonstrates the possibility of mutual beneficial arrangements even in centrally planned economies. Yugoslavia is a special case. It was the first Socialist country to permit minority participation by multinationals. A constitutional amendment of 1971 goes so far as

to offer a guarantee against expropriation and nationalization, once a joint venture contract has been concluded and
implemented.

The relationships between multinationals and the host
countries so far have varied in different countries. "The
institutions which have to deal with multinational corporations are frequently scattered in host countries. Policies are
not well coordinated and their execution is often feeble and
haphazard. There is a general need for the whole apparatus
affecting multinational corporations to be kept under review.
As a beginning, broad policy measures such as development
planning, objectives and strategy, and trade and fiscal policies
require a thorough review and appraisal. More specifically,
measures such as investment incentives and machinery for
dealing with multinational corporations also need to be
considered." [35]

The review process must be centralized in an agency
especially created for the purpose. Such agency must be
international and should be able to build up a nucleus of
competent people equipped to deal with technical, complex
problems facing multinationals and host governments. [36]

The present uncertainty and confusion stems from the fact
that there is no coordination nor even consultation among
the host countries. Several countries (Brazil, Chile, Colombia,
Mexico and Jamaica) require affiliates of the multinationals
to float shares on the local stock exchanges; other have
proposed local equity participation, leading in some cases to
total local ownership. [37] The International Chamber of Commerce has recommended that the host country should "take
appropriate measures, principally by encouraging the creation
or development of an effective capital market, to facilitate
the purchase of equity in domestic and foreign-owned enterprise by local interests." [38] Some multinational corporations
have opposed this suggestion based on their experience that

the presence of a narrow local capital market in many host countries eventually leads to the accumulation of such large shares in a few powerful, local hands, that local participation on a broad basis is rendered impossible. Furthermore, such a concentration would cause conflicts between local ownership interests, favoring a high dividend payment policy, and foreign interests which opt for reinvestment of profits and growth.[39]

In countries where some form of participation in the decision-making of the multinationals exists, like Iran, Iraq, and Saudi Arabia, the exercise of this role through a development corporation has facilitated coordination; but still, conflict and strain hinder maximum efficiency and cooperation.

To avoid future conflicts and confrontation the United Nations Study Group has recommended certain measures which will be examined in the next chapter.

Notes

1. United Nations, Department of Economics and Social Affairs, *Multinational Corporations in World Development*, 1973, pp. 71-72.

2. For example, Francois Mitterrand during his candidacy for President of France stated "We do not want a Europe of the stateless multinational conglomerates. You haven't made a social Europe, a Europe of the people. That will be my mission." *New York Times*, May 11, 1974, p. 3.

3. A Report of the United States Tariff Commission to the Committee on Finance. U.S. Senate, February, 1973, p. 145.

4. *New York Times*, March 5, 1974, p. 33.

5. United States Tariff Commission Report, January 16, 1973.

6. Senate Committee on Finance, February, 1973, p. 149.

7. 22 U.S.C. Section 2370 (e) (1) (1964).

8. For instance, Solitron's pulling out of Curacao. See *Island Territory of Curacao v. Solitron Devices, Inc.*, 489 F. 2d 1313 (1973).

9. Ibid., pp. 151-52.

10. A Report of the United States Tariff Commission to the Senate Committee on Finance, February, 1973, p. 133.

11. Ibid., p. 134.

12. Ibid., p. 138.

13. *Business International,* "The Effects of the United States Corporate Foreign Investment," 1960-1970, New York, 1972.

14. R. Helmann, *The Challenge of the United States Dominance of the Multinational Corporation*, New York, 1970, p. 60.

15. Ibid.

16. See Japan's Ministry of Trade and Industry, *Report on Foreign Owned Firms in Japan*, Tokyo, 1968.

17. See *Financial Times*, "United States Industry in Great Britain," January, 1972, and D. Van Den Buleke, *The Foreign Companies in Belgian Industry*, Ghent, Belgian Productivity Center, 1973.

18. United Nations Study, pp. 16, 17.

19. United Nations Study, p. 18.

20. Ibid.

21. E. Sidney Rolfe, *The Multinational Corporation*, Foreign Policy Association, February, 1970, p. 54.

22. United Nations Study, p. 75.

23. United Nations Study, p. 76. The Kuwait government on May 14, 1974, agreed to a joint venture with Gulf Oil and British Petroleum Corporation. The new agreement gives the Kuwait government a 60 percent share and provides that in 1979 there will be renegotiation of the present arrangement. Gulf and British Petroleum will receive a sum of $112 million in return for their 50-50 Kuwait oil interests being acquired by the government. A four-man committee composed of

two representatives of Kuwait and one each from British Petroleum and Gulf will administer the new corporation.

24. Andean Group.

25. The most recent studies have come from the Sub-Committee on Multinational Corporations of the Senate Committee on Foreign Relations, and the Sub-Committee on International Trade of the Senate Committee on Finance, and the United Nations Department of Economic and Social Affairs.

26. Emergency Committee for American Trade, *The Role of the Multinational Corporation in the United States' and World Economies*, Washington, D.C., 1973.

27. See International Chamber of Commerce, *Guidelines for International Investment* (Paris, 1972).

28. International Labor Office, *Multinational Enterprises and Social Policy*, Geneva, 1973, pp. 83-88.

29. Ibid., p. 89.

30. The Calvo Doctrine is named after a distinguished Argentinian jurist, Carlos Calvo. He argued that a state could not accept responsibility for losses suffered by aliens, and foreigners have no rights not accorded nationals. The attempts to embody this doctrine in Latin American laws and constitutions did not quite succeed. The arbitral decisions covering the doctrine are almost evenly split. William W. Bishop, *International Law*, Little, Brown, Boston, 1962, pp. 710-721.

31. United Nations Study, op. cit., p. 97.

32. R. Vernon, *Sovereignty at Bay: The Multinational Spread of the United States Enterprise*, New York, 1971, p. 279.

33. See P. Kindleberger, *American Business Abroad*, New Haven, Yale University Press, 1969, p. 68. Also Vernon, pp. 278, 279.

34. The United Arab Emirates, on May 12, 1974, took over the distribution of gasoline and oil products throughout its territory. One of the member regions, Abu Dhabi, in January, 1974, took over its local distribution from the group consisting of British Petroleum, the Caltex Petroleum Corporation, and Royal Dutch Shell (*New York Times*, May 15, 1974), p. 65.

35. United Nations Study, op. cit., pp. 83-84.

36. Ibid.

37. A. O. Hirsham, *How to Disinvest in Latin America and Why? Essays in International Finance, No. 6*, Princeton University Press, November, 1969.

38. The International Chamber of Commerce, op. cit., Article 3.

39. United Nations Study, op. cit., p. 84.

8.
An Agenda for Action

In the last chapter we discussed the sources of friction between the multinational enterprise and the national interest of the home and host countries. Our purpose in this discussion is to find a common ground to reconcile corporate objectives and public policy decisions.

In order to reconcile their differences we have to explore the factors which influence the operations of the multinational enterprises. The survival of the multinational corporation depends upon adequate return on investment capital and long-range maximization of profits. To achieve this goal it makes decisions some of which have positive and others negative impacts on the national and international welfare.

1. Concentration of resources and technological know-how, managerial skill and market information is the first characteristic of multinational enterprise.

2. Efficiency in resource allocation: This is achieved by "shifting at the margin" the location of production to reduce input costs of relatively mobile factors, particularly capital. Input combinations are rearranged as a result of multinational business operations, both within and between types of resources. The multinational corporation thus promotes globalization of trade, capital, resources, technology,

221

and managerial skills. That is one reason why most of the host countries are interested in the impact of the multinationals on their labor force, balance of payments, capital reinvestments and outflows, earning remissions, inflation and employment. They are interested in the trade impact of the foreign investment, in terms of reduction of imports and increase of exports, in new income and employment generated, taxes paid, labor and professionals trained, technology and managerial skill, prices and inflation. They are also concerned with the social effects of the incurred changes.[1]

3. Stability. Multinational corporations thrive on political, economic and social stability. They try to avoid risks which do not exist in their home operations. In areas of higher risks they aim at higher rate of return on invested capital. "Hedging foreign exchange risk and minimizing equity exposure in politically unstable countries are the source of friction between multinationals and the host countries."[2]

4. Control of the market. A true characteristic of a multinational is increased control of the market. This reduces the competition and raises complaints about the monopolistic practices of the multinationals. "Pressures to reduce competition and monopolize markets seem to be endemic in almost all forms of economic organization, and the multinational enterprise — operating from a strong competitive base — may cause increased concentration particularly in small markets characterized by comparatively weak indigenous firms."[3]

5. Economic control. In most of the developing nations the multinational is a major source of foreign exchange, government revenues, employer of resources and producer of industrial goods. It can disrupt governments' budgets, exert pressure on the labor market and control economic and financial institutions.

6. Social instability. Sizeable as the problem of social responsibility of multinationals is in the home countries, the

issues confronting them in the host countries are far more complex. "The firm operates in multiple social, political, and economic settings, each with a different historical pattern of development, set of current conditions, and collectively determined national goal structures."[4] Multinational enterprise may approach this problem in two ways. It can adopt a passive attitude as in the past. It can adopt an active position, whereby the firm becomes involved in the social and educational problems and creates an atmosphere of mutual interests with the people of the host country. In other words, what multinational business needs is a way to devise an optional response pattern for social issues — one that safeguards the firms' own interests, while minimizing the chance of conflict and competitive dislocations, and increasing mutual dependence.

An active multinational corporation, usually faces a set of social, political and economic problems in host countries quite different from those existing at home. The first difficulty is a lack of political and economic stability. In the developing nations conditions are changing. A firm conditioned by the home environment of keeping status quo is always resentful of frequent changes. It develops alliance with a small group of ultraconservatives and strives to control political and economic leaders in each host country whose policies serve to maintain conditions favorable to multinational objectives. This situation may continue for some time while opposition forces gather strength and revolt against both government and foreign corporations. The incidents of such cases are frequent in Latin America, Africa and the Middle East.

Therefore it would seem wise for multinationals to stay out of politics of the host countries and follow a policy of economic mutual dependence. "It is fundamentally up to each nation to establish the regulatory framework that will minimize the net social costs of multinational corporate involvement without at the same time sacrificing the associated economic benefits."[5]

Business Goals versus Government Goals

The next question asked is whether the multinational corporation in pursuing these objectives will escape national controls and so limit national economic development policies whether in the developed or developing countries. Since the pressures for controls largely come from the developing countries we shall examine in more detail in this chapter the relationships between multinational corporations and these countries although under current economic uncertainty home governments are increasingly concerned with the activities of multinational corporations.

Do national controls necessarily permit the implementation of national economic policies? Are there clear national economic policies? The objectives of national governments are clear: e.g., to create employment, to foster industrial development, to create additional monetary reserves through new exports, to choose which industries shall develop so as to avoid the excessive consumerism of the Western World, to bring in needed foreign technology, to train local cadres in business management. All these aims are laudable and understandable; the manner in which these objectives shall be achieved — and the transformation of desire into accomplishment — is far more difficult to enunciate.

Somehow in many discussions the role of the multinational corporation appears to be modified — and it becomes an agency of the development process within a national boundary. This is neither the function nor the objective of the business corporation, be it national or international.

The objective of the corporation is to develop or manufacture a product or products or provide a service which the public in a given nation wishes to have and is in an economic position to buy. It answers a need determined by the market place; it is not an eleemosynary institution. Its purpose is to return a profit as a result of an investment of capital. The capital is given to the corporation for purposes of earning a return.

If the providers of capital are willing to take the long view in so far as return is concerned (and it is foolish to invest in a foreign country, particularly a developing country without realizing that the road to profitability, much less profitability without need for further investment, is a long one) they nevertheless expect that the managers of the enterprise will not make an investment if there is little likelihood of return. Economic risk is a risk the entrepreneur is willing to face because he is able to evaluate it. Political risk, which investors in developing countries increasingly face, is not one which the business executive is truly able or conditioned to evaluate.

Since political risk may involve total loss of the investment, it is not one which the smaller business can afford to make. It is hardly surprising, therefore, that the corporations now willing to invest in the developing countries are those with sufficient assets and productive facilities elsewhere that loss of one segment of their business will not jeopardize the economic strength of the enterprise as a whole.

The more governments in the developing world seek to regulate or nationalize businesses, particularly if compensation is refused or delayed, the more apparent it becomes that only the largest business enterprises can afford the risk of doing business in those countries, thereby bringing about what those governments are most anxious to avoid. If cooperation and not confrontation is the desired end, then new rules governing foreign business investment are desperately needed.

One of the purposes of this discourse will be to examine whether there are alternative forms of investment in foreign countries — other than equity investment — which, given the political climate in the world today, will make foreign investment more welcome in the developing world. Conditions in these countries have changed markedly in the past ten years. Managers of enterprises are faced today with entirely new problems when considering an investment abroad. Nor are the "rules of the game" changing only in the socialist countries or the countries of the third or fourth worlds. Investments in the North Sea, for instance in the oil business, would require much more careful analysis if made today than three years ago in either Norwegian waters or those of the United Kingdom. As government services expand, in the developed as well as in the developing world, the needs for additional revenues grow exponentially. This can cause increased pressure for state ownership or demands by the government for a larger share of the fruits of industrial enterprise. Alternately, it can lead to collaboration between government and business to keep business profitable and thereby able to pay the higher taxes required to service increased government expenditures for social services. This is the situation in Sweden, for example.

If material physical resources are deemed to belong to the State and the State can give out and take back such resources at will regardless of contract, then what of other resources?

Already we are seeing questions raised as to the ownership of the resources of the human mind: the internationalization of patents, for example.[6] Most managers of enterprise, fortunately for local governments, are nearsighted when it comes to evaluation of political risk. Otherwise, they would be far more reluctant to invest in many parts of the world where political stability is absent.

Economic policies of government are expected to have

been developed through careful planning. Business understands and respects planning. International business growth is
often the result of careful planning.

Jean-Jacques Servan Schreiber, in his book *The American
Challenge*[7] surprised many American managers by indicating
how able they were when compared to their European coun-
terparts. He gave the impression that planning in the American
multinational gave companies a very real advantage over their
competitors. The Swedes and the Japanese have since proved
that American concepts — if they were American concepts —
can be increasingly well adapted by others.

In the case of Japan — which we hope to analyze in a later
volume — it is evident that the "Japanese Miracle" is due in
no small part to the close relationship which has existed
among the government, the banks and the major industrial
groups. In 1953, one of the Japanese negotiators of the Peace
Treaty between Japan and the United States was asked by his
American counterpart how a poor, backward, agricultural
country like Japan was going to make out now that American
aid was coming to an end.[8] His answer was that corporate income taxes would be cut by one third, that exports would be
favored by all possible means, and that in this manner, foreign
exchange would be earned in sufficient quantities to permit
the rapid industrialization of the country. What the Japanese
with limited natural resources were able to accomplish, many
other countries in a similar situation, given the will, can surely
do as well. It is the authors' contention that this lack of will
to accomplish may be due in part to the nature of the aid
programs which the developed world has granted to the developing countries.[9]

Mexico, burdened with one of the highest birth rates in
the world, through wise leadership in the 1960s transformed
itself from a poor underdeveloped status to a state rapidly
approaching developed status. It did this through careful

government planning, encouragement of the private sector, and wise policy on educational needs, so that as the infrastructure developed the people to manage it. In so doing, the Government, learning from its experience in the national oil company Pemex, encouraged development to come from the private sector wherever possible while giving tax advantages for adding to the country's infrastructure only to companies controlled by Mexican nationals.

Whether the focus of the recent United Nations economic charter,[10] directed as it is in favor of increased government regulation and control, will turn out to be helpful remains to be seen. History indicates rather that excessive government regulation can sap private initiative particularly in the development phase where hard work, innovative techniques, and a willingness to take risks are encouraged by an opportunity for substantial reward. This does not mean that planning is not essential. Each government needs to define its objectives and the methods by which it will achieve projected growth rates.

If a host country will lay down carefully prepared "rules of the game" concerning foreign investment and be prepared to live within such rules, the response from the MNCs will be positive even though another country similarly attractive as a production base might have fewer rules but less stability. It is a truism that most MNCs invest in a given country with the intent of making a growing commitment there. Not only is the cost of capital so high today but also the difficulty in obtaining managerial talent is so great that to make an investment on any other basis would be foolhardy indeed.

In discussing the transfer of technology we see that the investment must be upgraded constantly by new infusions of capital, because regardless of the attractiveness of wage rates in developing nations, changes in technology are constantly placing the initial reason for the investment in doubt. It is not only the high technology industries that are subject to constant change. The textile industry is a case in point. Swiss techniques in machinery design have forced companies in low-wage areas to install new machinery regardless of the effect on their work force.[11] Even in such an established old industry as the railroads, we are seeing a technological revolution about to take place. In agriculture, the needs of a growing world population can be expected to bring about new concepts and methods for raising yields and improving quality.

A major difference between planning in the MNC and planning by national government is that the time frame may be quite different.

In the modern multinational there is high continuity of management, where the chairman is likely to have selected the president who will succeed him — to be succeeded in turn by one of the vice presidents who is being groomed for the presidency. Under these conditions long range corporate strategy can be developed and implemented as required. There are, of course, numerous examples in business where the corporate strategy was quite wrong. The failure of management to understand the needs or wants of the buying public is all too evident in the case of the United States' automobile industry, the airlines and most railroads. Nevertheless, the time-frame for planning is there.

Except in a single party state, the time span for government planning is much shorter. A President in the United States has a four-year time frame. If the plan of his advisors is unlikely to yield the desired results within the period of his term, it has doubtful usefulness to him. The time frame of a member of Congress may be even shorter.

In developing countries, there is a great pressure on governments to find immediate answers to problems which may have existed for decades. In this area of planning for growth or planning for development, it is possible that the United

Nations may in time develop some constructive models which can then be adapted by individual governments. The MNCs cannot plan or even initiate government planning. However, once a government has calculated its objectives toward development goals, then the MNC, once it understands that it may have a role to play in such development, can participate fully for the benefit of all concerned.

Given such an approach the MNC can be expected to participate constructively because it is of necessity interested in the development of the host country. Otherwise internal markets will not develop and the MNC's troubles with government may multiply. We can, therefore, state that while an MNC cannot plan for a host country, it can *respond* to economic policies developed by the government if these are defined and maintained consistently.

The question of adequate government planning and determination of objectives for development is therefore of paramount importance. Nor is the need for better planning limited to developing countries. There is need for much better planning in the United States, for instance. The oil producing nations, beginning with Iran in 1952, warned the oil companies that they were dissatisfied with the concessions and wanted changes profitable to both parties. The oil company consortium and the CIA responded by overthrowing Dr. Mussaddegh and by establishing another twenty years of domination over the principal resource of the country.

In turn, however, the oil companies had warned the United States government in the late 1950's and again in the 1970's of the need for an energy policy in view of the runaway inflation in developed nations and the continued increase in oil consumption.[12] Yet it took the Arab embargo in 1973 during the October War to focus attention on the problem and 2 years later in late 1975 there was still no national energy policy and no apparent negotiations with oil producing nations. Once specific policy has been agreed upon within the ranks of government: the national and international companies engaged in the exploration, development, manufacture and distribution of energy sources will have to adjust their strategies and methods of operation to conform to natural energy depletion. This will in turn affect the future of many industries, including oil, gas, petrochemicals, chemicals, nuclear, coal, uranium, electrical, public utilities and any other industries which may directly or indirectly be concerned with either existing forms of energy or attempts at creating substitutes.

The need for careful governmental planning has recently been focused on energy because of the dependence of the developed world for oil on OPEC countries and in particular on the Persian Gulf States. Of immediate importance in this regard is the question of whether, in the oil consuming countries, the oil is to be imported by the multinational corporations as was true in the past, or whether since the OPEC cartel of producers is a cartel of governments, the governments of the principal consuming countries should themselves create a government cartel of importers thereby bypassing the current role of the private petroleum industry.

How can we avoid this type of government versus government confrontation? If the international oil companies are to be turned into public utilities because of government's new role in the exploration and development of crude, whose public utility are they to be: the producing government cartels or the cartels of governments of petroleum-consuming countries? Should oil exploration, refining and distribution be a government function, as is the case with public utilities, banks, communications, transportation, etc. in many parts of the world today? These are interesting questions to which there are no easy answers. Other questions immediately come to mind. If oil is to become a government monopoly, what about other natural resources? Can there be workable cartels in copper, uranium, tin, bauxite and other metals? Will producers' cartels require the institution of buyers' cartels at a government level?

Since the purpose of such cartels is to create price stability and a fair return to the producers and/or to the states in which the extraction takes place, would a better answer be to create through the IMF, the World Bank, or some new international agency, a fund which can in times of overproduction, purchase and warehouse the production of minerals to be sold to the consumers when required, in the meantime maintaining price stability and a guarantee of availability? [13] If this is done for metals what about food products particularly now that we know the world energy crisis is nothing compared to the impending world crisis in agricultural product demand, particularly proteins? [14]

These are all questions which must be resolved at the political level either through the international community or by regional groupings. It is a basic question of political and economic planning to be done at the government or inter-government level where the role of the multinational corporation is limited and subservient to political decision-making on an increasingly global rather than national level. In years to come, it is possible, although unlikely, that the oil embargo of October 1973 may be seen as the first step in a series of government decisions which eventually transformed the nature and role of the transnational corporation in essential industries — first in oil, then in mining, then in agricultural products, into a new form of internationally controlled state enterprises, the characteristics of which are yet to be determined. In this case the State-owned enterprise, as the oil business in France and Italy, may take on all the management characteristics of the privately owned multinational corporation.

The Effect of Controls on the Future Role of
Multinational Corporations

One of the basic questions we raised in the previous chapter
is this: will national policies established to govern international
trade and investment impair the operation of multinational
·corporations and prevent them from contributing as much as
they could to world income and productivity development?
Put another way, will the actions of individual home and host
governments toward foreign enterprise so discourage foreign
investment in the years to come that investment and trade
between the developed and developing world will continue to
diminish relative to trade and investment within the developed
world? In the authors' opinion this is a highly likely result if
the political climate within the developing nations continues
to be nonconciliatory and new efforts are not made by the
developed nations to understand the true concerns of the
developing nations.

If this is not to happen, it will be because developed countries on the one hand will have learned to approach foreign
direct investment with a new flexibility and respect for the
objectives of the developing nations. On the other hand, if
developing governments wish to industrialize and to make
available within their countries the manufacture of high technology products, the psychological climate within such governments should also be modified to understand and accept
better the objectives of the multinational enterprise which
controls the desired technology. By and large multinational
corporations tend to adapt to national objectives if these are
clearly stated.

If flexibility is the key attribute to be required of the
managers of the future, then perhaps stability (i.e., predicta-
bility) is what the manager looks for in the way of treatment
by the national government. This cannot and must not mean

that investments are forever frozen or that the state cannot nationalize what it chooses. It simply means that international enterprise is treated in the same manner as national enterprise and that methods will be found to compensate multinational corporations for what is taken on a basis which meets the requirements of what society has over a long period of developing civilization come to regard as law and equitable conduct. The need for acceptable mechanisms to settle disputes between multinational corporations and host countries is a delicate problem which requires careful consideration. It is one of the key areas of controversy in the United Nations Charter of Economic Rights and Duties of States. In the absence of approriate and even-handed methods for the settlement of disputes any foreign investment is discouraged or the risk left to speculators rather than investors.

The investment is then justifiable as a business risk only if the returns are so great as to earn a payout within months rather than years thereby taking away the major assurance the local government seeks, namely, that the investor plans to establish his business locally for the long pull, transferring his capital and his technology, training local cadres to run the business and eventually transferring the investment into local hands not only to operate but to participate in ownership. There are indications that such a change in psychological climate from the government side may be forthcoming.[15]

It is difficult for managers of multinational corporations to fully understand the present concern of national governments with the problem of ownership. Ownership of the large multinational corporations is increasingly international. To the management of such an enterprise it often makes little difference whether his stockholders are American, Canadian, European, Latin America, or perhaps now, Arabian. If the President of the multinational company is an American, he knows historically that in the period between the Civil War and

World War I, when industrial development of the United
States was progressing very rapidly, it was largely financed by
nationals of Great Britain and Germany who invested in the
railroads and public utilities, particularly in the western part
of the country.[16] Without foreign direct investment the development of the United States would not have taken place.

As a result of the transfer of wealth between nations in
World War I and the subsequent growth of national savings,
which followed, the stage was set for a reversal of capital
movement from the United States to Western Europe after
the end of World War II, which is referred to in detail in
chapter 2 of this work. Management of international enterprise is very much concerned with capital. If it is to plan the
growth of the business it must have capital with which to do
it. This is the sine qua non of corporate enterprise. Where the
funds come from is secondary.[17]

As businesses have grown, the impersonality of ownership
has become endemic. With the development of the practice
of indirect ownership, with the shares registered in the names
of banks, trust companies, brokers, in "street names," the investors become increasingly nameless and at many stockholders' meetings held once a year, generally with the exception of professional attendees, only a small proportion shows
up.

The separation of management and ownership — once so
close — is particularly evident in the American as opposed to
the European multinational company. As we pointed out in
chapter 2 foreign direct ownership in United States multinational corporations is principally by way of portfolio investment.[18] The switch in ownership of U.S. corporations
from individual shareholders or family holdings to institutions, investment trusts, mutual funds and pension trusts
compounds this trend. These shareholders seldom have any
desire to interfere with management. If they are not satisfied

with management they simply sell out. Foreign direct investment by United States investors is not portfolio investment. It is direct foreign investment by the multinational companies themselves and hence the investment is made to be retained and to be managed. This means that whereas United States managers of multinational corporations are only theoretically responsible to the owners, the managers of foreign affiliations within a corporate group are constantly answerable to top management corporate headquarters be it in New York, Chicago or San Francisco. This relationship between ownership and management has enabled the American multinational corporation to develop as it has and to take the business risks which have been taken in creating global enterprises. If stockholders, labor unions, customers and suppliers of the American multinational corporation had a more influential voice in management it is likely that such enterprises would have remained national rather than international in scope.

This is evident from an examination of family controlled businesses, even those of a sufficient size to make international development a worthwhile corporate objective. In these, internationalization is more of an unconscious happenstance than the result of planned strategy and such a company may find itself the focus of a takeover bid by another corporation with broader geographical understanding and aims.

An examination of accountability by management of American multinationals in terms of to whom, why, and how, may itself be worth looking into particularly with reference to the objectives of the home government — in this case the United States government — and the home country labor unions — which may through their pension trusts be increasingly active investors demanding accountability of corporate managers. Both the U.S. government and U.S. labor leaders may now insist on *decreased* foreign investment and a return to production at home.[19]

There is also increasing evidence of concern in the Congress of the United States which now regards the multinational in quite a different light from postwar executive and legislative branches of government, which were disposed to further internationalization of American business in order to counteract the spread of communism during a period of "cold war" political confrontation between incompatible ideological systems. Indeed, there are many in the Congress of the United today who look upon the transfer of American technology by the United States multinational corporations to the socialist countries with deep misgivings. There are twenty five bills pending currently in the Congress designed to affect in some manner the degree of foreign ownership of United States enterprises. And this has occurred in a period of supposed "détente."

Should the fragile political relationship between the United States and the Soviet Union and between the United States and China be exacerbated by political confrontation in the Middle East, Africa or South East Asia, the government of the United States may again revise its attitude toward investment by United States firms in the socialist countries particularly where defense items may be directly or indirectly involved.

To some of us who study these political relationships and the social framework within those countries which assures lesser rates of inflation and a lack of work stoppages, it is surprising that the domestic labor movement has not made more of an effort to discourage the transfer of productive facilities to Eastern-block countries. From the standpoint of the multinational corporation for which political and economic stability is so important, a guarantee of production for a period of years at fixed prices encourages the transfer of productive facilities, particularly in areas where a high labor content is required. It creates an appeal to make an investment of productive facilities even though management has no sympathy for a particular government.

Were it not for the fact that socialist country governments are more interested in the capital intensive industries which require high technology, the transfer might have been intensified, particularly in a period of growing inflation in the Western World. We shall discuss in more detail further on in the chapter how flexibility on the side of both parties has enabled joint enterprises to develop in the socialist world. The national government bends or bypasses its ideological requirements that all means of production must be owned by the state and the multinational corporation targets its requirements that the sole rights of management be entrusted to it or that the equity must be wholly or majority-owned.

Let us now examine whether multinational corporations can themselves in their conduct anticipate and answer some of the criticism leveled at the manner in which they conduct themselves and the methods used in structuring their foreign investment activities.

The U.N. Commission on Multinationals, established by the General Assembly found examples of political interference in the internal affairs of the host countries and suggested that a permanent commission and information and research center of the multinational should be established.[20] It recommended that: "The Commission will be the forum within the United Nations Systems for the consideration of issues relating to the MNC. The program of the work of the commission should be focused on the following areas:

1) Preliminary work with the purpose of formulating a code of conduct.

2) Establishment of a comprehensive information system.

3) Research on the political, economic and social effects of the multinationals' operations.

4) Organization and coordination of technical cooperation

programs of multinationals, at the request of the host countries.

The Information and Research Center must undertake the
following responsibilities and report to the second session of
the commission:

A) A comparative study of existing international codes of
conduct or guidelines drafted with the purpose of influencing
or regulating the operations and practices of multinational
corporations, including the study of relevant materials underlying such codes;

B) A comparative study of existing national and regional
legislation and regulation enacted with the purpose of regulating the operations and activities of multinationals;

C) Suggestions as to possible methods of intersessionals
work by the Commission which would further the task of
drafing a code of conduct;

D) To collect and analyse material relating to the evolution, development and formulation of a code of conduct;

E) To further understand the nature and political, economic and social effects of the activities of multinationals in
home and host countries and international relations, particularly between developed and developing nations;

F) To strengthen the capacity of host countries, in particular developing countries, in their dealings with multinationals.

Furthermore, the Information and Research Centers are
authorized to collect information in the following priority
areas, where very little information is available:

1) Transfer pricing and taxation.

2) Short-term capital movement by multinationals.

3) Restrictive business practices.

4) Corporate ownership and alternative forms of business
participation.

5) Market Concentration. In this case special considera-

tion should be given to acquisition of participation and merger.

6) Alternative forms of management and control.

7) Relative use by multinationals of home international and host countries financial markets in their operations and investments.

8) Social impact of multinational corporations.

9) Impact of multinationals on freedom of labor organizations, trade union rights, labor standards and working conditions.

10) The effect on *operations of multinationals* of the absence of a stable investment climate."

The Commission also recommended that the Information and Research Center should concentrate on the following areas which so far have been neglected by governments and corporations:

1. Studies on the role and effects of transnational corporations in sectors of economic activity that so far had been insufficiently covered by research projects, such as in the case of agricultural, extractive, land development, shipping, trade, banking, insurance, and tourism activities;

2. Obstacles to strengthening the bargaining capacity of governments in their relations with transnational corporations;

3. Lessons to be obtained from national and regional legislation, mechanism and arrangements that had permitted the strengthening of the bargaining capacity of governments in their relations with transnational corporations;

4. A study of the measures adopted by host countries to strenghten the competitive position of national enterprises vis-à-vis transnational corporations;

5. Studies described in paragraph 10 above to support the work directed towards the formulation of a code of conduct dealing with transnational corporations;

6. Studies of the political, economic and social impact of

the operations and activities of the transnational corporations.

Furthermore the Commission is asking all the host countries to notify the Information and The Research Center what their basic requirements for technical assistance are both in the field of manpower training and consultations, so that the Center can prepare a proposal for the next session of the Commission, taking into consideration the overall requirements of technical assistance and the availability of funds and experts from the United Nations. The ultimate responsibility for technical assistance to the developing nations should lie with the Research Center.

In the light of the United Nations recommendations we will examine below some specific areas in which some new thinking on behalf of multinational corporations might be useful. The following five areas are examined as particularly relevant:

1. Alternative forms of investment where foreign direct investment poses a problem. In this connection the channels through which international ownership disputes may be arbitrated are also examined.

2. The question of technology transfers.

3. Areas of conflict — social responsibility.

4. The question of communication.

5. Internationalizing management controls.

There are, of course, other areas of interest which will become increasingly important in the future and worthy of further study such as the question of restrictive trade practices and short term capital movements.

Alternate Methods of Investment.

As noted above there is increasing concern by governments in many countries about ownership of national business enterprises by foreigners. In the Cominform countries all private ownership of productive facilities whether domestic or foreign is forbidden. In Western Europe and the U.S.A., whose corporations have invested more than two hundred billion dollars all over the world, the question of ownership by foreign interests is also being raised.

In the developing countries, particularly those that have recently gained their political liberty, foreign direct ownership is increasingly regarded as a form of economic neocolonialism perpetrated by their former political masters. The recent concern of some members of Congress of the United States against possible takeovers of American businesses by Middle Eastern interests is but another instance of the same bias. When one thinks of how American companies have expanded their operations through acquisitions, particularly in Europe, Canada and the Middle East, it seems singularly ungracious for members of the legislative branch of the United States government to demand that the government regulate foreign investments in the United States. While no doubt most of these expressions of anxiety are for local political purposes, the number of proposals made in the Congress indicates the degree of concern.[21]

To many outside observers it is one more indication of the backward thinking of those in government. Nevertheless, we cannot dismiss this concern about foreign ownership of national businesses as mere emotional demagogery because it is a recurring theme and one which appears in both developed and developing countries.

Curiously enough, many businessmen appear relatively unconcerned about the threat of increased foreign competition through domestic ownership. The public reaction unless excited by the press is mild; it is the governments that appear to feel threatened.

Regardless of the reasons, since the question of foreign ownership may present a real problem, how can multinational corporations in their ventures abroad conduct themselves so as to eliminate or reduce the concern of governments regarding ownership. It is submitted that there are ways of approaching foreign investment so as to satisfy both the foreign investor and the host country government.

There are at least seven different ways of avoiding direct equity investment *if direct equity investment poses a problem.* They are:

   a) Joint ventures,

   b) Licensing arrangements,

   c) Cooperative agreements,

   d) Investment by contract which is either self-liquidating or restricted to certain functions to be performed by the multinational company,

   e) Production-sharing agreements,

   f) Profit-sharing agreements,

   g) Disinvestment patterns.

We start with the premise that when the management of a multinational corporation considers an investment abroad it thinks in terms of equity, i.e., holding the capital stock of a new corporation to be located in the host country. If it is an American multinational it will often ask for 100 percent ownership on the theory that minority partners are demanding and have very different investment objectives: e.g., their time horizon is short; they want a prompt return on their money; they do not want to reinvest earnings to build the business; they do not want to pay for parent company know-how, financial aid or engineering assistance; and they do not understand the needs of modern transnational business. The Europeans in general are more disposed to accept local partners. The Japanese in many cases, prefer to hold a minority interest in host countries outside Japan so as to allow domestic problems such as those involving labor unions to be handled by local majority interests. Being accustomed to working on the basis of concensus, they are not disturbed unduly by a "partnership" concept of business, nor are they apt to be concerned with global aspects of marketing. In Japan this is a specialized function of the trading companies and if the trading company is the investor it will expect to handle sales outside the host country as it does for all its other world-wide interests.

Does the concept of ownership necessarily require holding an equity interest? The answer, of course, is not in all cases. Joint Ventures (particularly in socialist countries):

To the legal and accounting advisors of multinational corporations, particularly the Americans, ownership usually means capital stock participation. It need not mean this in order to give the investor what he wants, and would have had, if he received a stock participation. The question immediately arises in the socialist countries because of the requirement there that all means of production belong to the State – or in the case of Yugoslavia, to the workers in the enterprise. There the problem is solved by a contract which provides for, as would a corporate statute, the duration of the new enterprise, the division of profits, the management, the supervisory board, the responsibility for production and marketing, etc. In other words all the basic business infrastructure that the charter and bylaws of a corporation would contain is provided for. No stock is issued. The parties are linked by contract. In other socialist countries, joint ventures with foreigners are treated under special laws, justified because they are limited in time and based upon the necessity of obtaining desired technology thereby. In these instances, since the State owns all means of production, it is evident that it can allow foreign participation limited by both time and function.

The advantage of joint ventures to the host country is clear: it is a method of acquiring foreign technology on a continuing basis thereby assuring the host government that its foreign partner which has a genuine continuing interest in the venture will bring in new technology as developed at home. This is important. As the technological time span continuously shortens, the necessity for continuity becomes an increasingly important consideration. The socialist countries have appreciated this factor and acted accordingly.

A contrary approach is that of the Andean Common Market Regulation 24 which provides that the foreign partner transfer almost all its interest in the venture to local investors. Under this arrangement the foreign investor has little incentive to keep the transferred technology current, to train local personnel for management responsibilities, or to increase the value of the investment by continued capital investment. It will be interesting to observe whether Regulation 24 works out satisfactorily in practice.

The joint venture also has advantages to the foreign investor because it is allowed to transfer equipment in return for its participation thereby avoiding the need for a cash contribution to secure its participating interest. Most joint ventures in the socialist countries provide that the return to the foreign investor will be paid out of the proceeds of foreign exchange earned by the venture. The State (or workers) receiving their return on local sales or sales with COMECON. Repatriation of capital and return on investment can and should be guaranteed in the socialist country joint venture by the appropriate government agency dealing with such matters whether it be the Foreign Trade Bank, the National Bank, or both. These guarantees have been scrupulously observed. In other parts of the world where political stability is not as great the rules of the game with respect to guarantees of payment of income or return of capital may change.

Licensing Arrangements

In Japan where the government has been very reluctant to allow foreign direct investment even on a joint venture basis, foreign technology has been acquired very successfully through licensing arrangements. Once the government accepts that the technology is needed, it requires that a license be obtained on a paid-up basis, but the government has been less concerned with the amount to be paid. Because of the engineering and scientific skills of its own people, the system has worked out well in Japan and we have seen repeated instances of licenses granted which result in a new invention patented and licensed back to the original licensor.

There may of course be problems associated with licensing from the host government's standpoint since the license may not mean that future technology will be forthcoming. Payment of foreign exchange is required for license fees. The license may provide for only limited geographical exploitation. From the point of view of the licensor, there may also be other serious problems. If the licensed product is to carry its name with or without that of the licensee, the licensor may find itself spending countless engineering hours improving manufacturing processes and product quality which may not be fully compensated or even provided for. In brief, licensing is useful but limited in time and worthwhile only to consider when the licensor can rely on the licensee's engineering know-how and friendly cooperation.

Cooperation Agreements

This type of agreement is also frequently used in trade between the multinational corporation and the socialist country governments. Under a cooperation agreement which is midway between a license and a joint venture, the foreign investor gives a license to manufacture and sell generally within the Comecon Countries and in addition transfers equipment necessary to manufacture the product in whole or in part. It is paid a licensee fee and a return calculated upon a number of products to be delivered to it either for further assembly or sale outside Comecon. If equipment is important, the government gets it without having to use foreign exchange which may be in very short supply. The foreign multinational gets products on an advantageous barter basis.

Problems in this type of agreement come from the foreign corporation's failure to make sure that manufacturing equipment needed goes in without duty and that products come out without duty. The foreign company must again be concerned with problems of quality control but since it is taking goods in return it must also take into account difficulties in meeting delivery dates, return of merchandise, etc., factors which can easily poison a business relationship. The interest of a cooperation agreement with a socialist country to the foreign corporation comes from the fact that the government can assure fixed prices for a period of years since there is no labor unrest, no unpredictable wage increases, and inflation may be hidden under fixed price agreements from one state enterprise to another.

Participation by Contract

We speak here of the method whereby the foreign multinational corporation with its unique knowhow performs certain services which may be in the form of management, engineering, construction, financial services, marketing services, production services or any other services which can, in the opinion of the host government or local enterprise, be handled more efficiently by the foreign multinational. The most common are the so-called turn-key construction contracts relating to installation of high technology facilities (oil refineries, petrochemical plants, etc.) or such services as road building, dam construction, etc. The job is contracted out and paid for and the foreign entrepreneur has no further interest in the investment except to the extent of its guarantee of workmanship, materials and satisfactory operating performance.

The contract may be on a fixed-fee or cost-plus basis. The government usually prefers the former because it knows what its commitment will be. Under current inflationary conditions the foreign contractor finds it hard to guarantee costs of labor and materials over the period of the contract particularly since the subcontractors will generally not work on this basis. If a fixed price is required the contractor must build into his price his estimate of inflation and other cost variants. There may be in addition patented products or processes involved in which case a license may be given requiring continued payments to be made to the contractor. The more difficult situations are those which require the contractor to perform continuing services.

The contractor may, for example, be required to manage an oil exploration and development project, a refinery, a smelter, a mining venture or other types of venture where the foreign corporation's continuing skill and knowledge is essential to the success of the enterprise. The difficulty here is what pressure the host country or host country investors can exert to make sure the job is properly done. If the results do not meet expectations, who is responsible? The contractor cannot be asked to guarantee results unless the defective condition is due to unsatisfactory materials, workmanship or design, but who is to make the determination? If the contracting multinational corporation is paid a fee to manage but has no participation in results it may shift its efforts to other projects in which it has a continuing equity participation.

Many variants of this contractual arrangement can be observed in the Middle East and other areas where management experience on complicated projects is limited. Time will indicate how well the contractual relationship works out where continued management services are required. Participation based on results achieved in addition to a fixed fee may prove to be the solution to the problem of continued interest. Of course, if the foreign multinational is given the right to distribute the product at a fixed cost price then its interest will be enhanced, but what about cost or production controls in this instance? The contracting company wants to assure product delivery and thus may not schedule production so as to minimize costs since overall profit is not its concern.

Production-sharing Agreements

Production-sharing agreements were first used in Indonesia. More recently they have been used as a method of structuring oil exploration and production arrangements in Egypt and also in Libya. In the opinion of many observers this type of contractual relationship will constitute the system of the future for joint enterprise in the oil field. In Egypt and in Libya, the multinational corporation in such an agreement puts up all the risk capital through the exploration and production phase, with the parties sharing thereafter on a fifty-fifty basis the cost of development and production. The duration of the exploration period and the production period is specified in the agreement. Work commitments in terms of minimum expenditures are provided for with withdrawal permitted at stated intervals. There are generally signature bonuses and later production bonuses to be paid by the contractor as nonrecoverable expenses. In these arrangements, other expenses by the contractor involved in exploration, development and production are recoverable out of 40 percent of the oil produced until fully paid. The initial 60 percent remaining (and after payout the full 100 percent) is divided 80 percent to the government and 20 percent to the foreign oil company contractor. The essence of the agreement, therefore, is that the host government takes no risk, gets periodic bonuses and an eventual 80 percent return on the results of exploration.

The oil company takes all the risk which can be justified on the basis of its technological expertise, but if the results are positive will get its expenses back (other than bonuses) and then 20 percent of the venture's profit. Nothing in these agreements is said of marketing. Each party markets its own share of the crude. In this sense these agreements differ from the normal profit-sharing arrangement used in mining ventures where the foreign multinational gets the right to market the product outside the host country.

It is interesting to compare the production sharing agreements with the recent decision of the government of the United Kingdom on the taxation of North Sea oil. There the government takes a royalty of 12½ percent (not dissimilar to the bonus system in production-sharing agreements). After repayment of 175 percent of the capital investment and an oil allowance of 1 million tons a year for ten years to encourage development of the smaller fields, the government gets 45 percent of revenues after expenses and allowances and thereafter the normal 52 percent corporation tax is applied. The net effect of this arrangement is to give the government close to the 80-20 split of production-sharing arrangements common in the Middle East. Whether in one country it is called taxation and in another production-sharing, the split is not dissimilar and is highly advantageous to the government which takes none of the risk of the enterprise. The company, of course, is very much interested in arranging the terms of contract in such a way as to obtain the maximum tax benefit, particularly if its home country allows tax credits.

Profit-sharing Agreements

In the profit-sharing agreement the foreign multinational

corporation again puts up all the risk capital to develop the property. The arrangement is frequently found in mining ventures where the government gives the foreign company the right to mineral exploration, development and exploitation within a certain area of the host country. The contract normally provides for a small lease payment on acreage covered by the contract, a royalty payment with minimums so that the government gets some return during the exploration period. Then during the exploitation period, the government is given a share of the profits, generally on a fifty-fifty basis.

Difficulties here center around a definition of profits, whether before or after depletion and depreciation. The multinational usually wants an allowance for depletion, the government says that there should be no depletion allowance because the ore belonged to the government and is not the property of the company. The claim for depreciation is more apparent. It is the company that buys and installs the equipment needed to develop the property or refine the ore and such property must be amortized as it will have to be replaced.

Another problem to be anticipated concerns the relationship between the multinational company and its affiliates. What if the parent company advances funds for the project? Are interest payments to be deducted from the venture prior to a determination of profits in which the host government shares? Are the interest payments reasonable? What of royalties paid to the contractor for patents and knowhow used in the process of developing the property? How are sales to affiliated companies to be handled in determining whether the price paid is a price equal to that which would be paid by an unrelated buyer? Is the cost of transport reasonable if the company provides transportation of the ore? We need not dwell on instances in the past when host governments have been taken advantage of by multinational companies engaged in the development of natural resources on a profit-sharing basis either through transfer price manipulation or excessive payments for services rendered by affiliated companies engaged in sales, marketing or transport. Today the managements of multinational companies tend to operate increasingly "in the open." We have only to see the effect of the reporting requirements of the Securities and Exchange Commission on commission payments to observe the increasing necessity for public disclosure of contract arrangements. Furthermore, expertise in host countries has grown and advice from international organizations or private consulting groups is now readily available, so that the risks to host countries of making unfavorable contracts for the development of their natural resources is much reduced. From the point of view of the company, avoidance of nationalization will stand the test of time. The percentage of eventual profit given to the host country is continuously being increased under host country demands. What is agreed upon under today's standards as a division of profits may therefore be rejected tomorrow. Yet the risk to the corporation has to be measured, and financing for the project assured, under current market conditions and risks.

It is very difficult to design a profit-sharing formula that will be considered fair in later years, when the results of the venture are known and the initial risks of failure forgotten. Perhaps the best way of designing a formula is to allow the contractor to recoup his capital investment with an allowance for what such capital would have earned if invested elsewhere — similar to the UK North Sea oil tax formula we noted earlier — and then allow for profit sharing on a basis which gives the company a greater percentage of profits if the eventual "take" from the property is smaller. Stated in other words, the more successful the exploitation, the greater will be the share allotted to the host government.

If the foreign company has been paid back for its investment with appropriate interest it appears reasonable to give the host country a substantially greater share of the return if the exploitation turns out more profitable than anticipated, because it is the country's resource that will have proved richer than anticipated. If results are benefited by greater expertise, input by the company might be expanded. Under such type of flexible arrangement any tendency to nationalize on the part of the host country or withdraw by the company may be lessened.

Another question relating to profit-sharing agreements is whether the government's share should be labeled as a tax or as a division of profit. Where the parent country allows the multinational a credit for foreign taxes paid, the company has an advantage in labeling the host country's participation as tax rather than as a share of profits, particularly if the host country's percentage is high. It is usually immaterial from the host government's standpoint how its profit share of the enterprise is labeled.

Disinvestment Patterns

A classic example here is the agreement between I.T.T., the American company, and the government of Indonesia with respect to operation of a communications satellite. In this case, the company invested its capital, put up the space station and then turned it over to the government in return for a long-term contract.

The advantages to both sides are obvious here: the government is obtaining a high technology public utility of the utmost necessity to the development of the country's infrastructure. The company builds the facility to its specifications, makes sure it functions as it should free of government controls, then transfers ownership in return for a twenty-year management contract, at the end of which period the facility can be government-operated.

There are, however, drawbacks to this type of government —multinational corporation relationship. Let us look at Resolution 24 of the Andean Common Market. This resolution provided very stringent regulations applying to both new and existing foreign investments and covering acquisitions, capital repatriation and remittance of profits, the prohibition of foreign investment in key sectors, technology, patent and trademark licenses and use of domestic credit facilities together with limits in interest rates payable to lenders abroad. Three types of investments are segregated: 1. foreign companies (those which have less than 51 percent national control or ownership); 2. mixed companies (51 percent-80 percent national control or ownership); 3. national companies (at least 80 percent national ownership with proportionate management control).

Briefly stated, foreign companies must divest majority ownership within a fifteen to twenty-year period in order to take advantage of the tariff regulations applicable within the Andean Common Market. A three-year period is allowed to make the decision on whether to meet the "fadeout" requirements. Local participation is provided for on a gradual basis: 15 percent upon initiation of production for new investments increasing gradually until 51 percent has been transferred by the fifteenth year (twenty years for Ecuador and Bolivia).

The state or state-owned coporations are given a priority on purchase. There are provisions for registration of all foreign capital. Markets considered "adequately served" by existing companies are excluded from new foreign participation and acquisition of existing companies is forbidden except where necessary to avoid bankruptcy. There are also regulations on concession agreements on mining ventures which must not exceed twenty years duration. New investments in banking and insurance are prohibited and existing foreign owned banks must be 80 percent locally owned if they are to continue after a time period to accept local deposits. The annual limit in profit repatriation is 14 percent of registered capital. Foreign borrowing is subject to authorization with interest rate limitations. There are also strict authorization procedures covering payments for technology as well as patents and trademarks. Generally, clauses restricting production or exports in such licensing agreements are forbidden.

The adoption of all those regulations by the Andean Common Market is understandable as an effort to develop local entrepreneurship and ownership, but how they will work out in practice remains yet to be seen since Resolution 24 was only adopted in late 1970. Entrepreneurship in many fields requires continued technology and knowhow to be successful. Whether owners of these intangible assets will respond favorably to such conditions also remains to be seen.

Application of Resolution 24 may result in efforts on the part of the foreign multinational to maximize profits during the period prior to local participation, to postpone the training of local nationals, and to postpone expenditures for capital items or for maintenance of plant and equipment. Nevertheless, these Regulations indicate a very definite intention on the part of developing countries to try to establish rules governing the activities of foreign multinationals.

It can be expected that similar regulations may be adopted in other parts of the world. A fully integrated multinational corporation may find it particularly hard to live with the rules relating to export sales as these may contravene already existing distribution arrangements in other parts of the world and the multinational corporation may, in due course, find itself forced to allow competition among its affiliates based in different geographical locations using the technology, knowhow, patents and trademarks developed by the same parent company. Governments are in effect saying here "if you believe in interdependence then affiliated companies based in our countries must be free to export anywhere in the world your technology for which they are paying a return." If this trend continues it must necessarily affect the marketing strategy of the multinational corporation because the owner of the technology will have less control over the global distribution of its products. It may mean that in the future marketing will have to be handled, on a world-wide basis by affiliated marketing companies similar to the Japanese trading companies which will buy from local producers under license and market anywhere under distribution agreements world-wide.

We have discussed above various methods of avoiding or complying with local or regional regulations having essentially to do with the problem of ownership. There are any number of variations of the seven methods outlined which can be negotiated to fit the requirements of individual government constraints or multinational corporation willingness to compromise. One thing is certain: in the give and take of investment negotiations with host governments the management of multinational corporations will have to bring to the negotiating table a new flexibility and on their part host governments will have to determine just how essential it is to produce locally rather than import the products of modern technology. In the final analysis the investment will only work out well if satisfactory to both parties over a period of time. If not, then the multinational will in due course pull out or the government make it impossible for it to stay either through the exercise of its sovereign right to seize or in a more sophisticated manner, to harass or tax away the MNC's privilege to remain in that country.

Can the multinational corporation protect itself in any other way against the threat of nationalization? As pointed out earlier, it can try a number of alternate routes to direct investment all of which have been tried in different parts of the world. Obviously, the best method is to provide for an arbitration clause to cover disputes in the basic investment authorization or agreement. In joint ventures in the socialist countries it is usual to provide for arbitration of disputes by the Arbitration Court of the International Chamber of Commerce either in Paris or in Zurich applying law acceptable to both parties. An alternative here is to use the International Center for Settlement of Investment Disputes. The difficulty, of course, is that a host government is understandably reluctant to allow some outside agency to pass on its acts as a derogation of its national sovereignty.

If an arbitration procedure cannot be set forth in the basic agreement, then the multinational corporation should consider whether it can obtain guarantees from agencies of its parent company's country, both as to convertibility (covering both income and eventual repatriation of capital) and as to expropriation.

Many countries have such guarantee programs which depend upon treaties between the host country and the parent company country for application. If in a given case such a guarantee is unavailable, the company can consider the advisability of making the investment with another company headquartered in a country that can provide an expropriation guarantee at least to the extent of the partner's investment.

In due course, it is hoped that an international investment insurance agency will be established as part of the World Bank system. Here again, however, the "rules of the game" leave much to be desired. It is universally recognized that national governments have the right to nationalize. Equally, it is generally recognized that upon nationalization, the government shall pay "adequate compensation" both with respect to modalities and amount. But what constitutes "adequate compensation"? The host country is likely to consider book value or at best updated book value. The corporation will look to a valuation based on its historic costs and profits on which future profits can be projected. Book value is a criterion seldom used in calculating the value of a company which is being acquired by another. The test here usually is future return on investment based upon past results and future potential. Nevertheless, even this test is necessarily a subjective test and fair valuations are very difficult to arrive at. Arbitration procedures are therefore probably the fairest method of arriving at a reasonable settlement.

Another method which companies have used is to try to internationalize the investment at inception either by participating with other companies or by inviting investment by such organizations as The International Finance Corporation which will take an equity position in certain instances, or the World Bank which may take a senior debt position in the enterprise. Host governments are noticeably reluctant to nationalize any investment in which such organizations may have a participation, first, because such organizations will already have determined that the investment is useful and fair; and secondly, because no country is likely to forego the goodwill of the World Bank and the IMF.

As far as the United States multinationals are concerned, they should, of course, consider guarantees from OPIC which with its predecessors have guaranteed some three thousand projects in eighty countries. [22]

The Transfer of Technology

Criticism of the multinational corporation in this area

centers around the charge that the multinational produces products in the developing countries which are either luxury items or unsuited to the needs of the consumer society in the host country, thereby using up much needed foreign exchange to produce unwanted and unneeded goods.

The answer to this problem seems clear. The national government can screen which industries it wants to have invest in the country and which products such industry shall manufacture. We tend to forget in this connection that certain products even though not destined for the local domestic market may be able to earn substantial foreign exchange thereby paying for needed imports. If such is the case then government's concern is not with manufacture of the product but with making sure that the foreign investor does not unduly limit exports.

The word "unduly" is purposely used. Governments cannot require in most instances that the foreign investor allow exports to other countries where he has a plant or a license. It may not want to import to its home country either for clear practical reasons: if it does it may be accused by labor unions in the home country of maintaining a "runaway plant." The recommendation of the UN Group of Eminent Persons appointed pursuant to Economic and Social Council Resolution 172 is helpful but difficult to implement. [23]

Other recommendations by this group on the question of technology transfers also create problems. Two such proposals relate to patents: one suggests that international organizations should work to revise the patent system and that a World Patent Bank be established. The purpose of the proposals is, of course, clear: reduce the cost of technology transfer to the developing countries.

There are four answers to these proposals: (1) The cost of research and development is very high and must be paid for out of profits made on the sale of these and other products (this in part paid by earnings from developing countries); (2) Research tends to be centralized because of cost factors and because researchers need to work where centers for testing, educational facilities, and exchange of information, etc. are available. This means that research tends increasingly to be done in the industrialized countries; (3) In the free enterprise system technology does not belong to the state but to individuals or to corporations. It is cearly recognized as a valuable asset, developed at substantial cost, even though it is not a tangible asset. Licenses will not be transferred without charge just because a developing country needs new technology; (4) Patents only serve to give the owner temporary lead-time in establishing a market for the product. Of far greater importance is the knowhow associated with the manufacture, testing and marketing of the product. As Senator Javits stated in his comments on the report of the UN Group of Eminent Persons " . . . it should be pointed out that what is actually reinforcing the position of the multinational corporations are two facts: first, technology becomes obsolete fairly rapidly and a constant new supply of up-to-date technology is essential — second, the knowhow concerning the capability of producing efficiently is much larger than the technology which patents protect."

It is true that other methods of technology transfer may be considered in lieu of foreign direct investment. We have discussed these in the preceding section of this chapter dealing with alternate means of investment. But the licensing of technology is only useful where there are already experienced businessmen within the country of the licensee who have the capability of producing items of the quality desired.

This is often difficult to do and under current conditions of rapid technological change it is often better to invite the foreign company in on at least a joint venture basis so as to obtain new technology as soon as it comes forth and not be limited to making products under license which are being replaced by more advanced products or processes.

We pointed out in this connection how well Japan has made use of patent license agreements. But Japanese technical ability was such that patents licensed to Japanese firms are often a few years later the subject of new inventions patented by the licensee and licensed back to the original licensor. Few developing countries have that type of engineering skill at the present time. Furthermore, the need is less in these countries for high technology requiring substantial capital investment and more for labor — intensive products or service investments where local manpower skills may play a major role. It is understandable that every government wishes to modernize its industrial production as rapidly as possible but every country cannot gainfully produce nuclear power, computers and electronic equipment. Spain rebuilt its lagging industrial infrastructure from foreign exchange largely earned from its tourist industry. International trade develops through diversity. Some of the greatest opportunities of tomorrow are in areas which may be generally neglected today: in agriculture, in tourism, in the development of substitute forms of energy, in harvesting energy from the sun.

In determining reasonable objectives for a country's development of its own resources, planning as we noted must play a key role. Such planning to be effective must not only focus on the natural advantages available within the country in terms of resources but on developing as rapidly as possible an educated elite of engineers, teachers, scientists, agronomists, bankers and lawyers and above all managers who will be able to convert the natural wealth of the country into a thriving economic infrastructure which is in some sort of balance.

What good does it do to have sophisticated nuclear technology in a country where the telephone does not work? How can you install a billion dollar petrochemical plant in an area where there are as yet no roads, no sources of transport, no communication facilities, and very few capable managers? Venezuela has been wealthy in resources for many years, yet its educational facilities to train men to use this wealth to develop the country is still lagging behind Mexico.

The success of the United States, the Soviet Union, Germany, Sweden, Japan, and now France, is in no small part due to the educational system which produced the scientists, engineers and businessmen to develop today's technology. Before such technology can be transferred, people must be trained to apply or utilize it. This is a slow and painful process of education. In the United States it has taken over 150 years to create a business climate where technological development is structured into the enterprise system.

Areas of Conflict – Social Responsibility

Some of the most interesting problems facing MNCs in the future relate to the question of social responsibility and relationships with labor unions and works councils.

We have seen how labor groups in developed countries express increasing concern with alleged transfers by MNCs of plants from home to host countries to take advantage of wage differentials.[24] There is a fundamental conflict of interest within the ranks of labor as between labor leaders in the developed countries and labor unions and governments (in some cases controlled by labor unions) in the developing countries. The former are concerned with unemployment in, and alleged job transfers from, the developed countries. The latter are anxious to create new jobs and raise wages in the host countries. Unfortunately labor in the developed countries largely ignore the fact that the golden age of relatively full employment in the United States, Western Europe, and Japan was during the decade of the expansion of multinational corporations, 1960-1971. During that period "the high foreign investment oriented industry increased its employment roles on a new basis — at more than twice the rate that the average U.S. manufactures did." [25]

The answer to the problem of labor conflicts is a difficult one: if wage differentials disappeared, obviously the MNC would be little disposed to establish productive facilities in the developing countries unless the available market for its products in such countries warranted it, or if the country was a part of a regional grouping, such as the Andean Common Market, thus making the investment advisable for larger market considerations. (We tend to forget that it is this market factor rather than wage differentials which usually determines whether or not the MNC makes an investment in a foreign country. That is the reason why 70 percent of the U.S. multinationals' investments are found in the developed countries with high wages.) So long as the pressure for additional sources of employment continues this fundamental conflict within the labor movement will persist. One way to solve it — though wholly satisfactory neither to host governments nor to the craft union in the developed country whose members will be affected — would appear to be to encourage in the developing nations the implantation of production facilities making goods with relatively little capital investment but a high labor content. Illustrative are such industries as tourism (hotels, etc.), textiles, shoes, wood-working, toys, and many other kinds of handicrafts. This, of course, would be in addition to the extractive industries, e.g., those requiring large inputs of energy where cheap energy is available, such as petrochemical plants, metal smelters, etc.

Understandably, developing nations' governments, preoccupied as they are with moving into the twenty-first century with production of high technology products, are reluctant to concentrate on labor-intensive products. Again this relates back to the question of host government object- ives and planning combined with a willingness to undertake development in a logical sequence — basic education and vocational training and simpler projects first — sophisticated technology later.

The Question of Communication

Analysis of the report to ECOSOC of the Group of Emin- ent Persons indicates very clearly that while the international business community may be headed by brilliant managers, planners, financiers, engineers and scientists, they need to do a much better job of communicating their objectives and atti- tudes to the outside world. Perhaps because of limited ac- countability under present conditions to the owners of large businesses, managers have all to frequently neglected this part of their role.

The presentations before the UN group reflected in some cases a lack of understanding of the purpose of the hearings and the very real concerns on the part of developing coun- tries for an examination of the role of the multinational cor- porations in host countries. While the questions of some panel members seemed at times more designed to present a political or social point of view than to elicit information pertinent to the inquiry, the nature of the inquiry was perfectly proper and reflected a genuine desire to find help in answers to complex and difficult questions. Even where the questioning was politically motivated, the witnesses could and should have given relevant answers presented in a forth- right, forceful manner.

One thing should by now be clear to the heads of multi- national enterprises. Under present trends someone in the enterprise must be prepared to answer for the actions of the enterprise be it to home government, host government, international organizations, labor unions or work councils, key employees, suppliers, customers and stockholders. The managements of large business enterprises — and many increasingly do [26] — need to spend considerably more time analyzing and responding to the questions increasingly asked by their constituencies.

If the owners of the business are no longer demanding mangement accountability as in the past, others are: home and host governments, labor unions, consumer groups (customers), financial institutions which provide the necessary capital, and environmentalists who are increasingly active. This is not an American phenomenon. Already in Europe, works councils in certain countries are beginning to ask very pertinent questions regarding the conditions under which plants are operated outside the home country, the investment made, the pay scales and even company profits.[27]

Under these circumstances, corporate executives must reflect on strategy and be prepared to explain very clearly and forcefully the reasons behind their investment decisions. Anyone watching the television documentary given in the United States in 1974 on the role of the international oil companies in the energy crisis could not have failed to note how often the senior executive interviewed appeared evasive or simply unprepared to answer the questions. In one instance, the president of one company, when asked why his company sent oil to Europe rather than the United States, answered: "Because we are a multinational" with no further explanation given in the interview. Since the working press, radio and television in many countries are often not favorably disposed towards private enterprise, it is even more important that areas of common concern be continuously monitored and answered, even though such actions could temporarily cause some unpleasant repercussions.

It is no wonder under these circumstances that multinational corporations which have done so much to bring about industrial development world-wide are under attack. It is also understandable that an executive who works twelve and fourteen hours a day running a world-wide industrial empire feels he has no time or need to explain his company's actions. It is nonetheless essential that someone in his organization be constantly seeking the opportunity to report on what the company is doing and why it is doing it. The failure of corporate communications will probably go down as one of the most surprising aspects of contemporary life when reviewed by history. If the suppliers of capital, the workers, the unions, the government, the youth are becoming disenchanted with the system of free enterprise, it is because those who benefit from it have not placed a higher priority to date on the importance of communicating to these constituents (in terms relevant to each of them) the very real values and benefits inherent in the system — as yet the most effective method devised to develop new technology, to finance it, and to manufacture and market world-wide the products which result from such technology on a favorable cost basis. A better perception by managers of social trends in the world appears evident.

Internationalizing Management Controls

We now come to the question of who runs the multinational corporation. We have indicated that the management is not accountable to its individual stockholders as a general rule. It may be stated that the larger the corporation the smaller its accountability to stockholders. What about the Board of Directors? In most instances nominees for Board position, to the extent that they are not from within management ranks, are proposed by management. How independent

therefore are Board members from management? What is
their interest if their work is done with a fee per meeting
which in many cases is minimal. Some have suggested that
the Boards of Directors of multinational corporations should
be restructured and that the government be allowed to appoint certain members.

It is likely that the recent scandals in the United States involving payment of illegal political contributions and bribery
of foreign officials by corporate executives using corporate
funds will result in new laws or regulations requiring committees of outside directors to review any such payments and
make full disclosure to the stockholders and to the Securities
and Exchange Commission.[28]

We have observed that there is a growing demand particularly in Europe, that work councils be represented on the
Board of Directors.

Certainly as a step in anticipation of eventual new government rules on the composition of Boards of Directors it would
appear to behoove managements of multinational corporations to consider adding to their Board of Directors one or
more persons from foreign countries or regions where the
corporation has major business investments. In certain cases,
a foreign advisory board to review policy matters may serve
the same purpose since the reason for such a group is primarily
to advise on policy questions and not to involve itself in day-
to-day operational decisions. Many multinational corporations
are now doing this, or planning to do so. Representatives
could be chosen on the basis of their ability to review and in-
terpret corporate policy with the regulatory authorities of
the host country of which they are nationals, to maintain
communications with outside shareholders, and to make
known to the press and to the public at large what the corporation is doing toward the development objectives within
the country. Conversely such an advisory board could be

helpful through its knowledge of "local" conditions by keeping operating management aware of problem areas in host country relationships before such problems become serious issues. Recently several American multinational corporations have enlarged their Board of Directors by adding an occasional black or a female to improve the breadth of management's vision. It would seem that much more should be done to make Boards more truly representative of those to whom the management of a multinational corporation is accountable. In a similar vein, there seems to be a very definite effort on the part of multinational corporations to increasingly staff their operations at the managerial level in host countries with nationals from those countries.

The Role of International Organizations

After pointing out the increased mutual suspicion with which some national governments regard multinational corporations and with which the multinationals in turn regard the recent record of some host governments in nationalizing foreign investment on the basis of what business regards as inadequate compensation, the previous chapter discussed the role which the community of nations proposed to play in defusing the problem. In 1975, the Group of Eminent Persons filed its report [29] and the Economic and Social Council of the United Nations presented the report to the General Assembly. [30] The General Assembly in turn has adopted the recommendation in the form of a Declaration [31] which calls for further implementation. The dialogue between multinational corporations and governments through the United Nations is therefore assured of a continuing forum. To this extent, action by the UN taken to date must be considered as positive. The sense of urgency which this continued investigation gives to the problem is reflected in action taken by economic or regional groupings such as EEC, OECD,[32] and business and labor advisory groups reporting to it as well as by the International Chamber of Commerce.[33]

In particular, the OECD and its business advisory group (BIAC) has begun some very meaningful efforts on some of the questions raised by the UN Group of Eminent persons.[34] As a high priority item there will be developed within OECD some guidelines for MNC behavior. In having a more homogeneous government composition the OECD is in a position to make some creative recommendations in the area of state-corporate relationships. On the theory that misunderstandings are often cleared up by an exchange of views and that lack of information is at the heart of any complex problem, the United Nations program for action may also help resolve some of the issues. Wherever such issues are directed at governments interests rather than at the relationships between governments and transnational corporations, then positive results ought to be expected since the United Nations is the proper forum. It may be difficult to legislate human behavior but conflicts can often be resolved where they can be identified, analyzed and discussed among the parties. If the UN in its ongoing examination of the multinationals can maintain a well-balanced factual and objective approach and concentrate on problems which can and should be solved in an international forum leading to agreements or treaties between sovereign states, then substantial positive progress can be made.

Some of the questions such as tax harmonization[35] and the role played by transfer pricing in the application of tax incidence can only be focused in the first instance through information obtained by an analysis of policies followed by individual multinational corporations in their global operations under constraints applied by government in diverse jurisdictions. Hopefully, such analysis can then be followed by preparation of appropriate tax treaties to be ratified by governments allocating a tax share of profits of multinational business between the various governments of countries where such companies are active on some basis satisfactory to all of them and not confiscatory to business.

Hopefully, such treaty models will contain provisions, including uniform tax incentives on the part of the capital exporting countries, to encourage the investment of funds in the poorer countries. The difficulty of treaty negotiations is, of course, obvious particularly in the present political and economic climate. To say that even on tax matters harmonization will be difficult to achieve is not to say it should not be tried. The discussion can be helpful even though only partial results are achieved. If the internationalization of business is accepted, as it now appears to be, then such business must be taxed on some basis of allocation as between the countries where the business is taking place. It has been suggested that the system of allocation as between states in the United States might be adapted to serve as a model for a tax harmonization treaty among nations. If nothing else, a single tax system applicable to international business transactions will be of great help to business planning without which business is quite unable to play its full role.

If some sort of uniform allocation basis were adopted it might also assure a fair distribution among governments of the taxable receipts of the enterprise. A perhaps simpler alternative, of course, might be to insist on arms-length pricing, but this is difficult between affiliated companies even in countries such as the United States where the Internal Revenue Service is increasingly alert to transfer pricing practices.

Other recommendations of the Group of Eminent Persons are politically oriented and equally directed at governments. One such recommendation is that home governments should not restrict transfer of production to the developing nations. Viewed in the light of the Burke-Hartke Bill this raises

interesting questions. If we are going to continue to face unemployment in the developed world there is an obvious potential conflict here that involves governments. As in the tax
questions, to which it is not unrelated, the problem can and
should be resolved as a result of government negotiations
which might well take place in the new forum created by the
United Nations. The International Chamber of Commerce
guidelines state on this point: "The government of the investor's country should, in formulating policies aimed at seeking
full employment, rely on stimulating domestic demand
through appropriate economic and social policies, rather than
in restrictions on the outflow of direct investment.[36]

Another recommendation which well indicates the political nature of the composition of the Group of Eminent
Persons, "Home and host countries should permit free entry
of unionists from other countries," is also directed to governments.

In this same area two other recommendations are somewhat startling: "Home countries should require MNCs to
maintain safety and health standards in host countries" — a
clear violation by the Group of its own criticism of entra-
territoriality. The same is true of its recommendation that
"Home countries should prevent MNCs from going into
countries where workers' rights are not respected." If the
United Nations is going to use its prestige in trying to force
home countries to use their multinational companies as a
weapon to require acceptance by host countries of political
and social pressures, then the effort of reestablishing good
relations between home governments and host countries will
collapse into empty political arguments.

Individual members of the Group of Eminent Persons expressed reservations or disagreements with the statements and
recommendations of the majority. Their comments should be
noted.[37]

As pointed out above, there is a need for constructive action on the part of this new international forum. In such fields as taxation, transfer pricing as it avoids taxation, competition policy, and methods of investment and security of investment, there is a need for the development of new policies by which governments and transnational companies can learn to live together in greater harmony. It remains to be seen whether the problem will be analyzed as an exercise in cooperation or confrontation.

Conclusion

Surely the growing interdependence of the economic world need not receive further substantiation in this book. In part what had made the modern multinational corporation possible has been the speed at which communication and travel can take place. Decisions taken in one country can be instantly implemented in another. Meetings of key executives from different parts of the world can take place frequently, supplemented by constant telephone and telex reviews. Effects of economic or monetary events can be anticipated. Capital can be made to flow from one country to another by cable transfers through multinational banks on immediate advice. Methods of protection against foreign exchange risk, exchange controls, or inability to raise local funds because of government action have been worked out as a result of the creation of the Eurocurrency market. The multinational corporations and the banks which serve them are thus equipped to mitigate the effects of economic action which individual national governments might take to counter inflation or protect currency from devaluation or revaluation. In this book we have discussed the industrial multinational corporation. But the role of the international banking institution is perhaps of equal significance.

As yet national governments and international organizations (although the OECD has prepared some interesting papers on Eurocurrency and Eurobond loans) appear to have paid little attention to the Eurocurrency bank, the growth of the Eurocurrency market, or the role of such banks in financing and giving supporting services to the multinational corporation. The Eurocurrency market headquartered in London disposes of some 120 billion dollars almost entirely free of government controls or reserve requirements, supervision or regulation.[38]

Governments, too, of course, make significant use of the Eurocurrency market, both those of developed countries and the developing countries.[39] Recently, OPEC funds in substantial quantities have found their way into the Eurocurrency market, and these funds, as those of the MNCs, will tend to move to those countries with stable currencies to the extent permitted by local regulation. Most of the OPEC funds are, however, short-term investments to be eventually reinvested elsewhere and banks are not looking to increase such deposits. The Eurocurrency market has in the past ten years played a key role in aiding the growth and development of the multinational corporation in its capital programs around the world; perhaps that is why there are more banks located in London than in New York. These international banks are in part American, in part French, British, Swedish, German, Japanese, Belgian, Dutch and Italian. The entire developed world is fully represented. Their activities may be carried on as individual banks or increasingly in banking consortiums which generally are diversified on a geographical basis.[40]

Freedom of such markets from government controls remains largely unquestioned despite the tendency of at least some of these banks to take foreign exchange risks, speculate in one currency against another and borrow short to lend long. It is curious that the multinational corporations have become objects of such concern to the international community that the banks which finance their operations are left unquestioned.

We thus have the phenomenon: here are a growing group of multinational companies, relatively well-managed, with efficient planning and a global approach to doing business, strong in technology, able in marketing, supported to the extent of their growing financial needs by a group of international banks based in London but with significant branches in the Bahamas, Panama and Singapore, themselves multinationals in scope and capacity. On the other side we have national governments jealous of their prerogatives, incapable of joint action, reluctant to act together even when faced with problems which can only be solved by joint action, with shifting strategies and growing needs.

If the multinational companies and banks are moving forward to satisfy the needs of the consuming public by accelerating capital investments in many different parts of the world, is it sound to say to them: stop, you must be regulated and controlled. Frontiers will continue to exist, the world's progress must not be limited by governments' desire to regulate, and particularly by governments which cannot act together even to the extent of managing their own economic affairs or the ratios between their currencies. Multinational companies did not destroy the Breton Woods system. Governments did! And now those same governments are disturbed because multinational companies seek to protect themselves from the ensuing monetary fluctuations.

There are many in these circumstances who would say: the tendency since World War II has been for governments to proliferate, for nationalist and socialist trends to predominate within the new nations (the so called Club of 77, for example), and for a gradual breakdown of the system of decision-making so painfully worked out at the end of the World War II.

As political relationships have deteriorated and governments have found increasing difficulty in working together separated as they are in many cases by unnatural borders, the multinational corporations, dealing with broad marketing concepts and entities rather than geographical enclaves have tried to bring to people internationally what they wanted and needed in the way of products and technology wherever permitted by home governments, local customs or currency regulations.

Would we, for example, be better off in the food crisis now almost certain to come, if governments allowed the price mechanism to operate freely and allowed the multinational companies to supply the goods so desperately needed free of border controls or distribution methods to assuage national sovereignty. If countries continue to regulate prices, control imports, and limit foreign investment will we not rapidly go back to the period of the 1930's where each country tried to protect its own economy on the premise that economic survival meant "beggar thy neighbor"? Philosophically speaking, is it not better to regard the efforts of multinational firms and banks as a step in the right direction, as a beginning along economic and commercial lines, to forge a world free of frontiers where men from diverse nations can work together for common goals? If supervision is needed, then should it not be at the international and not the national level, retaining only for national governments the right to decide who is allowed in and on what basis and for what purpose? William Jennings Bryan used to speak of a "cross of gold." Shall we have a "cross of national sovereignty and racial and ethnical politics?" One thing is clear: there will be no lack of new sovereignties and old prejudices in years to come.

In earlier chapters of this book we touched upon various reasons which encourage a national corporation to become a multinational particularly in terms of findings of the various U.S. government commissions appointed to study the problem in order to recommend what steps government could take to expand private investment abroad.[41]

It was pointed out that wage rates, tax advantages, and, to a much greater extent, accessibility of raw materials and market opportunities all figure among reasons why corporations make direct investments in foreign countries. Fundamentally, both national and multinational corporations prefer to export. They move abroad in order to maintain a market position or to get access to new markets which are only available if they produce outside the home country. As noted earlier, multinational corporations at the present time, when capital in the developed nations is relatively scarce and interest rates high, are reluctant to invest abroad unless a clear market opportunity or necessity exists. The current political climate toward multinationals in the developing countries is certainly not favorable to foreign direct investment. Unfortunately the same trend is now appearing in the developed countries. The climate in the socialist countries is currently more favorable, but negotiations of a participation in enterprises in such countries takes a great deal of time and forms of participation as noted are different from those negotiated elsewhere. It seems evident that not only will foreign governments in most developing countries not modify their approach to foreign direct investment but that rules in the future may make such investments even more risky and difficult than before despite the creation of new forms of cooperative agreements to eliminate ownership problems. At the same time pressure from labor unions in developed countries can be expected to make it more difficult for management of multinationals to establish new production facilities outside the home country. Worker participation statutes will probably make it more difficult in the future to invest abroad, particularly if plant closings or reductions in the home country may result. This will be true regardless of market opportunity or the impossibility of servicing such market from the home country.[42]

It may be stated therefore that if the climate in the host countries has changed vis-a-vis foreign direct investment so has the climate in home countries where there is increased pressure against the export of capital to be invested in competing facilities. Under conditions of declining production at home and consequent unemployment almost any new facility abroad tends to be considered by labor unions as a "runaway plant" regardless of sound underlying business reasons. If we are increasingly to reduce free trade by government action and live in a world of quotas, border closings, high tariffs and similar protectionist policies, we may well find multinational companies tending to bring home whatever manufacturing operations can be handled from the home country (or other developed countries with broad markets) regardless of loss of peripheral investments in the developing countries.

Those which still wish to establish a position in broader geographical areas may increasingly make such investments, particularly in developing countries, in a tripartite form where the home industry provides technological knowhow, engineering and/or management skills together with equipment, if special equipment is required, but the capital comes from Middle Eastern Funds and the developing country brings to the venture local capital, land and perhaps local market skills. As certain OPEC countries such as Kuwait, Libya, the United Arab Emirates, and Saudi Arabia build up receipts from oil exports faster than their own planned development can absorb, we may see increasing instances of this form of investment.[43]

In this way the developing country gets the technology it needs, the MNC is relieved of capital investment and the principal source of capital from OPEC countries considered to be in the developing stage and hence "noncolonialist" can obtain appropriate guarantees to protect the investment of all from potential eventual nationalization threats by the host country. Already Kuwait has established an insurance company for purposes of giving such guarantees and while priorities will remain for investments in Arab or Moslem countries there may be opportunities to structure new types of investment along this line in the developing countries generally. The future of Kuwait and Saudi Arabia as finance centers for developed and developing countries would appear sound unless the governments should decide to cut their oil production much more than at present as a means of saving their natural resources.

The report of the International Monetary Fund shows that the OPEC nations' share of loans and aid to the developing nations in 1974 was twice as much as the United States foreign aid. This responsible and humanitarian attitude of the developing nations is encouraging and promises a more cooperative future in areas of investment and development.

In chapters 1 and 2 we explained in detail how corporations which manufactured their products in the United States for export to other countries were encouraged by the government of the United States to establish manufacturing plants abroad in order to increase the employment base and needed capital for reestablishing industries ravaged by war. It has always been the policy of the United States government that private investment was preferable to public aid. Today private investment is questioned both in developing and developed countries at a time when there is so much need for capital, technology and managerial skill.

Perhaps there is an urgent need for the governments to understand that while they can promise gifts of money and food the establishment of plant facilities and the transfer of technology must come from individuals and corporations who must be able to see in such investment the likelihood of a return commensurate with the risk and justifying the effort. Governments can supply aid in times of need but they do not produce food or jobs or products; farmers and businessmen do. What is needed is not a policy of confrontation but a spirit of cooperation under which governments determine their development objectives and the programs to implement such objectives, businessmen engaged in international production and marketing then establish productive facilities which would bring mutual benefits to both the host nations and the investors.

Possibly one way to achieve this cooperation and harmony would be through the separation — both in law and in fact — of the multinational corporation from its national base. This could be achieved in two ways:

1. Expansion of the "Center for the Settlement of Investment Disputes" into a supranational organization, an agency of the United Nations and the International Court of Justice, with three branches:

a. *A Legislative Branch* which would work out a comprehensive set of rules by negotiation between the interested parties — experts acting for the corporations, other experts acting on behalf of the nations permitting the export of capital, and still others representing the host countries. These rules would make conditions uniform and predictable for taxes, the transfer of capital and technology across international boundaries, and from one jurisdiction to another.

b. *The Judicial Branch* — expansion of the machinery provided in the statutes of the International Court of Justice and in the 1966 Convention for the Settlement of Investment Dispute. The parties must accept judgment of the International Court to settle their dispute and thereby establish precedents for the avoidance of similar disputes in the future.

c. *An Administrative and Audit Branch* — to license the operation of world corporations agreeing to conform in their operations to the rules laid down by the legislative branch and to submit to the jurisdiction of the panels of experts set up under the judicial branch; to audit the transfer payment accounts of the world corporations; and to collect taxes to cover the cost of these operations.[44]

2. The other possible way for internationalization of multinationals is the model of the proposed European Company in the European Economic Community. This company created by special agreement of the European community nations would not be a part of any national legal system but would be operating under European Community laws. See Appendix C. There are a number of new ideas introduced with respect to the company structure. Thus, employees would be given certain rights and privileges to participate in the administration of the company, although these rights and responsibilities would not apply to the decision-making process at the management level. Disputes are settled through binding arbitration.[45]

Without a strong international authority disputes involving multinational corporations and host countries fall within national jurisdiction, which are often inadequate of conflicting. The convention on the Settlement of Investment Disputes provides a limited machinery for conciliation and arbitration but its work has thus far been very limited, chiefly on account of the nonparticipation of many countries, notably in Latin America, on the grounds that disputes in these territories should come under national jurisdiction.

The first case submitted for arbitration under the convention on the Settlement of Investment Disputes is that of Morocco against Holiday Inn. Since then many developing nations have included in their agreement a clause according to which all the disputes would be submitted to arbitration through the channel of the Settlement of Investment machinery. The possibility of a wider use of this machinery has been recommended by.the United Nations.

Multinationals as leaders of economic development thrive on political, economic and social stability. Their success depends upon concentration of resources, research, managerial skills and marketing knowhow. They avoid risks unless they foresee higher return on invested capital. Their success is assured by stability, long-range planning and freedom from government red-tape and harassment.

Since these issues are of great importance to the future of both host and home countries, open and dispassionate debate is vital. There must be regional and international forums (as suggested above), where both governments and corporations can present their cases and defend themselves against unfounded charges.

Some general agreement on a code of conduct for multinationals and host governments is difficult but it is not impossible. However, the tendency is that such a code must be in general terms, and its enforcement might be limited by nations' unwillingness to establish a strong agency to administer it. Moreover, there is hope that if the agency succeeds, it could gradually expand its activities and serve as a mediator for the settlement of the disputes.

Surely there are no inherent and insoluble conflicts between multinational corporations and nation states. Conciliation and cooperation are not only possible but necessary. The ultimate success and progress of multinational corporations requires international and enforcible rules that can assure both corporate accountability and government responsibility within the framework of long-range international economic and social goals.

Unless a new spirit guides the governments of developed and developing countries faced with growing populations, balance of payments and trade, deficits, high wages, low productivity and growing unemployment, the present system of trade and business may be crippled, chaos created and the solvency of many nations threatened. If that happens, then the increased flow of international trade which has played such a role in raising the standards of living around the world since World War II, may be reversed, and the world will be plunged into another depression and international anarchy.

Notes

1. Walter, Ingo, "A Guide to Social Responsibility of Multinational Enterprise" (manuscript to be published by New York University Press).

2. Ibid.

3. Ibid.

4. Ibid.

5. Ibid.

6. See *Business International*, "U.N. Agency Takes Aim at Technology Transfer Protection and Fees", July 4, 1975. pp. 209-11; contains a discussion of WIPO-World Intellectual Property Agency with its aim of developing a model law for developing countries on inventions and know-how to dilute the currently accepted patent protection accorded an investor.

7. New York: Atheneum, 1968.

8. Remarks made by Dr. Gingo Susuki, Chairman Associated Japanese Bank International, Ltd., London England, at monetary conference held by the Graduate Institute of International Studies, Fairleigh Dickinson University, Wroxton College Campus, England, June, 1973.

9. See N. Fatemi, T. Saint Phalle and G. Keefe, *The Dollar Crisis,* Rutherford N.J.: Fairleigh Dickinson University Press, 1963, pp. 257-8. See also Tibor Mende, *From Aid to Re-Colonization,* New York: Pantheon Books, 1973.

10. Resolution adopted by the Economic and Social Council 1913 (LVII) "The Impact of Transnational Corporations in the Development Process and on International Relations", December 11, 1974.

11. An example is the experience of OMNES, a textile manufacturer in Pereira, Columbia which uses sulzer machines from Switzerland to remain competitive with Japanese textile imports even though wage rates in Colombia are relatively low.

12. See James E. Akins, "The Oil Crisis: This Time the Wolf is Here" *Foreign Affairs*, April, 1973.

13. Proposals made by the United Nations Conference on Trade and Development (UNCTAD) Revised July, 1975. See report in *Financial Times*, July 8, 1975.

14. See Jean Mayer, "Coping with Famine", *Foreign Affairs*, October, 1974, p. 119; Also Lester R. Brown, *World Without Borders*, New York: Random House, 1972 esp. pp. 88-111.

15. See Ronald I. McKinnon, *Money & Capital in Economic Development*, Washington D.C.: The Brookings Institute, 1973. Also John Dunning, *International Investment — Selected Readings*, London: Penguin Books, 1972.

16. See "Proceedings of the Conference on Foreign Direct Investment in the United States", Institute for International and Foreign Trade Law, Georgetown University, 1972, esp. pp. 8-11. Also Nicholas Firth, *The Infiltrators*, London: Harmish Hamilton Ltd., 1971. See also for limitations on research in this area Arpan and Ricks "Foreign Direct Investments in the U.S. and Some Attendant Research Problems" *Journal of International Business Studies*. 1974, esp. p. 1.

17. See Robbins and Stobaugh, *Money in the Multinational Enterprise: a Study of Financial Policy*, New York; Basic Books, 1973.

18. Tables pp. 64-65.

19. See discussion in chapter 3.

20. See Note 8, supra. An Information and Research Center on Transnational Corporations has now been established and reports to the U.N. Commission on Transnational Corporations consisting of 48 members appointed by the General Assembly. Priority has been established for the Center to establish a Code of Conduct for transnational corporations.

21. See Senate Hearings currently held in the Senate of the United States by the subcommittee on Multinationals for the Foreign Relations Committee. These Hearings are certain to create additional problems for multinational corporations in their relations with host governments.

22. The Overseas Private Investment Corporation (OPIC) was authorized as an independent agency pursuant to an Act of December 30, 1969 supplemented by Executive Order 11579 dated January 1, 1971. The law is contained in 83 Stat. 805; 22 U.S.C. 2191 et seq. For additional background see A. A. Fatouros, *Government Guarantees to Foreign Investment*, New York: Columbia University Press, 1962.

23. See discussion contained in ICC Document No. 191/81 "Comments by the ICC on Part Two of the Report to the United Nations Economic and Social Council of the Group of Eminent Persons on Multinational Enterprises" Chapter IX - Competition and Market Structure, pp. 25-29.

24. See detailed discussion of the subject in Chapter 3 beginning on p. 59 and particularly p.70.

25. Business International, *The Effects of U.S. Corporate Foreign Investment 1960-72,* New York, 1974, p. 56.

26. Two examples of multinational corporations which have attempted to put in writing a Code of Social Responsibility are Caterpillar Tractor Co. in the United States and Ciba-Geigy in Switzerland. Clark Equipment Company makes up a periodic balance sheet showing host countries what the corporation has done for the country. For a detailed statement of the form used see *Business International,* June 20, 1975 at p. 198.

27. Of particular interest is the Belgian legation which requires detailed information to be given by management of certain size companies to their Work Councils (Conseil d'Entreprise). National Law of September 20, 1948 as amended. Royal Decree of November 17, 1973 extends rights to information and gives Works Councils the power to call in experts to evaluate information.

28. See J.K. Galbraith, "Apres General Motors? ", *Enterprise,* March 14, 1975, pp. 38-41.

29. Department of Economic and Social Affairs, United Nations, *The Impact of Multinational Corporations on Development and on International Relations,* E/5500/Rev.1; St./ESA/6 United Nations, 1974.

30. Economic and Social Council Resolution 1913 (IVII) of December 5, 1974.

31. Resolution 3281 (XXIX) of December 12, 1974 on The Charter of Economic Rights and Duties of States.

32. Resolution of the Council of OECD Establishing a Committee on International Investment and Multinational Enterprises (adopted by the Council at its 376th meeting on 21st January, 1975).

33. See ICC Document No. 191/79 Rev. "Comments on Part I of the Report to the United Nations Economic and Social Council of the Group of Eminent Persons on Multinational Enterprises" adopted June 10, 1974 and Document No. 191/81 "Comments by the ICC on Part Two of the Report to the United Nations Economic and Social Council of the Group of Eminent Persons on Multinational Enterprises". See also ICC "Guidelines for International Investment", October, 1974, and "A New Challenge to Private Enterprise", United States Council of the ICC, April, 1975.

34. Pursuant to the Resolution of the Council of OECD referred to in Note 32.

35. See John F. Chowne, *Taxation and Multinational Enterprise* London, Longman, 1974.

36. ICC, *Guidelines for International Investment,* October, 1974, Chapter VI, Section 2a.

37. See document referred to in Note 31.

38. See Geoffrey Bell, *The Eurodollar Market and the International Financial System,* New York; Macmillan, 1973, Paul Einzig, *The Eurodollar System,* New York, St. Martin Press Fifth Edition, 1973, H. Prochnow, ed. *The Eurodollar,* New York; Rand McNally & Co., 1970.

39. See detailed review "Multibank Consortia" *Financial Times,* January 9, 1974; "The Multibanks of Europe: A Dramatic Experiment", *Worldwide P & E Planning,* May/June, 1971; Charles Ganoe, "Banking Consortia: Are They Here to Stay", *Columbia Journal of World Business,* July/August, 1972; Michael von Clemm, "The Rise of Consortium Banking", *Harvard Business Review,* May/June, 1971.

40. These are the socalled "speculators" which government leaders frequently refer to without identifying them except as the mythical "gnomes of Zurich". See R. Vicker, *Those Swiss Money Men,* New York; Scribner's 1973.

41. See chapters 1 and 2, supra.

42. An interesting example is the current discussion within Volkswagen on the advisability of establishing a manufacturing or assembly plant in the United States and the role of Works Council's representatives in the decisions at the Supervisory Board level.

43. For instance the chemical complex currently under way in Morocco involving two German firms, a Polish State enterprise, German and American banks and Kuwait and Moroccan capital.

44. Burchill, C.S., *World Federalist Magazine,* The Multinational Corporation, p. 10, 1974.

45. The Commission of the European Communities proposal is contained in a special supplement to *European Community Bulletin,* No. 8, 1970 and No. 5, 1975. For further reference see C. Schmitthoff, *London Times,* July 30, 1975, p. 21.

Appendix A
Excerpts from Recent Resolutions of United Nations Bodies Relevant to the Issue of Multinational Corporations

1. **Economic and Social Council resolution 1721 (LIII).** The impact of multinational corporations on the development process and on international relations.

"The Economic and Social Council,

"Recalling, that, according to the Charter of the United Nations, the creation of conditions of stability and well-being is necessary for peaceful and friendly relations among nations based on respect for the principle of equal rights and self-determination of peoples,

"Recognizing the growing interdependence of economic and social development in the various parts of the world,

"Aware that economic and social conditions are continually undergoing changes which require regular scrutiny to ensure unimpeded and equitable progress towards the attainment of an integrated world economy within the framework of the International Development Strategy for the Second United Nations Development Decade,

"Taking note of the statement in the *World Economic Survey, 1971* which says, with reference to the multinational corporations, that 'while these corporations are frequently effective agents for the transfer of technology as well as capital to developing countries, their role is sometimes viewed with awe, since their size and power surpass the host country's entire economy. The international community has yet to formulate a positive policy and establish effective machinery for dealing with the issues raised by the activities of these corporations',

286

"*Noting also* the resolution adopted at the fifty-sixth session of the International Labour Conference, concerning the social consequences of the activities of multinational corporations and the convening by the Governing Body of the International Labour Office of a meeting concerning the relationship between multinational undertakings and social policy,

"*Noting further* that, in resolution 73 (III) on restrictive business practices adopted at the third session of the United Nations Conference on Trade and Development, considering the possible adverse impact of restrictive business practices, including among others those resulting from the increased activities of multinational enterprises, on the trade and development of developing countries, the Conference decided that an *Ad Hoc* Group of Experts on Restrictive Business Practices should be set up to make a further study of restrictive business practices followed by enterprises and corporations which have already been identified and which are adversely affecting the trade and development of the developing countries, including among others such practices which may stem from cartel activities, business restrictions practised by enterprises and multinational corporations, export prohibitions, agreements on market distribution and allocation, the typing of the supply inputs including raw materials and components, restrictions specified in contracts for the transfer of technology, arbitrary transfer pricing between the parent company and its affiliates, and monopoly practices,

"1. *Requests* the Secretary-General, in consultation with Governments, to appoint from the public and private sectors and on a broad geographical basis a study group of eminent persons intimately acquainted with international economic, trade and social problems and related international relations, to study the role of multinational corporations and their impact on the process of development, especially that of the developing countries, and also their implications for international relations, to formulate conclusions which may possibly be used by Governments in making their sovereign decisions regarding national policy in this respect, and to submit recommendations for appropriate international action, the study group to consist of not less than 14 nor more than 20 persons;

"2. *Recommends* that the study group appointed by the Secretary-General be informed of the conclusions of the *Ad Hoc* Group of Experts on Restrictive Business Practices established by the United Nations Conference on Trade and Development at its third session, and the comments on them of the Trade and Development Board's Committee on Manufactures, so that, among the various aspects of the problem, the important one referred to the *Ad Hoc* Group of Experts can be taken into account in the global study of multinational corporations envisaged in paragraph 1 above;

"3. *Recommends* further that the study group take advantage of and take into account research being carried out in this field by other international organizations, particularly that of the Governing Body of the International Labour Office as a result of the resolution concerning the social consequences of the activities of multinational corporations adopted at the fifty-sixth session of the International Labour Conference;

"4. *Further requests* the Secretary-General to support the report of the study group, together with his own comments and recommendations, to the Economic and Social Council at its fifty-seventh session at the latest and to inform the Council at its fifty-fifth session of the progress made in the implementation of the present resolution."

2. **General Assembly resolution 2626 (XXV).** International Development Strategy for the Second United Nations Development Decade. Adopted by the General Assembly on 24 October 1970.

"(50) Developing countries will adopt appropriate measures for inviting, stimulating and making effective use of foreign private capital, taking into account the areas in which such capital should be sought and bearing in mind the importance for its attraction of conditions conducive to sustained investment. Developed countries, on their part, will consider adopting further measures to encourage the flow of private capital to developing countries. Foreign private investment in developing countries should be undertaken in a manner consistent with the development objectives and priorities established in their national plans. Foreign private investors in developing countries should endeavour to provide for an increase in the local share in management and administration, employment and training of local labour, including personnel at the managerial and technical levels, participation of local capital and reinvestment of profits. Efforts will be made to foster better understanding of the rights and obligations of both host and capital-exporting countries, as well as of individual investors."

3. **United Nations Conference on Trade and Development resolution 56 (III).** Foreign private investment in its relationship to development. Adopted on 19 May 1972.

"1. *Affirms* the sovereign right of developing countries to take the necessary measures to ensure that foreign capital operates in accordance with the national development needs of the countries concerned, including measures to limit the repatriation of profits;

"2. *Expresses* its concern not only at the total amount of the financial outflow brought about by private foreign investment but also at its excessive utilization of local financial resources as well as the effects of certain marketing contracts among foreign companies that disrupt competition in the domestic markets, and their possible effects on the economic development of the developing countries;

"3. *Recognizes* that private foreign investment, subject to national decisions and priorities, must facilitate the mobilization of internal resources, generate inflows and avoid outflows of foreign reserves, incorporate adequate technology, and enhance savings and national investment;

"4. *Urges* developed countries to take the necessary steps to reverse the tendency for an outflow of capital from developing countries, by fiscal or other appropriate measures, such as tax exemption of reinvestments of profits and other earnings accruing to private capital investments."

4. United Nations Conference on Trade and Development resolution 73 (III). Restrictive business practices. Adopted on 19 May 1972.

"1.*Recommends* that:

"(a) Every effort should be made with the view to alleviating and, where possible eliminating, restrictive business practices adversely affecting the trade and development of developing countries;

"(b) Co-operation among developed and developing countries through an exchange of information and consultations and other means could contribute to the alleviation and, where possible, elimination of restrictive business practices adversely affecting both the developed and developing countries;

"(c) Attention should be paid to the possibility of drawing up guidelines for the consideration of Governments of developed and developing countries regarding restrictive business practices adversely affecting developing countries;

"2. *Calls* upon the UNCTAD secretariat to pursue further its studies in this field and to give urgent consideration to formulating the elements of a model law or laws for developing countries in regard to restrictive business practices;

"3. *Further calls* upon all member countries in particular the developed countries and competent international organizations, such as the World Intellectual Property Organization and the International Chamber of Commerce, to extend their fullest co-operation to the UNCTAD secretariat in this regard;

"4. *Decides* to establish an *Ad Hoc* Group of Experts on Restrictive Business Practices consisting of an adequate number of governmental and non-govermental experts to be nominated by the Secretary-General of UNCTAD after consultations with Governments. This Expert Group will be responsible to the Committee on Manufactures, to which it shall submit its report as soon as possible;

"5. The terms of reference of the *Ad Hoc* Group of Experts shall include the following, bearing in mind that the work shall be carried out in the context of liberalization and expansion of trade in manufactures and semi-manufactures of interest to developing countries;

"(a) The identification of all restrictive business practices including among others those resulting from activities of multinational corporations and enterprises which adversely affect the trade and development of developing countries with a view to submitting recommendations to the Committee on Manufactures for alleviating and, where possible, eliminating, such practices;

"(b) Further study of restrictive .business practices followed by enterprises and corporations, which have already been identified, and which are adversely affecting the trade and development of developing countries, including among others such practices which may stem from: cartel activities; business restrictions practised by enterprises and multinational corporations; export prohibitions; agreements on market distribution and allocation; the tying of the supply of inputs including raw materials and components; restrictions specified in contracts for the transfer of technology, arbitrary transfer pricing between the parent company and its affiliates; monopoly practices;

"(c) In addition to the practices already referred to in the present resolution in carrying out its studies and submitting its recommendations to the Committee on Manufactures, more attention than in the past should be given to such practices, among others, applied by enterprises and corporations and adversely affecting the trade and development of the developing countries, as those in relation to licensing arrangements and related agreements referring to the use of patents and trade-marks; market sharing; pricing policy and participation of firms of developing countries in industrial projects of multinational corporations;

"(d) In carrying out its studies and submitting its recommendations to the Committee on Manufactures, the Group of Experts shall give special consideration to the position of the least developed among the developing countries;

"(e) It shall examine the possibility of drawing up guidelines for the consideration of Governments of developed and developing countries regarding restrictive business practices adversely affecting developing countries;

"(f) It shall take fully into account those studies which have been and are being carried out by the other international organizations of relevance to work in this area, and shall work in close co-operation with them;

"(e) It shall examine the possibility of drawing up guidelines for the consideration of Governments of developed and developing countries regarding restrictive business practices adversely affecting developing countries;

"(f) It shall take fully into account those studies which have been and are being carried out by the other international organizations of relevance to work in this area, and shall work in close co-operation with them;

"6. *Requests* the Committee on Manufactures to consider the Expert Group's report and recommend appropriate remedial action on restrictive business practices;

5. **United Nations Conference on Trade and Development resolution 39 (III). Transfer of technology. Adopted on 16 May 1972.**

"3. *Invites* the developing countries to establish institutions, if they do not have them, for the specific purpose of dealing with the whole range of complex questions connected with the transfer of technology from developed to developing countries, and takes note of the wishes of the developing countries, that these institutions should *inter alia*:

"(a) Be responsible for the registration, deposit, review and approval of agreements involving transfer of technology in the public and private sectors;

"(b) Undertake or assist in the evaluation, negotiation or renegotiation of contracts involving the transfer of technology;

"(c) Assist domestic enterprises in finding alternative potential suppliers of technology in accordance with the priorities of national developing planning;

"(d) Make arrangements for the training of personnel to man institutions concerned with the transfer of technology;

"4. *Invites* the developing countries to take the specific measures they deem necessary to promote an accelerated transfer of adequate technology to them under fair and reasonable terms and conditions;

"5. *Recommends* that developed market-economy countries facilitate an accelerated transfer of technology on favourable terms to developing countries, *inter alia*, by:

"(a) Providing capital and technical assistance and developing scientific and technological co-operation;

"(b) Endeavouring to provide possible incentives to their enterprises to facilitate an accelerated transfer of their patented and non-patented technology to developing countries on fair and reasonable terms and conditions and by assisting these countries in using effectively imported techniques and equipment;

"(c) Assisting developing countries to absorb and disseminate imported technologies through the provision of necessary information and technical assistance, such as training in planning and management of enterprises and in marketing, as well as other forms of scientific and technological co-operation;

"(d) Endeavouring to provide their enterprises and their subsidiaries located in developing countries with possible incentives to employ wherever possible local labour, experts and technicians as well as to utilize local raw materials, to transfer specifications and technological processes used in production to local enterprises or competent organizations, and also to contribute to the development of know-how and expertise by training staff in the developing countries;

"(e) Designating institutions able to provide information to developing countries concerning the range of technologies available;

"(f) Assisting through their over-all co-operation programmes in the application of technology and in its adaptation to the production structures and economic and social requirements of developing countries at their request;

"(g) Taking steps to encourage and promote the transfer of the results of the work of research institutes and universities in the developed countries to corresponding institutions in developing countries;

"(h) Participating actively in the identification of restrictive business practices affecting the transfer of technology to developing countries with a view to alleviating and, where possible, eliminating these practices in accordance with paragraph 37 of the International Development Strategy for the Second United Nations Development Decade;

"6. *Recommends* that the socialist countries of Eastern Europe, in accordance with their economic and social systems, undertake to facilitate the accelerated transfer of technology on favourable terms to developing countries *inter alia* through agreements on trade, economic and scientific and technical co-operation;"

"11. *Recommends* that the international community, in recognition of the special position of the least developed among the developing countries should:

"(a) Assist such countries, for instance by the establishment and/or consolidation of information centres and applied technology institutes;

"(b) Furnish on easier terms the specialized institutions of such countries with the results of research relevant to their economic development;

"(c) Give special consideration to the terms, conditions and costs of transfer of technology to such countries;"

6. General Assembly resolution 3016 (XXVII). Permanent sovereignty over natural resources of developing countries. Adopted on 18 December 1972.

"1. *Reaffirms* the right of States to permanent sovereignty over all their natural resources, on land within their international boundaries as well as those found in the sea-bed and the subsoil thereof within their national jurisdiction and in the superjacent waters;

"2. *Further reaffirms* its resolution 2625 (XXV) of 24 October 1970, containing the Declaration on Principles of International Law concerning Friendly Relations and Co-operation among States in accordance with the Charter of the United Nations, which proclaims that no State may use or encourage the use of economic, political or any other type of measures to coerce another State in order to obtain from it the subordination of the exercise of its sovereign rights and to secure from it advantages of any kind;

"3. *Declares* that actions, measures or legislative regulations by States aimed at coercing, directly or indirectly, other States engaged in the change of their internal structure or in the exercise of their sovereign rights over their natural resources, both on land and in their coastal waters, are in violation of the Charter and of the Declaration contained in resolution 2625 (XXV) and contradict the targets, objectives and policy measures of the International Development Strategy for the Second United Nations Development Decade;

"4. *Calls upon* Governments to continue their efforts aimed at the implementation of the principles and recommendations contained in the aforementioned resolutions of the General Assembly and, in particular, of the principles enunciated in paragraphs 1 to 3 above;

"5. *Takes note* of the report of the Secretary-General on permanent sovereignty over natural resources and requests him to supplement it with a further detailed study on recent developments, taking into account the right of States to exercise permanent sovereignty over their natural resources, as well as the factors impeding States from exercising this right;

"6. *Requests* the Economic and Social Council to accord high priority, at its fifty-fourth session, to the item entitled 'Permanent sovereignty over natural resources of developing countries', together with the report of the Secretary-General and the present resolution, and to report to the General Assembly at its twenty-eighth session."

7. **Economic and Social Council resolution 1737 (LIV).** Permanent sovereignty over natural resources of developing countries. Adopted on 4 May 1973.

"1. *Reaffirms* the right of States to permanent sovereignty over all their natural resources, on land within their international boundaries, as well as those of the sea-bed and the subsoil thereof within their national jurisdiction and in the superjacent waters;

"2. *Emphasizes* that both the exploration and the exploitation of such natural resources shall be subject in each country to national laws and regulations;

"3. *Declares* that any act, measure or legislative provision which one State may apply against another for the purpose of suppressing its inalienable right to the exercise of its full sovereignty over its natural resources, both on land and in coastal waters, or of using coercion to obtain advantages of any other kind, is a flagrant violation of the Charter of the United Nations, contradicts the principles adopted by the General Assembly in its resolutions 2625 (XXV) and 3016 (XXVII) and obstructs the attainment of the goals and objectives of the International Development Strategy for the Second United Nations Development Decade, and that to persist therein could constitute a threat to international peace and security;

"4. *Recognizes* that one of the most effective ways in which the developing countries can protect their natural resources is to promote or strengthen machinery for co-operation among them having as its main purpose to concert pricing policies, to improve conditions of access to markets, to co-ordinate production policies and, thus, to guarantee the full exercise of sovereignty by developing countries over their natural resources;

"5. *Urges* the international financial organizations and the United Nations Development Programme to provide, in accordance with the priorities established in national development plans, all possible financial and technical assistance to developing countries at their request or for the purpose of establishing, strengthening and supporting, as appropriate, national institutions to ensure the full utilization and control of their natural resources;

"6. *Requests* the Secretary-General to complete the study of the political economic, social and legal aspects of the principle of permanent sovereignty over natural resources referred to in Council resolution 1673 D (LII) and to include therein the aspects of the permanent sovereignty of States over their natural resources of the sea-bed and the subsoil thereof within the limits of national jurisdiction and in the superjacent waters;

"7. *Further requests* the Secretary-General to submit to the General Assembly at its twenty-eighth session, through the Economic and Social Council, the study referred to in paragraph 6 above."

8. United Nations Conference on Trade and Development resolution 75 (III). Export promotion. Adopted on 19 May 1972.

"*The United Nations Conference on Trade and Development,*

"*Bearing in mind* the International Development Strategy for the Second United Nations Development Decade and, in particular, paragraph 36 thereof,

"*Recognizing* that promotion of the exports of developing countries is a necessary complement to removal of the external obstacles to those countries' exports,

"*Noting* with appreciation that the large-scale technical assistance project financed by the United Nations Development Programme for training and advisory services to preference-receiving countries in the implementation of the generalized system of preferences has already become operational,

"1. *Recognizes* that developing countries should actively continue and intensify the implementation of appropriate measures for export promotion:

"2. *Urges* developed countries, due consideration being given to measures undertaken for the reduction and, if possible, elimination of tariff and non-tariff barriers to the exports of developing countries, to take measures to promote the exports of developing countries through the provision of technical and financial assistance to developing countries for the purpose of:

"(a) Studies and research including exchange of commercial information on a continuous basis on the export prospects for products from developing countries;

"(b) Standardization, packaging, design and quality control of products from developing countries;

"(c) Organizing international trade fairs with a view to securing increased export opportunities for products from developing countries;

"(d) Formulating and implementing programmes for training executives and experts at all levels in the field of trade promotion;

"3. *Requests* the appropriate international organizations to provide technical and financial assistance to developing countries in the field of export promotion;

"4. *Urges* developed countries to consider measures to facilitate exports from developing countries through appropriate means, such·as, where possible, the establishment of national centres in developed countries for the promotion of imports from developing countries or other import facilitation measures;

"5. *Recognizes* with appreciation the financial and other support given by the developed countries to the UNCTAD/GATT International Trade Centre and recommends that such support should, if possible, be increased;

"6. *Requests* developed countries and the international organizations concerned to continue to lend their technical and financial support to the work programmes of regional, subregional and national trade promotion centres in order to enable them, in co-operation with other agencies, to collect and disseminate commercial information on a continuing basis, and to supplement the export efforts of developing countries to promote trade with developed countries and among themselves;

"7. *Requests* developed countries and the international organizations concerned to assist, where necessary, in creating or strengthening national trade promotion centres and associations thereof in the developing countries in order to achieve the objectives stated in paragraph 6 above;

"8. *Recommends* to developing countries to co-operate among themselves in order to intensify the export promotion of their products in the markets of developing and developed countries;

"9. *Recommends* regional trade promotion centres to assist developing countries in taking advantage of the trade opportunities resulting from regional and subregional co-operation plans and of the export possibilities in such cases where aid is provided in untied form;

"10. *Requests* the Secretary-General of UNCTAD together with the Director-General of GATT to continue their efforts to ensure that the International Trade Centre is fully equipped to enable it, in co-operation with the Food and Agriculture Organization of the United Nations and the United Nations Industrial Development Organization, to pursue effective and co-ordinated programmes of assistance to developing countries in the field of export promotion and to pay particular attention to the problems of the least developed countries;

"11. *Urges* developed countries to take into account the special market situations prevailing in developing countries and the special needs of developing countries for adopting certain export promotion measures as part of their efforts to achieve diversification and promotion of their exports;

"12. *Requests* developed countries and international financial organizations, including the regional development banks, recognizing the need for developing countries to improve their export financing facilities, to give active consideration to means to bring about such an improvement."

9. United Nations Conference on Trade and Development resolution 45 (III). Charter of the economic rights and duties of States. Adopted on 18 May 1972.

"1. *Decides* to establish a working group composed of Government representatives of 31 member States, to draw up the text of a draft charter. The Working Group shall be appointed as soon as possible by the Secretary-General of UNCTAD in consultation with States members of the Conference;

"2. *Decides* that the Working Group shall use as basic elements in its work:

"(a) The general, special and other principles as approved by the Conference at its first session;

"(b) Any proposals or suggestions on the subject made during the third session of the Conference;

"(c) All documents mentioned above and other relevant resolutions adopted within the framework of the United Nations, particularly the International Development Strategy for the Second Development Decade;

"(d) The principles contained in the Charter of Algiers and the Declaration of Lima;

"3. *Further decides* that the draft prepared by the Working Group shall be sent to States members of the Conference in order that they can forward their suggestions, it being understood that the Working Group shall reconvene to elaborate the draft charter further in the light of comments and suggestions to be received from Governments of member States;

"4. *Recommends* to the Trade and Development Board, that it examine, as a matter of priority, at its thirteenth session, the report of the above-mentioned Working Group, and the comments and suggestions made by member States of the Conference and transmit it with its comments to the General Assembly at its twenty-eighth session;

"5. *Invites* the General Assembly, upon receipt of the above-mentioned report of the Trade and Development Board, and the views expressed by Governments during the consideration of the item in the General Assembly, to decide upon the opportunity and procedure for the drafting and adoption of the charter."

10. **Resolution concerning the Social Problems Raised by Multinational Undertakings adopted at the fifty-sixth session of the General Conference of the International Labour Organisation.**

"*The General Conference of the International Labour Organisation,*

"*Considering* that one of the striking features of economic evolution in recent years is the increasingly rapid development of multinational undertakings and international conglomerates of undertakings,

"*Considering* that this evolution, while offering certain possibilities, raises new social problems, the extent of which will increase, as regards employment, conditions of work and industrial relations,

"*Considering* that because of the international character of these social problems the International Labour Organisation is eminently qualified to deal with them,

"*Considering* that the Sixth Asian Regional Conference of the International Labour Organisation (Tokyo, 1968) agreed to recommend that the Governing Body of the ILO should consider at one of its forthcoming sessions the question of labour-management relations, including multinational undertakings,

"*Considering* that the Ninth Conference of American States Members of the ILO (Caracas, 1970) invited the Governing Body of the ILO to place on the agenda of an early session of the Inter-American Advisory Committee of the ILO the question of the effects of the policies of multinational corporations on working and living conditions in the countries where they operate,

"*Considering* the resolution (No. 73) on multinational corporations adopted by the Metal Trades Committee at its Ninth Session (Geneva, January 1971),

"*Noting* that the Governing Body of the ILO decided at its 182nd (March 1971) Session to provide for an appropriation for the organization of a technical meeting on the possibilities of action by the ILO regarding the relationships between multinational undertakings and social policy,

"1. *Notes* with satisfaction the decision of the Governing Body of the ILO to consider holding a technical meeting on the possibilities of action by the ILO regarding the relationship between multinational undertakings and social policy, to be attended by a large number of employers' and workers' representatives;

"2. *Expresses* the wish that this meeting should be held as soon as possible;

"3. *Requests* the Governing Body to decide, in the light of the conclusions reached at this meeting, what action the ILO should take on the question, including its examination by the International Labour Conference at a future session."

Note: A number of reports of the Secretary-General are also relevant to the issue of multinational corporations. See, for instance, *The impact of multinational corporations on the development process and on international relations: Progress report of the Secretary-General* (E/5334 and E/5381); *The International Development Strategy. First over-all review and appraisal of issues and policies, report of the Secretary-General* (United Nations publication, Sales No.: E.73.II.A.6), Direct investment, pp. 67-69; *World Economic Survey, 1971. Current Economic Developments* (United Nations publication, Sales No.: E.72. II.C.2), Capital movements, p. 10; *Promotion of private foreign investment in developing countries: report of the Secretary-General* (E/5114), paragraphs 15-19; *Permanent sovereignty over natural resources: report of the Secretary-General* (E/5170). See also the summary records of the discussions on multinational corporations at the fifty-third and fifty-fourth sessions of ECOSOC (E/SR.1831-1834, 1836; E/AC.6/SR.585-587; E/AC.6/SR.630-632; E/SR.1858).

Appendix B
Tables

TABLE 1
The 650 Largest Industrial Corporations*
of the Market Economies, by Country
and by Size–1971
(sales in millions of dollars)

Country*	Number of corporations with sales† of					
	Over 10,000	5,000- 10,000	1,000- 4,999	500- 999	300- 499	Total
United States	3	9	115	115	116	358
Japan	–	–	16	31	27	74
United Kingdom	–	1	14	22	24	61
Federal Republic of Germany	–	–	18	10	17	45
France	–	–	13	9	10	32
Canada	–	–	2	7	8	17
Sweden	–	–	2	6	5	13
Switzerland	–	–	4	2	2	8
Italy	–	–	4	2	–	6
Netherlands	–	1	1	2	2	6
Belgium	–	–	1	2	2	5
Australia	–	–	1	1	2	4
South Africa	–	–	–	1	2	3
Spain	–	–	–	–	3	3
Argentina	–	–	–	1	1	2
Austria	–	–	–	–	2	2
India	–	–	–	1	1	2
Brazil	–	–	1	–	–	1
Luxembourg	–	–	1	–	–	1
Mexico	–	–	1	–	–	1
Netherlands Antilles	–	–	–	1	–	1
Zaire	–	–	–	–	1	1
Zambia	–	–	–	–	1	1
Netherlands- United Kingdom	1	1	–	–	–	2
United Kingdom-Italy	–	–	1	–	–	1
TOTAL, number of corporations	4	12	195	213	226	650
TOTAL, sales	76,131	83,807	379,297	147,703	86,069	773,007

Source: Centre for Development Planning, Projections and Policies of the Department of Economic and Social Affairs of the United Nations Secretariat, based on the listing in *Fortune*, July and August 1972, of the 500 largest industrial corporations in the United States and the 300 largest industrial corporations outside the United States.

* Countries are arranged in descending order of total number of corporations listed.

† Sales are based on figures adjusted by *Fortune* and are not necessarily identical with those reported by corporations.

TABLE 2
Foreign Content of Operations and Assets of Manufacturing Corporations of Market Economies with Sales of Over $1 Billion, 1971

Rank (a)	Company	Nationality	Total sales (millions of dollars)	Foreign Content as Percentage of					Number of subsidiary countries(c)
				Sales (b)	Production	Assets	Earnings	Employment	
1	General Motors	USA	28,264	19(j)	–	15(g)	19(j)	27(e)	21
2	Standard Oil (N.J.)	USA	18,701	50(j)	81(e)	52(h)	52(j)	–	25
3	Ford Motors	USA	16,433	26(j)	36(h)	40(h)	24(j)	48(e)	30
4	Royal Dutch/Shell Group	Neth./UK	12,734	79(j)	–	–	–	70(j)	43
5	General Electric	USA	9,429	16(j)	–	15(h)	20(j)	–	32
6	International Business Machines	USA	8,274	39(j)	–	27(h)	50(j)	36(e)	80
7	Mobil Oil	USA	8,243	45(j)	–	46(h)	51(j)	51(h)	62
8	Chrysler	USA	7,999	24(j)	22(e)	31(h)	–	24(e)	26
9	Texaco	USA	7,529	40(j)	65(e)	–	25(e)	–	30
10	Unilever	Neth./UK	7,483	80(j)	–	60(h)	–	94(i)	31
11	International Telephone and Telegraph Corp.	USA	7,346	42(j)	60(h)	61(h)	35(j)	72(h)	40
12	Western Electric	USA	6,045	–	–	–	–	–	–
13	Gulf Oil	USA	5,940	45(j)	75(e)	38(h)	21(j)	–	61
14	British Petroleum	UK	5,191	88(j)	–	–	–	83(j)	52
15	Philips' Gloeilampen-fabrieken	Neth.	5,189	–	67(h)	53(h)	–	73(i)	29
16	Standard Oil of Calif.	USA	5,143	45(j)	46(j)	9(h)	43(h)	29(h)	26
17	Volkswagenwerk	FRG	4,967	69(j)	25(j)	–	–	18(i)	12
18	United States Steel	USA	4,928	–	–	–	–	–	–
19	Westinghouse Electric	USA	4,630	–	–	–	–	–	–
20	Nippon Steel	Japan	4,088	31(k)	–	–	–	2(k)	5

21	Standard Oil (Ind.)	USA	4,054	—	—	16(e)	—	—	24
22	Shell Oil (subsidiary of Royal Dutch/Shell)	USA	3,892	—	12(h)	12(g)	—	—	—
23	E.I. du Pont de Nemours	USA	3,848	18(j)	17(j)	—	—	—	20
24	Siemens	FRG	3,815	39(j)	—	—	—	23(j)	52
25	ICI (Imperial Chemical Industries)	UK	3,717	35(j)	42(h)	25(h)	—	27(j)	46
26	RCA	USA	3,711	—	—	—	—	—	18
27	Hitachi	Japan	3,633	—	—	—	—	—	—
28	Goodyear Tire and Rubber	USA	3,602	30(g)	—	22(g)	30(g)	—	22
29	Nestle	Switz.	3,541	98(j)	—	90(h)	—	96(h)	15
30	Farbwerke Hoechst	FRG	3,487	42(j)	17(i)	—	—	—	43
31	Daimler-Benz	FRG	3,460	44(j)	12(j)	28(j)	—	—	12
32	Ling-Temco-Vought	USA	3,359	—	—	—	—	—	—
33	Toyota Motors	Japan	3,308	31(k)	—	1(k)	—	11(g)	6
34	Montedison	Italy	3,270	37(h)	—	—	—	—	14
35	British Steel	UK	3,216	—	—	—	—	—	18
36	BASF	FRG	3,210	47(j)	17(j)	16(h)	—	18(j)	14
37	Procter and Gamble	USA	3,178	25(j)	—	—	25(j)	—	24
38	Atlantic Richfield	USA	3,135	—	—	—	—	—	12
39	Mitsubishi Heavy Industries	Japan	3,129	—	—	—	—	—	—
40	Nissan Motor	Japan	3,129	28(k)	—	1(k)	—	6(g)	10
41	Continental Oil	USA	3,051	—	—	20(d)	—	—	27
42	Boeing	USA	3,040	—	—	—	—	—	—
43	Union Carbide	USA	3,038	29(j)	25(h)	26(h)	22(e)	43(h)	34
44	International Harvester	USA	3,016	25(j)	19(h)	26(h)	10(g)	32(e)	20
45	Swift	USA	2,996	16(j)	—	—	—	—	—

TABLE 2
Foreign Content of Operations and Assets of Manufacturing Corporations of Market Economies with Sales of Over $1 Billion, 1971

Rank (a)	Company	Nationality	Total sales (millions of dollars)	Sales (b)	Production	Assets	Earnings	Employment	Number of subsidiary countries (c)
					Foreign Content as Percentage of				
46	Eastman Kodak	USA	2,976	33(k)	20(h)	27(k)	19(j)	40(k)	25
47	Bethlehem Steel	USA	2,964	2(e)	—	—	—	—	—
48	Kraftco	USA	2,960	—	—	—	—	—	16
49	Fiat	Italy	2,943	36(j)	—	43(j)	—	—	25
50	August Thyssen-Hütte	FRG	2,904	21(j)	—	—	—	—	17
51	Lockheed Aircraft	USA	2,852	3(d)	—	—	—	—	10
52	Tenneco	USA	2,841	—	—	—	—	—	14
53	British Leyland Motors	UK	2,836	14(j)	—	—	—	12(j)	33
54	Renault	France	2,747	41(k)	—	—	—	—	23
55	AEG-Telefunken	FRG	2,690	29(j)	8(j)	—	—	10(j)	31
56	Matsushita Electric Industrial	Japan	2,687	23(k)	—	—	—	1(k)	27
57	Bayer	FRG	2,649	54(j)	19(j)	—	—	16(j)	3
58	Greyhound	USA	2,616	—	—	—	—	—	—
59	Tokyo Shibaura Electric	Japan	2,553	13(k)	—	1(k)	—	15(k)	22
60	Firestone Tire and Rubber	USA	2,484	—	—	—	26(e)	24(d)	33
61	Litton Industries	USA	2,466	17(j)	—	—	—	—	13
62	Pechiney Ugine Kuhlmann	France	2,462	12(k)	—	—	—	—	29

#	Company	Country							
63	Occidental Petroleum	USA	2,400	46(j)	—	—	—	—	21
64	Cie Francaise des Petroles	France	2,395	49(k)	—	—	—	—	28
65	Dunlop Pirelli Union	Italy/UK	2,365	52(k)	—	—	87(k)	—	28
66	Phillips Petroleum	USA	2,363	—	42(e)	—	—	—	37
67	Akzo	Neth.	2,307	84(i)	—	18(h)	—	66(i)	19
68	General Foods	USA	2,282	21(j)	—	—	3(e)	—	20
69	British-American Tobacco	UK	2,262	93(j)	100(l)	82(j)	92(h)	84(j)	54
70	General Electric	UK	2,218	24(j)	10(h)	—	—	13(j)	36
71	North American Rockwell	USA	2,211	—	—	—	—	—	—
72	Rhone Poulenc	France	2,181	47(i)	24(h)	—	—	—	27
73	Caterpillar Tractor	USA	2,175	53(j)	14(h)	25(g)	—	17(d)	14
74	ENI	Italy	2,172	—	—	—	—	18(i)	39
75	National Coal Board	UK	2,159	—	—	—	—	—	—
76	Nippon Kokan	Japan	2,122	29(k)	—	—	—	1(k)	4
77	BHP (Broken Hill Proprietary)	Austla.	2,100	—	—	—	—	—	—
78	Singer	USA	2,099	37(j)	—	54(h)	75(j)	66(h)	30
79	Monsanto	USA	2,087	24(j)	—	25(d)	31(j)	—	23
80	Continental Can	USA	2,082	—	—	—	—	—	11
81	Borden	USA	2,070	7(d)	—	12(d)	13(d)	—	—
82	McDonnell Douglas	USA	2,069	40(j)	25(h)	—	—	—	—
83	Dow Chemical	USA	2,053	35(j)	34(h)	—	45(j)	22(d)	24
84	W.R. Grace	USA	2,049	22(j)	—	—	39(j)	60(e)	18
85	Ruhrkohle	FRG	2,043	—	—	—	—	—	—
86	United Aircraft	USA	2,029	11(d)	—	—	—	—	—
87	Rapid American	USA	1,991	—	—	—	—	—	—
88	Union Oil of Calif.	USA	1,981	—	—	—	—	8(d)	—
89	International Paper	USA	1,970	10(l)	—	—	—	—	11
90	Gutehoffnungshütte	FRG	1,962	38(i)	—	—	—	—	19

TABLE 2

Foreign Content of Operations and Assets of Manufacturing Corporations
of Market Economies with Sales of Over $1 Billion, 1971

Rank (a)	Company	Nationality	Total sales (millions of dollars)	Foreign Content as Percentage of					Number of subsidiary countries (c)
				Sales (b)	Production	Assets	Earnings	Employment	
91	Xerox	USA	1,961	30(j)	—	—	38(j)	38(j)	23
92	Honeywell	USA	1,946	35(k)	—	20(d)	—	24(d)	24
93	Sun Oil	USA	1,939	—	—	—	—	—	21
94	Saint-Gobain-Pont-à Mousson	France	1,914	19(x)	—	—	—	—	13
95	American Can	USA	1,897	—	—	—	—	—	24
96	General Dynamics	USA	1,869	—	—	—	—	—	16
97	Ciba-Geigy	Switz.	1,843	98(i)	—	—	⊢	71(h)	37
98	Krupp-Konzern	FRG	1,843	23(j)	3(j)	—	—	3(i)	15
99	Minnesota Mining and Manufacturing	USA	1,829	36(j)	30(h)	29(h)	29(h)	40(h)	29
100	Beatrice Foods	USA	1,827	4(d)	—	—	5(d)	—	13
101	ELF Group	France	1,825	—	—	—	—	—	—
102	Mannesmann	FRG	1,823	41(j)	11(j)	—	—	12(j)	15
103	R.J. Reynolds Industries	USA	1,816	—	—	—	—	—	—
104	Cities Service	USA	1,810	—	—	—	—	—	25
105	Citroën	France	1,792	33(k)	—	—	—	—	13
106	Bolse Cascade	USA	1,786	—	—	—	—	—	—
107	Ralston Purina	USA	1,746	—	—	—	—	—	26
108	Sperry Rand	USA	1,739	34(j)	—	28(h)	—	42(h)	27
109	Coca-Cola	USA	1,729	31(j)	—	30(d)	11(d)	—	11
110	Burlington Industries	USA	1,727	4(h)	—	8(h)	—	—	—

#	Company	Country								
111	Cie Générale d' Electricité	France	1,699	20(k)	–	–	–	–	–	14
112	Courtaulds	UK	1,696	22(j)	–	–	–	–	16(j)	31
113	Armco Steel	USA	1,696	–	–	3(d)	–	–	11(d)	–
114	Consolidated Foods	USA	1,689	36(k)	–	–	–	–	–	10
115	Peugeot	France	1,685	–	–	–	–	–	–	–
116	Uniroyal	USA	1,678	27(j)	–	30(h)	75(j)	–	–	20
117	American Brands	USA	1,627	–	–	–	–	–	–	–
118	Ashland Oil	USA	1,614	1(d)	–	4(d)	2(d)	–	2(d)	17
119	Bendix	USA	1,613	49(e)	14(h)	10(h)	–	–	–	20
120	Robert Bosch	FRG	1,607	39(j)	8(j)	–	–	–	20(j)	23
121	ARBED	Lux.	1,604	–	–	–	–	–	–	–
122	Textron	USA	1,604	26(d)	–	–	–	–	–	13
123	U.S. Plywood-Champion Papers	USA	1,600	–	–	–	–	–	–	–
124	Brown Boveri	Switz.	1,599	76(j)	–	–	–	–	82(h)	11
125	Sumitomo Metal Industries	Japan	1,598	37(k)	–	–	–	–	–	3
126	Gulf and Western Industries	USA	1,566	–	–	–	–	–	–	14
127	TRW	USA	1,544	–	–	–	–	–	–	16
128	Associated British Foods	UK	1,525	32(j)	–	–	–	–	24(j)	–
129	National Steel	USA	1,522	–	–	–	34(j)	–	–	14
130	Owens-Illinois	USA	1,508	–	–	10(d)	9(d)	–	27(d)	15
131	CPC International	USA	1,500	50(j)	46(h)	27(h)	51(j)	–	–	22
132	Michelin	France	1,500	50(i)	–	–	–	–	–	13
133	Rheinstahl	FRG	1,483	23(i)	–	–	–	–	–	–
134	Kobe Steel	Japan	1,466	–	–	–	–	–	–	–
135	National Cash Register	USA	1,466	45(j)	41(h)	35(h)	60(h)	–	–	42

Rank (a)	Company	Nationality	Total sales (millions of dollars)	Foreign Content as Percentage of					Number of subsidiary countries (c)
				Sales (b)	Production	Assets	Earnings	Employment	
136	United Brands	USA	1,449	–	–	–	–	–	–
137	Georgia-Pacific	USA	1,447	–	–	–	–	–	–
138	Aluminium Co. of America	USA	1,441	–	–	7(d)	–	–	28
139	Hoesch	FRG	1,431	26(i)	–	–	–	–	14
140	Alcan Aluminium	Canada	1,431	–	–	42(h)	–	–	33(g)
141	American Home Products	USA	1,429	19(d)	–	14(d)	14(d)	–	27
142	American Standard	USA	1,410	36(j)	28(h)	30(h)	33(j)	–	21
143	U.S. Industries	USA	1,407	45(e)	–	–	5(e)	–	–
144	Hoffmann-LaRoche	Switz.	1,402	80(j)	–	–	–	83(h)	–
145	Standard Oil (Ohio)	USA	1,394	–	–	–	–	–	–
146	Republic Steel	USA	1,385	–	–	–	–	–	–
147	GKN (Guest, Keen and Nettlefolds)	UK	1,377	16(j)	–	31(j)	38(j)	21(j)	27
148	KF (Kooperativa Förbundet)	Sweden	1,376	9(i)	–	–	–	–	13
149	FMC	USA	1,354	9(d)	–	–	–	–	19
150	Petrofina	Belgium	1,350	90(i)	–	–	–	–	21
151	Amerada Hess	USA	1,349	–	–	–	–	–	–
152	Warner-Lambert	USA	1,346	36(j)	33(h)	32(h)	33(g)	–	47
153	Getty Oil	USA	1,343	–	–	–	–	–	19
154	Reed International	UK	1,330	–	–	–	–	–	13
155	Allied Chemical	USA	1,326	–	–	–	–	6(d)	14

	Company	Country							
156	Colgate-Palmolive	USA	1,310	52(j)	—	50(h)	88(d)	70(d)	55
157	Raytheon	USA	1,308	6(d)	—	—	13(h)	13(h)	18
158	Genesco	USA	1,307	—	—	—	—	—	13
159	B.F. Goodrich	USA	1,300	—	—	—	—	—	24
160	Weyerhaeuser	USA	1,300	—	—	2(d)	—	—	12
161	Mitsubishi Electric	Japan	1,294	—	—	—	—	—	—
162	Taiyo Fishery	Japan	1,292	13(k)	—	—	—	21(k)	25
163	American Cynamid	USA	1,283	18(j)	—	18(d)	20(h)	17(d)	27
164	Signal Companies	USA	1,281	—	—	—	—	—	16
165	Ishikawajima-Harima Heavy Industries	Japan	1,280	32(k)	—	—	—	13(k)	8
166	Whirlpool	USA	1,274	—	—	(4(d))	—	—	—
167	Inland Steel	USA	1,254	—	—	—	—	—	—
168	Columbia Broadcasting System	USA	1,248	—	—	—	—	—	—
169	Metallgesellschaft	FRG	1,248	22(j)	—	—	—	—	19
170	Thomson Brandt	France	1,246	23(k)	6(j)	—	—	—	17
171	PPG Industries	USA	1,238	19(j)	—	—	—	—	10
172	Celanese	USA	1,236	—	—	22(h)	18(e)	—	21
173	American Motors	USA	1,232	—	—	9(d)	—	—	10
174	Pepsi Co.	USA	1,225	34(d)	—	—	—	52(d)	25
175	Pemes (Petróleos Mexicanos)	Mexico	1,214	—	—	—	—	—	—
176	Philip Morris	USA	1,210	—	—	—	—	—	11
177	Volvo	Sweden	1,196	69(k)	26(h)	—	—	—	13
178	Deere	USA	1,188	—	—	—	—	—	14
179	Marathon Oil	USA	1,182	—	—	—	—	4(d)	—
180	Imperial Tobacco Group	UK	1,173	5(j)	—	—	—	11(j)	13

Rank (a)	Company	Nationality	Total sales (millions of dollars)	Foreign Content as Percentage of					Number of subsidiary countries (c)
				Sales (b)	Production	Assets	Earnings	Employment	
181	Kawasaki Steel	Japan	1,162	27(k)	–	–	–	14(k)	18
182	Hawker Siddeley Group.	UK	1,151	36(j)	–	40(j)	–	18(j)	20
183	Borg-Warner	USA	1,148	–	–	–	–	–	21
184	Carnation	USA	1,148	–	–	–	–	–	–
185	Olin	USA	1,145	–	–	–	–	–	18
186	Idemitsu Kosan	Japan	1,145	25(e)	–	–	–	–	–
187	Johnson and Johnson	USA	1,140	–	–	27(e)	25(d)	40(d)	18
188	General Mills	USA	1,120	–	–	–	–	–	–
189	Teledyne	USA	1,102	–	–	–	–	–	–
190	Mitsubishi Chemical Industries	Japan	1,095	–	–	–	–	–	–
191	Reynolds Metal	USA	1,093	54(l)	28(h)	32(d)	4(d)	–	–
192	Usinor	France	1,092	18(j)	–	–	–	–	–
193	Rio Tinto-Zinc	UK	1,087	74(j)	–	82(j)	71(j)	71(j)	20
194	Italsider	Italy	1,080	–	7(h)	–	–	–	–
195	British Insulated Callender's Cables	UK	1,080	35(j)	–	–	55(j)	36(j)	17
196	Nabisco	USA	1,070	–	–	–	–	–	16
197	Wendel-Sidelor	France	1,067	37(k)	–	–	–	–	–
198	Bristol-Myers	USA	1,066	–	–	–	–	–	15
199	Combustion Engineering	USA	1,066	–	–	–	–	–	12
200	Salzgitter	FRG	1,061	–	–	–	–	–	12

No.	Company	Country	Sales						
201	Standard Brands	USA	1,057	5(d)	–	9(d)	10(d)	–	26
202	Mead	USA	1,056	–	–	–	–	–	13
203	Kennecott Copper	USA	1,053	–	–	–	–	–	13
204	Norton Simon	USA	1,052	–	–	–	–	–	–
205	Petróleo Brasileiro (Petrobras)	Brazil	1,044	74(l)	–	–	–	–	–
206	Ogden	USA	1,043	–	–	–	–	–	–
207	Eaton	USA	1,036	23(h)	–	25(h)	22(h)	35(e)	–
208	Henkel	FRG	1,033	–	–	–	–	29(j)	8
209	Campbell Soup	USA	1,032	–	–	–	8(d)	–	7
210	Massey-Ferguson	Canada	1,029	90(g)	62(g)	84(g)	–	–	22
211	Iowa Beef Processors	USA	1,015	–	–	–	–	–	–

Source: Centre for Development Planning, Projections and Policies of the Department of Economic and Social Affairs of the United Nations Secretariat, based on table 1; Belgium's 500 largest companies (Brussels, 1969); Entreprise, No. 878, 6-12 July, 1972; Rolf Jungnickel, "Wie multinational sind die deutschen Unternehmen?" in Wirtschafts dienst, No. 4, 1972; Wilhelm Grotkopp and Ernst Schmacke, Die Grossen 500 (Düsseldorf, 1971); Commerzbank, Auslandsfertigung (Frankfurt, 1971); Bank of Tokyo, The President Directory 1973 (Tokyo, 1972); Financial Times, 30 March 1973; Vision, 15 December 1971; Sveriges 500 Största Företag (Stockholm, 1970); Max Iklé, Die Schweiz als internationaler Bankund Finanzplatz (Zürich, 1970); Schweizer Bankgesellschaft, Die Grössten Unternehmen der Schweiz (1971); Financial Times, 15 May 1973; J.M. Stopford, "The foreign investments of United Kingdom firms", London Graduate School of Business Studies, 1973, (mimeo); Multinational Corporations, Hearings before the Subcommittee on International Trade of the Committee on Finance, United States Senate, 93rd Congress, First Session, February/March 1973; Nicholas K. Bruck and Francis A. Lees, "Foreign content of United States Corporate activities", Financial Analyst Journal, September-October 1966; Forbes, 15 May 1973; Chemical and Engineering News, 20 December 1971; Moody's Industrial Manual, 1973; Sidney E. Rolfe, The International Corporation, (Paris, 1969); Charles Levinson, Capital, Inflation and the Multinationals (London, 1971); Yearbook of International Organizations, 12th ed., 1968-1969, and 13th ed., 1970-1971; Institut für Marxistische Studien und Forschung, Internationale Konzerne und Arbeiterklasse (Frankfurt, 1971); Heinz Aszkenazy, Les grandes sociétés européennes (Brussels, 1971); Mirovaja ekonomika i mezdunarodnyje otnosenija, No. 9, 1970.

a. Corporations are ranked in descending order of sales.
b. Total sales to third parties (non-affiliate firms) outside the home country.
c. Countries in which the parent corporation has at least one affiliate, except in the case of Japan, where the number of foreign affiliates is reported.

d. 1964.   g. 1967.   j. 1970.
e. 1965   h. 1968.   k. 1971.
f. 1966   i. 1969.   l. 1972.

Table 3
Multinational Corporations of Selected Developed Market Economies:
Parent Corporations and Affiliate Networks by Home Country, 1968-1969

Home Country*	Total Parent		Parent Corporations with Affiliates in				Affiliates	
	Number	Percentage	1 Country	2-9 Countries	10-19 Countries	Over 20 Countries	Minimum Number†	Percentage
United States	2,468	33.9	1,228	949	216	75	9,691	35.5
United Kingdom	1,692	23.3	725	809	108	50	7,116	26.1
Federal Rep. of Germany	954	13.1	448	452	43	11	2,916	10.7
France	538	7.4	211	275	42	10	2,023	7.4
Switzerland	447	6.1	213	202	26	6	1,456	5.3
Netherlands	268	3.7	92	149	20	7	1,118	4.1
Sweden	255	3.5	93	129	24	9	1,159	4.2
Belgium	235	3.2	137	88	8	2	594	2.2
Denmark	128	1.8	54	69	4	1	354	1.3
Italy	120	1.7	57	54	3	6	459	1.7
Norway	94	1.3	54	36	4	–	220	0.8
Austria	39	0.5	21	16	2	–	105	0.4
Luxembourg	18	0.2	10	7	1	–	55	0.2
Spain	15	0.2	11	4	–	–	26	0.1
Portugal	5	0.1	3	2	–	–	8	–
Total	7,276	100.0	3,357	3,241	501	177	27,300	100.0

Source: Centre for Development Planning, Projections and Policies of the Department of Economic and Social Affairs of the United Nations Secretariat, based on Yearbook of International Organisations, 13th ed., 1970-1971.

* Countries are arranged in descending order of number of parent corporations.

† "Minimum number of affiliates" refers to the number of "links" between parent corporations and host countries. Two or more affiliates of a particular corporation in a given foreign country are counted as one "link".

Table 4
Market Economies: Stock of Foreign Direct Investment
(Book Value), 1967, 1971
(millions of dollars and percentage)

Country(a)	1967		1971(b)	
	Millions of Dollars	Percentage Share	Millions of Dollars	Percentage Share
United States	59,486	55.0	86,001	52.0
United Kingdom	17,521	16.2	24,019	14.5
France	6,000	5.5	9,540	5.8
Federal Rep. of Germany	3,015	2.8	7,276	4.4
Switzerland	4,250(c)	3.9	6,760	4.1
Canada	3,728	3.4	5,930	3.6
Japan	1,458	1.3	4,480(d)	2.7
Netherlands	2,250	2.1	3,580	2.2
Sweden(e)	1,514	1.4	3,450	2.1
Italy	2,110(f)	1.9	3,350	2.0
Belgium	2,040(f)	0.4	3,250	2.0
Australia	380(f)	1.9	610	0.4
Portugal	200(f)	0.2	320	0.2
Denmark	190(f)	0.2	310	0.2
Norway	60(f)	0.0	90	0.0
Austria	30(f)	0.0	40	0.0
Other(g)	4,000(g)	3.7	6,000	3.6
Total	108,200	100.0	165,000	100.0

Source: Centre for Development Planning, Projections and Policies of the Department of Economic and Social Affairs of the United Nations Secretariat, based on table 11; Organisation for Economic Co-operation and Development, *Stock of Private Direct Investments by DAC Countries in Developing Countries, End 1967* (Paris, 1972); United States Department of Commerce, *Survey of Current Business*, various issues; Bundesministerium für Wirtschaft, *Runderlass Aussenwirtschaft*, various issues; Handelskammer Hamburg, *Deutsche Direktinvestitionen in Ausland* (1969); Bank of England, *Quarterly Bulletin*, various issues; Hans-Eckart Scharrer, ed., *Förderung privater Direktinvestitionen* (Hamburg, 1972); Toyo Keizai, *Statistics Monthly*, vol. 32, June 1972; Canadian Department of Industry, Trade and Commerce, "Direct investment abroad by Canada, 1964-1967" (mimeo) (Ottawa, 1971); Skandinaviska Enskilda Banken, *Quarterly Review*, No. 2, 1972.

Note: According to the Organisation for Economic Co-operation and Development, *op. cit.*, " ... by the stock of foreign investment ... is understood the net book value to the direct investor of affiliates (subsidiaries, branches and associates) in LDC's ... Governments of DAC member countries decline all responsibility for the accuracy of the estimates of the Secretariat which in some cases are known to differ from confidential information available to the national authorities ... Any analysis of detailed data in the paper should therefore be done with the utmost caution ... ", p. 4.

a. Countries are arranged in descending order of book value of direct investment in 1971.

b. Estimated (except for United States, United Kingdom, Federal Republic of Germany, Japan and Sweden) by applying the average growth rate of the United

States, United Kingdom and Federal Republic of Germany between 1966 and 1971.

c. Data from another source for 1965 ($4,052 million) and 1969 ($6,043 million) seem to indicate that the 1967 and 1971 figures are probably relatively accurate. See, Max Iklé, *Die Schweiz als internationaler Bank und Finanzplatz* (Zurich 1970).

d. *Financial Times*, 4 June 1973. ⎯⎯⎯⎯

e. The figures for Sweden are for 1965 and 1970 instead of 1967 and 1971 and they are in current prices for total assets of majority-owned manufacturing subsidiaries.

f. Data on book value of foreign direct investment are only available for developing countries. Since the distribution of the minimum number of affiliates between developing countries and developed market economies correlates highly with the distribution of book value, the total book value has been estimated on the basis of the distribution of their minimum number of affiliates. For Australia, the average distribution of the total minimum number of affiliates has been applied.

g. Estimated, including developing countries.

Table 5
Average Size* of United States and United Kingdom Foreign
Affiliates by Area, in Selected Years
(thousands of dollars)

Area	United States			United Kingdom	
	1950	1957	1966	1965	1968
Developed market economies	1,221	2,299	2,413	1,822	2,105
Canada	1,825	3,171	3,172	2,903	3,282
Western Europe	769	1,564	1,885	920	1,063
European Economic Community	651	1,371	1,867	925	1,172
United Kingdom	1,219	2,342	2,449	–	–
Japan	333	1,350	1,424	551	771
Southern hemisphere	1,019	1,846	1,657	2,429	2,879
United States	–	–	–	3,001	3,867
Unallocated				5,372	3,954
Developing countries†	2,083	2,548	2,096	1,600	1,575
Africa	840	1,344	2,158	1,479	1,412
Asia	1,956	2,615	2,037	1,506	1,424
Western hemisphere	2,220	2,639	2,106	2,027	2,299
Unallocated	. . .	8,748	4,710	467	5,298
Total	1,589	2,472	2,350	1,742	1,919

Source: Centre for Development Planning, Projections and Policies of the Department of Economic and Social Affairs of the United Nations Secretariat, based on United States Department of Commerce, *United States Direct Investments Abroad, 1966, Part I: Balance of Payments Data*, (Washington, D.C.,

1970) and *Survey of Current Business*, various issues; United Kingdom Department of Trade and Industry, *Trade and Industry*, various issues.

* Book value of foreign direct investment divided by number of affiliates.

† The developing countries comprise the countries and territories of Africa (other than South Africa), Asia and the Pacific (other than Australia, China, the Democratic People's Republic of Korea, the Democratic Republic of Viet-Nam, Japan, Mongolia, New Zealand and Turkey) and Central and South America and the Caribbean (other than Puerto Rico and the United States Virgin Islands).

Table 6
United States Multinational Corporations:
Number of Foreign Affiliates
by Area, 1950, 1957 and 1966

Area	1950		1957		1966		Aver. annual rate of growth (%)	
	Number	Percentage distribution	Number	Percentage distribution	Number	Percentage distribution	1950-1957	1957-1966
Developed market economies	4,657	62.8	6,105	59.4	15,128	65.0	3.9	10.6
Canada	1,961	26.4	2,765	26.9	4,360	18.7	2.9	5.2
Western Europe	2,236	30.1	2,654	25.8	8,611	37.0	2.5	14.0
European Economic Community	1,003*	13.5	1,225	11.9	4,063	17.5	2.9	14.3
United Kingdom	695	9.4	842	8.2	2,310	9.9	2.8	11.9
Israel	44	0.6	44	0.4	103	0.4	–	9.9
Japan	57	0.8	137	1.3	531	2.3	13.3	16.2
Southern hemisphere	359	4.8	505	4.9	1,523	6.5	5.0	13.0
Developing countries	2,760	37.2	4,048	39.4	7,718	33.2	5.6	7.4
Africa	175	2.4	270	2.6	683	2.9	6.4	10.9
Asia†	524	7.1	727	7.1	1,599	6.9	4.8	9.2
Western Hemisphere	2,061	27.8	3,051	29.7	5,436	23.3	5.8	6.6
Unallocated	–	–	119	1.2	436	1.9	–	15.5
Total	7,417	100.0	10,272	100.0	23,282	100.0	4.8	9.5

Source: Centre for Development Planning, Projections and Policies of the Department of Economic and Social Affairs of the United Nations Secretariat, based on United States Department of Commerce, *United States Direct Investments Abroad, 1966, Part I: Balance of Payments Data* (Washington, D.C., 1970).

* Excluding Luxembourg.

† Including Turkey and Oceania (other than Australia and New Zealand).

Table 7
Ownership Patterns of Foreign Affiliates
in Selected Developed Market Economies
(number, value in millions of dollars and percentage)

Affiliates in:	Wholly Owned (more than 95%)	Majority Owned (50-95%)	Minority Owned (less than 50%)
Australia(a)			
Manufacturing			
Number	1,641	516	148
Percentage	71.2	22.4	6.4
Value	140.2	455	171
Percentage	69.1	22.5	8.4
Mining			
Number	44	15	13
Percentage	61.1	20.8	18.1
Value	178	82	20
Percentage	63.7	29.2	7.0
Austria(b)			
Number	720	345	225
Percentage	55.8	26.7	17.4
Value	162	44	38
Percentage	66.3	18.1	15.6
Belgium(c)			
Value	1,422	216	283
Percentage	74.0	11.2	14.7
France(d)			
United States-owned			
Number	181	94	43
Percentage	56.9	29.6	13.5
Others			
Number	66	93	40
Percentage	33.2	46.7	20.1
Federal Republic of Germany(e)			
Number	5,020	1,108	1,633
Percentage	64.7	14.3	21.0
Value	4,720	535	674
Percentage	79.6	9.0	11.4
Japan(f)			
United States-owned			
Number	16	28	23
Percentage	23.9	41.8	34.3

Table 7 (continued)
Ownership Patterns of Foreign Affiliates
in Selected Developed Market Economies
(number, value in millions of dollars and percentage)

Affiliates in:	Wholly Owned (more than 95%)	Majority Owned (50- 95%)	Minority Owned (less than 50%)
Others			
Number	10	15	8
Percentage	30.3	45.5	24.2
New Zealand(f)			
Number	421	120	33
Percentage	73.4	20.9	5.7
United Kingdom(g)			
United States-owned			
Number	384	52	105
Percentage	71.0	9.6	19.4
Value	2,726	517	370
Percentage	75.4	14.3	10.2
Others			
Number	277	51	62
Percentage	71.0	13.1	15.9
Value	1,278	480	63
Percentage	70.2	26.3	3.5

Source: Centre for Development Planning, Projections and Policies of the Department of Economic and Social Affairs of the United Nations Secretariat, based on Australian Bureau of Census and Statistics, "Overseas participation in Australian mining industry, 1967" and "Overseas participation in Australian manufacturing industry, 1962-1963 and 1966-1967" (mimeos), (Canberra); Oskar Grünwald and Ferdinand Lacina, *Auslandskapital in der österreichischen Wirtschaft* (Vienna, 1970); Banque Nationale de Belgique, *Bulletin d'Information et de Documentation*, vol. 2, October 1970; Société d'Editions Economiques et Financières, *Les Maisons Financières Françaises* (Paris, 1966); Deutsche Bundesbank, *Monthly Report*, January 1972; Bank of Tokyo, *The President Directory*, 1973 (Tokyo, 1972); Roderick S. Deane, *Foreign Investment in New Zealand Manufacturing* (Wellington, 1970); United Kingdom Board of Trade, *Board of Trade Journal*, 26 January 1968.

a. 1966-1967 for manufacturing; 1967 for mining. "Wholly owned" is defined as 75 per cent or more owned. "Value" is in terms of value of production.

b. 1969. Limited liability companies only. "Wholly owned" is defined as 100 per cent owned. "Value" is in terms of nominal capital.

c. 1960-1967. "Wholly owned" is defined as 100 per cent owned. "Value" is in terms of book value.

d. 1965.

e. End of 1970. "Wholly owned" is defined as 90 per cent or more owned. "Value" is in terms of nominal capital.

f. 1964. "Wholly owned" is defined as 100 per cent owned.

g. End of 1965. "Wholly owned" is defined as 100 per cent owned. Branches are included. "Value" in terms of book value.

Appendix C

Statute European Companies

Commission Proposal

1301. On 13 May 1975, the commission transmitted to the Council the amended Proposal for a Council Regulation on the Statute for European Companies.[1] Both the European Parliament[2] and the Economic and Social Committee[3] have given their opinions on the original proposal.[4]

The original proposal has been significantly amended, in particular because of the advice given by the Parliament, and there have been extensive consultations with all interested circles since then.

The need for a European legal framework

1302. The rapidly changing economic situation in the world and the increase in competition faced by European Companies has created the urgent necessity that European concerns be able to operate on the scale of the Community as a whole.

The looser economic trading arrangements of the 50's and 60's will not enable the Community to meet the greater challenge of the 70's and 80's. The durability and adaptability of the Community will depend on more solid structural foundations, of which a common legal framework constitutes a significant ingredient.

The Statute for a European Company is an important part of that framework and is designed to enable companies more easily to adapt to the Community dimension, and to stimulate economic activity. It is, moreover, a sophisticated instrument, which offers protection for the legitimate interests of all concerned in the running of enterprises. Use of the Statute is optional, and it is not designed to replace the existing national systems.

It will be particularly attractive to transnational companies, offering them a new European form with a transparent structure and clear obligations in relation to shareholders, creditors, employees and society as a whole. Small and medium-sized firms will, moreover, be able to use the form, by virtue of the scaled-down capital requirements of the amended Proposal, or in cooperation with larger undertakings.

Contents of the amended proposal

Access and formation

1303. The Company is envisaged as being used by companies incorporated in different Member States for three basic purposes:
(i) cross-frontier mergers of those companies
(ii) the formation of holding companies under European law by those companies
(iii) the formation of joint subsidiaries under European law by those companies.
As in the original Proposal, only companies limited by shares can use the first two methods. Owing to pressure from industry, and in accordance with the opinion of the European Parliament, however, the availability of the European Company to form a joint subsidiary has been considerably extended, and now includes all companies with legal personality, cooperatives, and other legal persons governed by the law of the Member States whose object is to carry on economic activities.
The minimum capital required for eligibility has now been reduced from 500,000 u.a. to 250,000 u.a. in the case of merger or the formation of a holding company, and from 250,000 to 100,000 u.a. as regards a joint subsidiary.
European companies must be set up under the judicial control of the European Court of Justice, and entered in a European Commercial Register. They may have several offices anywhere in the Community.

Employee participation

1304. The connection between economic interests and the other requirements of people in contemporary society are becoming increasingly apparent. In the context of the company, in particular, the employee has interests which are at least as substantial as those of managers and shareholders. These interests include work satisfaction, health and physical condition, and all those factors which pertain to the personal dignity of employees and their autonomy as human beings.
The extent to which employees should be able to influence company decisions has consequently become a problem of paramount interest within all Member States. It has, moreover, become increasingly rele-

vant because of the accentuated degree of economic and social change in the present world. This has for example profound implications as regards supplies of energy and raw material resources, which have led to significant alterations in the economic environment of enterprises. The need for industrial reorganization has increased, while the prospects of immediate wage increases have become more limited. Consequently, conflicts of interests between different groups have developed more acutely.

Such a period of heightened economic and social tension gives rise to a greater need for effective mechanisms whereby those involved in industry can respond quickly and sensibly to the requirements of the situation with a minimum of wasteful confrontation. In this context, the decision-making machinery of the enterprise can make an important contribution, and the Community can and should play an important role in making practical proposals. The proposed Regulation therefore includes provisions on employee participation which are tailored to the needs of the European Company. They fall into three broad sections, which are necessarily interlinked, namely the formation of European Works' Councils, the composition of the Supervisory Boards, and the Conclusion of European Collective Agreements.

The European Works' Council

1305. A 'European Works' Council' must be set up in all European Companies with establishments in different Member States. The competence of the European Works' Council extends to the right to be informed on matters relating to the running of the undertaking; it must be consulted prior to important economic decisions and must give its approval to decisions by the Board of Management which directly affect employees. As a result of the Opinion of the European Parliament, it must now approve in particular a Social Plan which the Board of Management must in future draw up to deal with the social problems following, for example, the closure of an establishment.

Election to the Works' Council is by all employees on the basis of proportional representation; in accordance with uniform European electoral provisions candidates may be proposed by Trade Unions or groups of employees.

Composition of the Supervisory Board

1306. The Supervisory Board of a European Company which appoints the Management Board is to consist as to one third of representatives of shareholders, one third of representatives of employees, and as to one third of members co-opted by these two groups who are to be independent of both shareholders and employees, and represent 'general interests'. This composition was adopted by a large majority in the European Parliament. Election procedures are similar to those of the European Works' Councils.

This system has the advantage of avoiding deadlocks which might be created by a 50:50 representation of shareholders and employers.

The concept 'general interests' is intended to cover all interests affected by the activity of the European Company other than those of employees or shareholders directly involved, and is not more specifically defined in terms of concrete example. These representatives must, in addition to having no links with the shareholders or employees, possess 'the necessary knowledge and experience'. If the required majority is not reached amongst the first two groups for the election of this third group, the group is appointed by an Arbitration Board consisting of one representative each of shareholders and employees, and a third member co-opted by the first two.

Collective agreements

1307. The conditions of employment with a European Company may be governed by a European Collective Agreement, applied to all members of a trade union party to the agreement. Alternatively, collective agreements arrived at in the context of one Member State may also be reached.

It is expressly provided that where there is a collective agreement, the powers of the European Works' Council do not extend to matters covered by it. Moreover, the European Works' Council cannot conduct negotiations or conclude agreements on employees' conditions unless so empowered by a European Collective Agreement.

Groups of companies

1308. Groups of companies — that is groupings of legally independent companies under unified management — have acquired such economic importance that they cannot be ignored in the provisions.

The statute protects shareholders outside the group ('outside shareholders') and the creditors of dependent group undertakings. This protection takes the form of annual compensation as a dividend guarantee as well as an obligation on the controlling undertaking either to offer the outside shareholders payment in cash or an exchange for their shares of shares in the controlling undertaking.

Where the controlling undertaking provides the necessary protection, it can issue instructions to the management of a dependent undertaking in order to implement a unified business policy. These instructions must be complied with even if they adversely affect the interests of the dependent undertaking. These are the proposals put forward in 1970, and have broadly received the approval of the European Parliament.

Employees in group undertakings are also protected. When the European Company is a controlling group company, a Group Works' Council is formed in which the employees of all the group undertakings are represented and which has similar powers to those of the European Works' Council in matters affecting the group. Employees in all group undertakings may participate in the election of the Supervisory Board.

Taxation

1309. In tax matters, the European Company is subject to the law of the State in which business is actually conducted. Preferential treatment for tax purposes for European Companies cannot be entertained, since distortions in competition might arise if European Companies were not given the same treatment as companies constituted under national law.

Notes

1. Supplement 4/75 — Bull. E.C.

2. OJ C124 of 10.10.1970 and Bull. EC 8-1970 Supplement.

3. OJ C93 of 7.8.1974.

4. OJ C131 of 13.12.1972.

Bibliography

Ball, G.W. "Cosmocrop: The Importance of Being Stateless." *Columbia Journal of World Business* (November-December 1967).

Bancroft, J. *The Multinational Corporation: A Background Survey.* International Relations Foreign Affairs Division, Congressional Research Service, Washington, D.C., Library of Congress (December 1972).

Barlow, E.R., and Wender, I. *Foreign Investment and Taxation.* Englewood Cliffs, N.J.: Prentice Hall, 1955.

Behrman, J.N. "Foreign Investment Muddle: The Perils of Ad Hoccery." *Columbia Journal of World Business* (Fall 1965).

――――. *National Interests and the Multinational Enterprise.* Englewood Cliffs, N.J.: Prentice Hall, 1970.

――――. *U.S. International Business and Governments.* New York: McGraw-Hill, 1971.

Business International. *The Effects of U.S. Corporate Foreign Investment, 1960-1972.* New York: 1974.

Denison, E., and Poullier, J.P. *Why Growth Rates Differ.* Washington, D.C.: Brookings, 1967.

Diebolt, W. *The United States and the Industrial World.* New York: Praeger, 1972.

Dunning, J.H., ed. *The Multinational Enterprise.* London: George Allen & Unwin, Ltd., 1971.

Emergency Committee on American Trade. *The Role of the Multinational Corporation in the United States and World Economies.* Washington, D.C.: 1972.

Fabian, Y., and Young, A. *R & D in OECD Member Countries: Trends and Objectives.* Paris: 1971.

Fatemi, N.S., deSaint Phalle, T., and Keefe, G. *The Dollar Crisis.* Rutherford, N.J.: Fairleigh Dickinson University Press, 1963.

Fisher, B.S. "The Multinationals and the Crisis in United States Trade and Investment Policy. *Boston University Law Review*, vol. 53, p. 308 (1973).

Gilpin, R. *The Multinational Corporation and the National Interest.* Washington, D.C.: U.S. Government Printing Office, 1973.

Goldberg, P., and Kindleberger, C.P. "Toward a GATT for Investment: A Proposal for Supervision of the International Corporation." *Law and Policy in International Business* (Summer 1970).

Gray, G. *Report to the President on Foreign Economic Policies.* Washington, D.C.: U.S. Government Printing Office, 1950.

Hazen, W.N. "U.S. Foreign Trade in the Seventies." *Columbia Journal of World Business* vol. 6 (September-October 1971).

Hellman, R. *The Challenge to U.S. Dominance of the International Corporation.* New York: Dunellen, 1970.

Hirsham, A.O. "How to Disinvest in Latin America and Why." *Essays in International Finance* No. 76, Princeton, International Finance Section (November 1969).

Hufbauer, G.C. and Adler, F.M. *Overseas Manufacturing Investment, The Balance of Payments.* Washington, D.C.: Department of Treasury, 1968.

Hymer, S.H. "The Efficiency (Contradictions) of Multinational Corporations." *American Economic Review* vol. 60, no. 2 (May 1970).

Hynning, C.J. "Balance of Payments Controls by the United States." *International Lawyer* vol. 2, p. 400 (1968).

International Chamber of Commerce. *Guidelines for International Investment.* Paris: 1972.

International Economic Policy Association. *The United States Balance of Payments: From Crisis to Controversy.* Washington, D.C.: 1972.

International Labour Office. *Multinational Enterprises and Social Policy.* Geneva: 1973.

Keesing, D. "The Impact of Research and Development on United States' Trade." *Journal of Political Economy* (February 1967).

Kindleberger, C.P. *American Business Abroad.* New Haven, Conn.: Yale University Press, 1969.

Krause, L.B. "The International Economic System and the Multinational Corporation." Philadelphia. *Annals* (September 1972).

Krause, L.B., and Dam, D. *Federal Tax Treatment of Foreign Income.* Washington, D.C.: Brookings, 1964.

Mikesell, R.F. *Promoting United States' Private Investment Abroad.* Planning Pamphlet No. 101, National Planning Association. Washington, D.C.: 1957.

National Association of Manufacturers. *New Proposals for Taxing Foreign Income.* New York: 1972.

—————. *U.S. Stake in World Trade: The Role of the Multinational Corporation.* New York: 1971.

National Foreign Trade Council. *Economic Implications of Proposed Changes in the Taxation of U.S. Investments Abroad.* New York: 1972.

National Planning Association. *U.S. Foreign Economic Policy for the 1970s': A New Approach to New Realities.* Washington, D.C.: 1971.

Organization for Economic Co-operation and Development. *Company Tax Systems in OECD Member Countries.* Paris: 1973.

———. *Gaps in Technology: General Report.* Paris: 1968.

———. *Market Power and the Law: Report o the OECD Committee of Experts on Restrictive Business Practices.* Paris: 1970.

. Social Affairs Division, *Programme for Employers and Unions, Regional Trade Union Seminar on Internationl Trade.* Paris: 1971.

Paley, W.S. *Resources for Freedom.* A Report to the President. Washington, D.C.: June 1952.

Pavitt, K. "Technology in Europe's Future." *Research Policy* vol. 1 (August 1972).

———. "Technology, International Competition and Economic Growth." *World Politics* (January 1973).

Peterson, P.G. *The United States in the Changing World Economy.* Vols. 1 & 2. Washington, D.C.: U.S. Government Printing Office, 1971.

Randall, C.B. *Report to the President and the Congress.* Commission on Foreign Economic Policy. Washington, D.C.: January 1954.

Robock, S.H., and Simmonds, K. "International Business: How Big is it? The Missing Measurement." *Columbia Journal of World Business* (May-June 1970).

Rockefeller, N.A. *Partners in Progress.* A Report to the President by the U.S. International Development Advisory Board. New York: Simon and Schuster, 1951.

Rolfe, S.E. *The Multinational Corporation in the World Economy.* New York: Praeger, 1970.

Rose, S. "Multinational Corporation in a Tough New World." *Fortune* (August 1973).

Ruttenberg, S. "Needed: A Constructive Foreign Trade Policy." *AFL-CIO* (1971).

Servan-Schreiber, J.J. *The American Challenge.* New York: Atheneum, 1968.

Solandt, O.M. "Science, Policy and Canadian Manufacturing Industries." *The Canadian Forum* (January-February 1972).

Teplin, M.F. "U.S. International Transactions in Royalties and Fees: Their Relationship to the Transfer of Technology." *Survey of Current Business* (December 1973).

United Nations Conference on Trade and Development. *Restrictive Business Practices in Relation to the Trade and Development of Developing Countries.* Geneva: 1973.

United Nations, Department of Economics and Social Affairs. *Multinational Corporations in World Development.* New York: 1973.

U.S. Chamber of Commerce. *United States Multinational Enterprise Survey*. Washington, D.C.: 1972.

U.S. Commission on International Trade and Investment Policy. *United States International Economic Policy in an Interdependent World*. Washington, D.C.: U.S. Government Printing Office, 1971.

U.S. Council of Economic Advisors. *International Economic Report of the President*. Washington, D.C.: U.S. Government Printing Office, 1974.

U.S. Department of Commerce, Office of International Investment. *Report to the Secretary*. January 1972.

U.S. Department of Commerce. *Policy Aspects of Foreign Investment*. Washington, D.C.: U.S. Government Printing Office, January 1972.

U.S. Department of State. *The U.S. Role in International Investment*. Washington, D.C.: December 1973.

U.S. House of Representatives, Committee on Ways and Means. *Multinationals: Perspectives on Trade and Taxes*. Washington, D.C.: U.S. Government Printing Office, 1973.

U.S. Senate, Committee on Finance. *Multinational Corporations*. A Compendium of Papers Submitted to the Subcommittee on International Trade, 93rd Congress, 1st Session. Washington, D.C.: U.S. Government Printing Office, 1973.

U.S. Senate, Committee on Foreign Relations. *Report of the Committee on Foreign Relations*. 93rd Congress, 1st Session. Washington, D.C.: 1973.

U.S. Senate, Committee on Labor and Public Welfare. *The Multinational Corporation and the National Interest*. 93rd Congress, 1st Session. Washington, D.C.: U.S. Government Printing Office, 1973.

U.S. Tariff Commission. *Economic Factors Affecting the Use of Items 807.00 and 806.30 of the Tariff Schedules of the United States*. Washington, D.C.: U.S. Government Printing Office, 1970.

———. *Implications of Multinational Firms for World Trade and Investment and for United States Trade and Labor*. Report to the Committee on Finance, U.S. Senate, 93rd Congress, 1st Session. Washington, D.C.: U.S. Government Printing Office, 1973.

Vagts, D.F. "The Multinational Enterprise: A New Challenge for Transnational Law." *Harvard Law Review* vol. 83, no. 739 (1970).

Vernon, R. "International Investment and International Trade in the Product Cycle." *Quarterly Journal of Economics* (May 1966).

———. *Sovereignty at Bay*. New York: Basic Books, 1971.

Vernon, R., ed. *The Technology Factor in International Trade*. New York: National Bureau of Economic Research, 1970.

Wells, L.T., ed. *The Product Life Cycle and International Trade*. Boston: Harvard Business School, 1972.

Wilkins, M. *The Emergence of Multinational Enterprise: American Business Abroad from the Colonial Era to 1914*. Cambridge: Harvard University Press, 1970.

Index